Fodor's Family

BOSTON WITH KIDS

1st Edition

Where to Stay and Eat
for All Budgets

Must-See Sights
and Local Secre

D0967459

Ratings You Can Trust

Excerpted from *Fodor's Boston*

Fodor's Travel Publications New York, Toronto, London, Sydney, Auckland

www.fodors.com

FODOR'S FAMILY BOSTON WITH KIDS

Editor: Eric B. Wechter
Writer: Lisa Oppenheimer

Production Editor: Carrie Parker
Editorial Contributors: Pam Bair, Louisa Kasdon, Susan MacCallum-Whitcomb, Erin Murray, Erin Riley, Sarah Pascarella, Andrew Rimas, Diane Wright
Maps & Illustrations: David Lindroth, *cartographer*; Bob Blake and Rebecca Baer, *map editors*; William Wu, *information graphics*
Design: Fabrizio La Rocca, *creative director*; Guido Caroti, *art director*; Ann McBride, *designer*; Melanie Marin, *senior picture editor*
Cover Photo Top: Kindra Clineff/Index Stock Imagery/Jupiter Images; Bottom: Jerry Horbert/Shutterstock
Production Manager: Amanda Bullock

COPYRIGHT

Copyright © 2009 by Fodor's Travel, a division of Random House, Inc.

Fodor's is a registered trademark of Random House, Inc.

All rights reserved. Published in the United States by Fodor's Travel, a division of Random House, Inc., and simultaneously in Canada by Random House of Canada, Limited, Toronto. Distributed by Random House, Inc., New York.

No maps, illustrations, or other portions of this book may be reproduced in any form without written permission from the publisher.

1st Edition

ISBN 978–1–4000–0886–5

ISSN 1943-0132

SPECIAL SALES

This book is available for special discounts for bulk purchases for sales promotions or premiums. Special editions, including personalized covers, excerpts of existing books, and corporate imprints, can be created in large quantities for special needs. For more information, write to Special Markets/Premium Sales, 1745 Broadway, MD 6-2, New York, New York, NY 10019, or e-mail specialmarkets@randomhouse.com.

AN IMPORTANT TIP & AN INVITATION

Although all prices, opening times, and other details in this book are based on information supplied to us at press time, changes occur all the time in the travel world, and Fodor's cannot accept responsibility for facts that become outdated or for inadvertent errors or omissions. **So always confirm information when it matters,** especially if you're making a detour to visit a specific place. Your experiences—positive and negative—matter to us. If we have missed or misstated something, **please write to us.** We follow up on all suggestions. Contact the Boston with Kids editor at editors@fodors.com or c/o Fodor's at 1745 Broadway, New York, NY 10019.

PRINTED IN THE UNITED STATES OF AMERICA

10 9 8 7 6 5 4 3 2 1

Be a Fodor's Correspondent

Your opinion matters. It matters to us. It matters to your fellow Fodor's travelers, too. And we'd like to hear it. In fact, we *need* to hear it. When you share your experiences and opinions, you become an active member of the Fodor's community. Here's how you can help improve Fodor's for all of us.

Tell us when we're right. We rely on local writers to give you an insider's perspective. But our writers and staff editors also depend on you. Your positive feedback is a vote to renew our recommendations for the next edition.

Tell us when we're wrong. We update most of our guides every year. But things change. If any of our descriptions are inaccurate or inadequate, we'll incorporate your changes in the next edition and will correct factual errors at fodors.com *immediately*.

Tell us what to include. You probably have had fantastic travel experiences that aren't yet in Fodor's. Why not share them with a community of like-minded travelers? Share your discoveries and experiences with everyone directly at fodors. com. Your input may lead us to add a new listing or a higher recommendation.

Give us your opinion instantly at our feedback center at www. fodors.com/feedback. You may also e-mail editors@fodors.com with the subject line "Boston with Kids Editor." Or send your nominations, comments, and complaints by mail to Boston with Kids Editor, Fodor's, 1745 Broadway, New York, NY 10019.

Happy Traveling!

Tim Jarrell, Publisher

CONTENTS

ABOUT THIS BOOK

Our Ratings

We wouldn't recommend a place that wasn't worth your time, but sometimes a place is so unique that superlatives don't do it justice: you just have to be there to know. These sights, properties, and experiences get our highest rating, **Fodor's Choice**, indicated by orange stars throughout this book. Black stars highlight sights and properties we deem **Highly Recommended**, places that our writers, editors, and readers praise again and again for consistency and excellence.

Credit Cards

Want to pay with plastic? **AE, D, DC, MC, V** following restaurant and hotel listings indicate whether American Express, Discover, Diners Club, MasterCard, and Visa are accepted.

Restaurants

Unless we state otherwise, restaurants are open for lunch and dinner daily. We mention dress only when there's a specific requirement and reservations only when they're essential or not accepted—it's always best to book ahead.

Hotels

Hotels have private bath, phone, TV, and air-conditioning and operate on the European Plan. We always list facilities but not whether you'll be charged an extra fee to use them.

Many Listings

★	Fodor's Choice
★	Highly recommended
⊠	Physical address
✛	Directions
⌂	Mailing address
☎	Telephone
🖷	Fax
⊕	On the Web
✉	E-mail
🎟	Admission fee
☉	Open/closed times
Ⓣ	Metro stations
🖃	Credit cards

Hotels & Restaurants

🏨	Hotel
⌨	Number of rooms
⌂	Facilities
🍽	Meal plans
✕	Restaurant
⌨	Reservations
⃠	Smoking

Outdoors

⛳	Golf
⛺	Camping

Other

⇨	See also
✉	Branch address
☞	Take note

WHAT'S WHERE

1 Beacon Hill. A collection of local landmarks and quaint, gaslit streets, as well as the Boston Common.

2 The Old West End. The Museum of Science and TD Banknorth Garden will appeal to science fans and sports fans respectively.

3 Government Center. Faneuil Hall, a restored market, has something for every family member. On weekends, see the frenetic and colorful street vendors at Haymarket.

4 The North End. Boston's oldest residential neighborhood is crammed with historic sites and scores of authentic Italian restaurants.

5 Charlestown. At this end of the Freedom Trail you'll find the Bunker Hill Monument and the USS *Constitution*.

6 Downtown Boston. Shopping, dining, and fun are found in Downtown Crossing, sprawling Chinatown, and the waterfront.

7 The Back Bay. Chic Back Bay is home to some of Boston's most characteristic skyscrapers, as well as upscale shops and eateries on Newbury Street.

8 The South End. The ultrahip enclave due south of Chinatown is another locale for a great meal. Look for an active arts community and multicultural population.

9 The Fenway. Home to the revered Fenway Park as well as the Museum of Fine Arts and Isabella Stewart Gardner Museum.

10 South Boston & the Streetcar Suburbs. The Institute of Contemporary Art is in South Boston. Outlying

Dorchester has the John F. Kennedy Library, and Jamaica Plain has the Arnold Arboretum.

11 Cambridge. Funky Harvard Square, and the cool Harvard Museum of Natural History are favorites for families.

BAD WEATHER PLANS

When the weather doesn't cooperate in Boston, a traveler can be left high and dry (or cold and wet!). The stifling heat of summer and the snow and frigid temperatures of winter can push you inside with equal insistence. Fortunately, when conditions are less than ideal, there are great options to keep you and your brood comfortably occupied. The following sights—all close to transportation and dining—provide maximum fun with minimum exposure to the elements.

The **Museum of Science** is a great place for inquisitive minds. It offers a wide selection of exhibits and live presentations, as well as an IMAX theater, a planetarium, and lasers. Tickets are valid throughout the day but shows are additional. The on-site café offers an assortment of casual eateries. On Friday evenings the Science Street Café features live jazz and a fixed-price menu. On-site parking is available but expensive. A more economical option is the subway—the Green Line Science Park Station (not wheelchair accessible) drops you across the street. Other lines, coupled with a short walk, will also get you there.

Messy weather? Then head to the **Children's Museum** and get even messier with the very hands-on activities offered at the Art Studio. Bring a change of clothes—you may need them. Exhibits include the New Balance Climb, the Science Playground, and everything in between (and under and through!). There's even a PlaySpace for children ages 0 to 3 and their caregivers. For dining, there's the newly opened Au Bon Pain, or visitors are permitted to bring food from "home." A number of restaurants are also within easy walking distance. Museum hours span most of the day, and Fridays have extended hours. Daily admission is reasonable and visitors are permitted to leave and reenter. Parking is not available at the museum, but several lots can be found close by. Or take the Red Line to South Station for a 5- to 10-minute walk.

The **New England Aquarium** is rife with opportunities to explore the world under the sea. The aquarium features endless live exhibits, an IMAX theater, and hands-on areas. Presentations, shows, classes, and lectures are offered daily. The on-site café has an extensive selection of snacks and meals, and plenty of restaurants are within walking distance. The aquarium hours are long. Daily admission permits reentry and covers everything but the IMAX theater and whale watch. The aquarium is off the subway Blue Line and is also accessible via commuter boat and car. There is no on-site parking but several paid lots are nearby.

IF YOUR KIDS LIKE

Gizmos, Gadgets & Play

No place does gizmos and gadgets like the Museum of Science. Just about everything here is meant to be pushed, pulled, or otherwise maneuvered—sometimes even hopped on (thank you Musical Stairs!). When they've had enough of the "playground" learning about fulcrums and gravity, steer the kids over to the 3-D Virtual Fish Tank and let them create computer-generated fish—and then instruct them to eat their friends' fish. It's positively addictive. Kids who like a little pretend play in the mix will adore the Boston Children's Museum, where, among other things, they can jump into one of Marc Brown's Arthur books, or turn air into music via Airplay, an exhibit created by the museum in conjunction with Blue Man Group. Look also for a place to explore science via soap bubbles, plus a Construction Zone for building and an art studio for creating.

Sports

In Boston, baseball isn't a sport—it's a religion, and Fenway Park is the place of worship. The ratio of number of fans to number of Fenway seats (roughly a billion to about 36,000) has led owners to find more and more creative ways to squeeze in seats, plopping them everywhere, even atop the Green Monster. Maybe that's why it's such a boisterous crowd. Baseball-loving kids who can't make a game will at least want to pay homage to this grande dame on a tour. And, don't forget the BBall and Hockey shrine. The original Gah-den is no more, but the Boston Celtics and Bruins now play beneath the umbrella of their new arena, the TD Banknorth Garden. Tickets are notoriously hard to come by. But, you can see the stadium via the Sports Museum of New England where, if you come early on a game day, you might just catch players warming up.

Getting Out on the Water

From April through October, the New England Aquarium boats head off to Stellwagen Bank (30 mi off-shore) looking for humpbacks, fin-backs, and diminutive (at least in whale terms) minkes. While these supersize mammals come mainly to feed, some seem happy to perform. If you're lucky, one might breach, blow, or give you a wave with its massive flipper. There are also ferries traveling around the Boston Harbor Islands area, and self-propelled adventures via Charles River Canoe & Kayak. Families with shorter attention spans (or a tendency for seasickness) may be just as happy to go short and sweet on one of the water taxis to and from the Charlestown Navy Yard.

QUINTESSENTIAL BOSTON

Explore History

History via textbook? So blasé. History via exploration? So cool! In Boston, the past is the city's present, with the historic Freedom Trail a focal point of any visit. The path was paved by long-ago revolutionary patriots, a two-plus-mile trek that, along cobblestones and red bricks, past gas lamps and historic halls, can feel like a time-travel adventure. Among the don't-miss stops: the Old North Church, the very spot where, according to Longfellow, "a lantern aloft in the belfy arch" hung as a signal on the night of Paul Revere's famous ride.

Stroll the Charles

There is just nothing like walking along the Charles River. The path (known officially as the Dr. Paul Dudley White Charles River Bike Path, but it's a good bet there's not a single local who can identify it as such) is the perfect place to blow off steam. Sunny days, you'll be in good company, as university track teams come in packs, followed by moms with jog strollers, corporate types getting a workout, and assorted power striders and dog walkers. On July 4, the Hatch Shell becomes the most boisterous Independence Day party on earth. In October keep an eye to the water for those college crew teams, no doubt training for the annual Big Kahuna of regatta fests, the Head of the Charles.

Get on Board a Swan

You haven't truly done Boston until you've trod into the Public Garden and taken your place on the ornithological vehicles lovingly known as the Swan Boats. For kids, the big birds—around since 1877— are literally a page out of a storybook, made famous by the release of Robert McCloskey's Make Way for Ducklings in 1941. Rides offer a 15-minute tour of the lagoon, courtesy of the amiable (and hearty) operators who motor the vehicles by foot. While you're in the garden, waddle on over to the Duckling sculpture where you can visit with Mrs. Mallard and her famous offspring. Or, be really adventurous, and take a walk in their webprints, via the Historic Neighborhoods Foundation's Make Way for Ducklings Tour.

Ride the T

Sure, it may not have the renown of the Cable Cars of San Francisco or the grit of the New York City Subway. But the "T," as it's known to the locals, is a must-do experience. The vehicles are pretty cool, emerging from their underground city holes to become suburban trolley cars. Kids will want to get a seat up front behind the driver where they can see all the action—and, don't forget to ask about Charlie.

FOR FREE

Boston may be a metropolis of fancy hotels and restaurants to match, but it's also a bastion of free stuff. The Freedom Trail alone has 13 sites that admit guests free of charge. Freebies include Faneuil Hall, the USS *Constitution* and the State House. Better yet, the latter has free 90-minute tours for visitors who'd like a guided walk, plus free MP3 tours (downloadable at ⊕*www.boston.com/travel/boston*) for high-tech-loving families who prefer to go it alone.

Additional theme routes—some scenic, some historic—include the Black Heritage Trail, the Irish Heritage Trail, and HarborWalk, and all can be enjoyed at no charge. Ditto for outdoor attractions like the city's major monuments, memorials, parks, and public gardens. Boston's to-die-for cemeteries (such as the Granary Burying Ground, a preferred resting place for patriots) also have no price tag attached.

If you're lucky enough to be in town for July 4, head over to the Esplanade, where the country's biggest celebration—featuring the Pops—is free of charge. Summer Fridays, look to the Hatch Shell for family movies under the Free Friday Flicks program.

For a free, scenic view of Boston, visit the patio at the Museum of Contemporary Art. The museum itself offers free admission on Thursday evenings. Other major sites also waive admission at set times, including the Museum of Fine Arts (Wednesday evenings). The Isabella Steward Gardner Museum, meanwhile, is always free for art lovers under 18—as well as for anyone who happens to be named Isabella. Friday evenings, admission into the Children's Museum can be had for $1 per person.

WHEN TO GO

Weather wise, late spring and fall are the optimal times to visit Boston. Aside from mild temperatures, the former boasts blooming gardens throughout the city; and the later (specifically from mid-September to early November) sees the surrounding countryside ablaze with brilliantly colored foliage. At both times, however, you should expect crowds. Autumn, for instance, draws hordes of hopeful leaf-peepers. Students must be factored into the mix as well. More than 250,000 of them flood into Boston and Cambridge each September; then pull out again in May and June. So hotels and restaurants, especially during move-in, move-out and graduation weekends, can be packed.

The good news is that this is a four-season destination. Summer brings sailboats to Boston Harbor, concerts to the Esplanade, and café tables to assorted sidewalks. It also brings the most reliable sunshine. If you're dreaming of a classic shore vacation, summer is prime. Of course, others also know this—which makes advance planning imperative.

Even winter has its pleasures. The cultural season heats up when it's cold, and Boston sports a festive glow over the holidays, thanks to the thousands of lights strung around the Common, Public Gar-

> ### QUICK FORECASTS
>
> Check the coded lights atop the Berkeley Building overlooking Copley Square: Steady blue means clear view; flashing blue, clouds due; steady red, rain ahead; flashing red, snow instead . . . except in baseball season when it means the Sox game is canceled!

den, and Commonwealth Avenue Mall. During the post-Christmas period, temperatures continue to fall. But penny pinchers will be pleased to know that lodging prices do, too.

Exploring
Boston

WORD OF MOUTH

". . . Walk over the pedestrian walk-way to the Charles River—kids get a kick out of walking 'over the highway' sometimes—and you can see the hatch shell, Museum of Science from there, and look down the other way to Longfellow Bridge, etc. It is fun just to walk along the Charles if weather is good."

—escargot

Updated
by Lisa
Oppen-
heimer

BOSTON'S A CITY OF MANY IMAGES. Sitcom fans may still think of it fondly as a charming, eccentric place with a little bar where everybody knows your name. Sports lovers know Boston for its diehard fans and champion teams such as the Red Sox, Celtics, and Patriots. History buffs know it for those other patriots, Colonial-era statesmen who helped spark the American Revolution. And then there's that accent, and all the talk about Hahvad Yahd (Harvard Yard) and paaking the cah (parking the car), which has caused legions of film stars to try (and mostly fail) to emulate the native tongue.

Beantown wears all forms of notoriety as a badge of honor. Numerous odes to the city's past are enmeshed in the region's present, from the building where colonists plotted the Boston Tea Party to the very spot where some of the first shots of the Revolution were fired. It's all easily accessible, with the most historic portions of the city so quaint and unspoiled, it's almost as if a corporate operator had moved in to create "Historic Boston: The Theme Park." History Hub-style might mean biking the path of the Minutemen or climbing in the footsteps of the man who signaled Paul Revere for his famous ride. Spring and summer finds famous patriots like Ben Franklin and Paul Revere "reincarnated" as tour guides. And, there's more— from museums, to art, sports, theater, and academia, Boston certainly offers enough landmarks, attractions, and history to hold your family in thrall for the entirety of your visit.

BEACON HILL & BOSTON COMMON

Gas lamps and 19th-century architecture are the draw of this lovely spot. There's history everywhere here, not to mention Beacon Hill's possible claim to Most Beautiful Neighborhood in the city. And for kids, there's nothing like the sprawling acreage of the Boston Common.

While Beacon Hill is home to the heart of the state legislature (the Massachusetts State House is at the top of the hill), the Common—so named because of its origin as common grazing ground for cattle—is a focal point of recreation. Here is where you'll find Bostonians catching some rays or jogging along the paths, while the littlest ones run around the on-site playground or dip piggies in the amphibian-less Frog Pond. History surrounds you. The State House, which offers free tours, looms large, and monuments to the city's grand past preside over the pathways. As for Beacon

TOP EXPERIENCES

Boston Common (bounded by Beacon, Charles, Tremont, and Park). A stroll through the park on any day finds Bostonians lost in conversation or mid-game tossing a Frisbee to human or canine.

Loews complex (175 Tremont Street). The place is a veritable theme park of movie going and though it's in Boston, there's something distinctly Hollywood about it.

Massachusetts State House (Beacon Street at Park Street). See your public servants in their natural habitat. The beautiful building with the large gold dome offers free weekday tours, but they must be scheduled in advance.

Old Town Trolley Tour. Touristy? Yes, but the guides are a font of information and the on/off privileges make getting around the city a snap.

Street itself, the redbrick elegance and narrow streets are so beautiful and well-preserved, you may think you've stumbled onto a 19th-century movie set.

A good place to begin an exploration of Beacon Hill is at the Boston Common Visitor Information Center *(⇨below)*, where you can buy a map or a complete guide to the Freedom Trail.

Ranger-led tours leave from the **National Park Service Visitor Center** (✉*15 State St.* ☎*617/242–5642* ⌨*www.nps.gov/bost* Ⓣ*State St.*) from mid-April through November.

PLANNING YOUR TIME

Beacon Hill, one of the more compact areas of Boston, can be explored in an afternoon; add an extra few hours if you wish to linger on the Common or in the shops on Charles Street, enjoy pizza and pastries, or tour the Black Heritage Trail. In winter the cobblestone streets can be difficult to navigate, but the neighborhood is especially pretty during the holidays—the Common is alive with Christmas lights, and on Christmas Eve carolers and bell ringers fill Louisburg Square. Other seasons bring other pleasures, from cherry blossoms on the Common in spring to free summer concerts on the nearby Esplanade.

Numbers in the margin correspond to the Beacon Hill &
Boston Common map.

WHERE CAN I FIND . . . IN BEACON HILL/ BOSTON COMMON?

A Quick Meal		
The Upper Crust	20 Charles Street	Yummy slices of pizza that you can smell from the street.

A Good Grocery Store		
Deluca's Market	11 Charles Street	The spot for your pâté, cheeses, or just good ol' milk and cookies.

Good Coffee		
Café Vanille	70 Charles Street	Large selection of delicious brews and tasty desserts.
Panificio Bakery	144 Charles Street	Cozy neighborhood hangout and old-fashioned Italian café. Goodies made on the premises.

A Fun Store		
The Red Wagon	69 Charles Street	Top-notch games, toys, and clothes for wee ones.

A Fun Playground		
Playground at Frog Pond	Boston Common	Ample sliding, climbing, and running around—what could be better?

A Clean Public Bathroom		
Visitor Information Center	147 Tremont Street	Dependable and free

WHAT TO SEE

★ Fodor'sChoice **Boston Common.** The oldest public park in the United States, Boston Common started as 50 acres where the freemen of Boston could graze their cattle. The **Central Burying Ground** (⊠*Boylston St. near Tremont, Beacon Hill* Ⓣ*Park St.*) is the final resting place of Tories and Patriots alike, as well as many British casualties of the Battle of Bunker Hill. The Burying Ground is open daily 9–5. On Tremont Street near Boylston stands the 1888 **Boston Massacre Memorial.** The Common's highest ground, near the park's Parkman Bandstand, was once called Flagstaff Hill. It's now surmounted by the **Soldiers and Sailors Monument,** honoring Civil War troops. The Common's only body of water is the **Frog Pond,** a tame and frog-free concrete depression used as a children's wading pool during steamy summer days and for ice-skating in winter. It marks the original site of a natural pond that inspired Edgar Allan Poe to call Bostonians "Frogpondians."

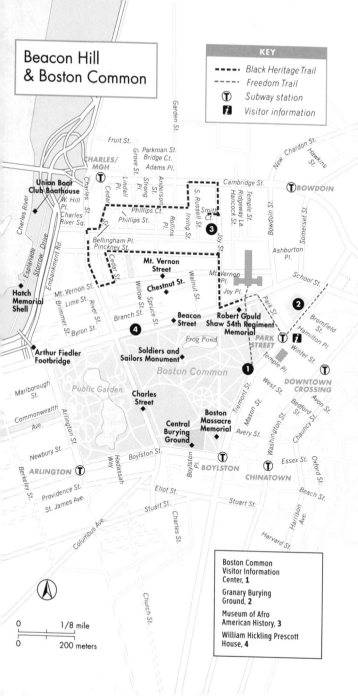

Beacon Hill
& Boston Common

KEY

- - - - Black Heritage Trail
- - - - Freedom Trail
(T) Subway station
(i) Visitor information

Garden St.

Fruit St.
New Chardon St.
Hawkins St.

CHARLES/ MGH

Parkman St.
Bridge Ct.
Adams Pl.

(T) BOWDOIN

Charles St.
W. Hill Pl.

Grove St.
Lindall Pl.
Anderson St.
Strong Pl.
S. Russell St.

Cambridge St.
Temple St.
Ridgeway La.
Hancock St.
New Hancock St.
Bowdoin St.
Somerset St.

Union Boat Club Boathouse

Charles River Sq.

Cedar St.
Phillips Ct.
Phillips St.
Rollins Pl.
Irving St.
Smith Ct.
Joy St.

③

Ashburton Pl.

Charles River

Esplanade

Bellingham Pl.
Pinckney St.
Cedar St.

School St.

Storrow Drive

Embankment Rd.

Mt. Vernon St.
Lime St.
River St.
Byron St.

Mt. Vernon Street

Chestnut St.

Willow St.
Spruce St.
Walnut St.

Mt. Vernon Pl.
Joy Pl.

Bromfield St.
Hamilton Pl.

Hatch Memorial Shell

②

Brimmer St.

Branch St.

Beacon Street

④

Robert Gould Shaw 54th Regiment Memorial

Park St.

(T) PARK STREET

(i)
Winter St.

Arthur Fiedler Footbridge

Soldiers and Sailors Monument

Frog Pond

①

Temple Pl.

DOWNTOWN CROSSING

(T)

Boston Common

Public Garden

West St.
Mason St.

Avon St.
Bedford St.
Chauncy St.

Marlborough St.

Charles Street

Tremont St.
Washington St.

Commonwealth Ave.

Charles Street

Central Burying Ground

Boston Massacre Memorial

Avery St.

Essex St.
Oxford St.

Newbury St.
Berkeley St.

Arlington St.
Hadassah Way

Boylston St.

Boston Pl.
Boylston St.

(T) BOYLSTON

CHINATOWN

Beach St.

(T) ARLINGTON

Providence St.
St. James Ave.

Eliot St.

Stuart St.

Harrison Ave.

Columbus Ave.

Stuart St.

Charles St.

Church St.

Harvard St.

N

0   1/8 mile
0   200 meters

Boston Common
Visitor Information
Center, 1

Granary Burying
Ground, 2

Museum of Afro
American History, 3

William Hickling Prescott
House, 4

On the Beacon Street side of the Common sits the splendidly restored **Robert Gould Shaw 54th Regiment Memorial**. It commemorates the 54th Massachusetts Regiment, the first Civil War unit made up of free blacks, led by the young Brahmin Robert Gould Shaw. He and half of his troops died in an assault on South Carolina's Fort Wagner; their story inspired the 1989 movie *Glory*. This magnificent memorial makes a fitting first stop on the Black Heritage Trail (⇨ *"The Black Heritage Trail" box, below*). Historic significance aside, the Common has plenty of room to simply throw a ball or push a stroller. Climbing, sliding, and playing in the sand are the inherent joys of the good-size playground near Frog Pond. ✉*Bounded by Beacon, Charles, Tremont, and Park Sts., Beacon Hill* Ⓣ*Park St.* All ages

❶ **Boston Common Visitor Information Center.** This center, run by the Greater Boston Convention and Visitors Bureau, is on the Tremont Street side of Boston Common. It's well supplied with stacks of free pamphlets about Boston, including a useful guide to the Freedom Trail, which begins in the Common. This is the place to pick up the Greater Boston Convention & Visitors Bureau's inexpensive ($1.50) and indispensable *Kids Love Boston* book. ✉*147 Tremont St., Beacon Hill* ☎*888/733–2678* ⊕*www.bostonusa.com* ☉*Weekdays 8:30–5, weekends 9–5* Ⓣ*Park St.* All ages

❷ **Granary Burying Ground.** If you found a resting place here at the Old Granary, as it's called, chances are your headstone would have been impressively ornamented with skeletons and winged skulls. Your neighbors would have been impressive, too: among them Samuel Adams, John Hancock, Benjamin Franklin's parents, and Paul Revere. As cemeteries go, this one is particularly cool, made more cool by the fact that it's home to Elizabeth Veroose, the woman widely considered to be Mother Goose. ✉*Entrance on Tremont St., Beacon Hill* ☉*Daily 9–5* Ⓣ*Park St.* 9 + up

★ Fodor'sChoice **Museum of African American History.** Ever since
❸ runaway slave Crispus Attucks became one of the famous victims of the Boston Massacre of 1770, the African-American community of Boston has played an important part in the city's history. The Museum of African American History was established in 1964 to promote this history. The umbrella organization includes a trio of historic sites: the Abiel Smith School; the African Meeting House; and the African Meeting House on the island of Nantucket, off the coast of Cape Cod. Park Service personnel lead tours of the

THE FREEDOM TRAIL

More than a route of historic sites, the Freedom Trail is a 2½-mi walk into history, bringing to life the events that exploded on the world during the Revolution. Follow the route marked on your maps, and keep an eye on the sidewalk for the red stripe that marks the trail. Kids can make the adventure more entertaining by picking up a free *Junior Ranger Activity Book* from visitor centers either at 15 State Street (near the Old State House) or in the Charlestown Navy Yard. Each has activities and questions, plus spaces to collect stamps from historic locations. You can also sign on for the privately run **Boston By Little Feet Freedom Trail** tour (*617/367–2345*).

It takes a full day to complete the entire route comfortably. The trail lacks the multimedia bells and whistles that are quickly becoming the norm at historic attractions, but on the Freedom Trail, history speaks for itself. When you're finished head to the Charlestown water shuttle, which goes directly to the Downtown area, and congratulate yourself: you've just completed a unique crash course in American history.

Black Heritage Trail starting from the Shaw Memorial. The museum is the site of activities, including lectures, children's storytelling, and concerts focusing on black composers. ⊠*46 Joy St., Beacon Hill* ☎*617/725–0022* ⊕*www.afroam museum.org* ⊡*Free, $5 suggested donation* ☉*Mon.–Sat. 10–4* Ⓣ*Charles/MGH.* 9 + up

❹ **William Hickling Prescott House.** A modest but engaging house museum has been installed in this 1808 Federal structure. Now the headquarters for the Massachusetts Society of Colonial Dames of America, the house was the home of noted historian William Hickling Prescott from 1845 to 1859, with period furniture, including the former study with Prescott's desk and "noctograph," which helped the nearly blind scholar write. (He was blinded in one eye by a flying crust of bread during a food fight at Harvard.) The house also has a fine costume collection. Of all local house tours, this is the most accessible way to introduce kids to local architecture. Tours range from about 30 to 45 minutes, but amiable tour guides will tailor the experience to suit young attentions spans. ⊠*55 Beacon St., Beacon Hill* ☎*617/742–3190* ⊕*www.nscda.org/ma/william_hickling_ prescott_house.htm* ⊡*$5* ☉*Tours May–Oct., Wed., Thurs., and Sat. noon–4* Ⓣ*Park St., Charles/MGH.* 12 + up

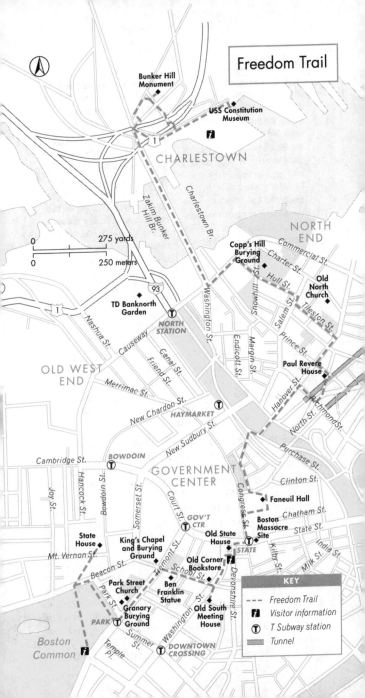

TOP OLD WEST END EXPERIENCES

Charles River. Stand atop the footbridge over Storrow Drive and watch the boats—on a sunny day the river teems with all sorts of watercraft, making it one of the most beautiful sights in the city. Or take a stroll along the banks of the Charles. You'll be in good company alongside moms with strollers, business folks on a jog, and hundreds of university students out running with their teams and classmates.

Museum of Science. Tinker with all the cool gizmos. Make a day of it and stop by the Planetarium, the Imax Theater, and the aptly named Science Playground.

Sports Museum of New England. Check out the shoe that launched the New England Patriots into history. If you come early on a game day, you might just catch a basketball or hockey team warming up.

THE OLD WEST END

Just a few decades ago, this district resembled a typical medieval city. The biggest surviving structures in the Old West End with any real history are two public institutions, Massachusetts General Hospital and the former Suffolk County Jail, which dates from 1849 and was designed by Gridley Bryant. The onetime prison is now part of the luxurious, and wryly named, Liberty Hotel.

Behind Massachusetts General and the sprawling Charles River Park apartment complex is a small grid of streets recalling an older Boston. In addition to the TD Banknorth Garden (home away from home for loyal Celtics and Bruins fans), the innovative Museum of Science is one of the more modern attractions of the Old West End. The newest addition to the area's skyline is the Leonard P. Zakim Bunker Hill Bridge, which spans the Charles River just across from the TD Banknorth Garden.

Numbers correspond to the Old West End map.

WHAT TO SEE

❷ **Leonard P. Zakim Bunker Hill Bridge.** Dedicated in October 2002, the Zakim Bridge is the newest Boston landmark, part of the "Big Dig" construction project. The 1,432-foot-long bridge, designed by Swiss bridge architect Christian Menn, is the widest cable-stayed hybrid bridge ever built and the first to use an asymmetrical design. One of the best spots to view the bridge is from the Charlestown waterfront across the river. The best viewing is at night, when the illuminated bridge glows blue. ⊠*Old West End.* All ages

WHERE CAN I FIND . . . IN OLD WEST END?

A Quick Meal		
Finagle a bagel	277 Cambridge Street	Mass General employees throng here for their quick supply of a bagel and all the fixings.
A Good Grocery Store		
Whole Foods Market	161 Cambridge Street	Dependable, if a bit pricey, chain with all your staples, plus prepared foods, and a place to eat them.
Good Coffee		
Au Bon Pain	242 Cambridge Street	Come to the Boston-launched chain for the coffee, but stay for a chocolate or raisin croissant.
A Fun Store		
The Pro Shop	TD Banknorth Garden, 100 Legends Way	All your sports-team gear, plus memories of the old, beloved Boston Garden.
A Public Bathroom		
Massachusetts General Hospital	55 Fruit Street	Basic bathrooms are on the first floor of this world-famous hospital.

★ Fodor'sChoice **Museum of Science.** With 15-foot lightning bolts
❸ in the Theater of Electricity and a 20-foot-long *Tyrannosaurus rex* model, this is just the place to ignite any child's scientific curiosity. More than 550 exhibits cover astronomy, astrophysics, anthropology, progress in medicine, computers, the organic and inorganic earth sciences, and much more. The emphasis is on hands-on education. In the "Science in the Park" exhibit, for example, children can learn the physics behind everyday play activities such as swinging and bumping up and down on a teeter-totter.

The **Charles Hayden Planetarium** (☎617/723–2500) produces exciting programs on astronomical discoveries. Laser light shows, with laser graphics and computer animation, are scheduled Thursday through Sunday evenings. The shows are best for children older than five. Admission to the planetarium is $4 if you paid the admission for the museum and $9 for the planetarium alone. The **Mugar Omni Theater** (☎617/723–2500) five-story dome screen allows the

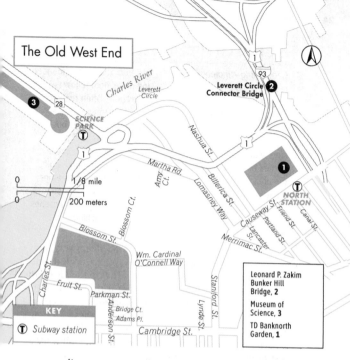

The Old West End

Charles River

Leverett Circle

Leverett Circle Connector Bridge **2**

3

28

SCIENCE PARK Ⓣ

Nashua St.

1

Martha Rd.

Amy Ct.

Billerica St.

Lonasney Way

Ⓣ NORTH STATION

Causeway St.

Friend St.

Portland St.

Canal St.

Lancaster St.

Merrimac St.

0   1/8 mile
0   200 meters

Blossom Ct.

Blossom St.

Wm. Cardinal O'Connell Way

Stanford St.

Charles St.

Fruit St.

Parkman St.

Anderson St.

Bridge Ct.

Adams Pl.

Lynde St.

Cambridge St.

> Leonard P. Zakim Bunker Hill Bridge, **2**
>
> Museum of Science, **3**
>
> TD Banknorth Garden, **1**

KEY

Ⓣ Subway station

---

audience to practically experience the action on screen. Try to get tickets in advance online or over the phone. Admission for shows is $9 (or $4 if you paid the admission for the museum). Call or check the museum's Web site for showtimes. ⊠*Science Park at Charles River Dam, Old West End* ☎*617/723–2500* ⊕*www.mos.org* ⊠*Exhibit halls, $19 ages 12 and up, $16 children 3–11* ⊙*July 5–Labor Day, Sat.–Thurs. 9–7, Fri. 9–9; after Labor Day–July 4, Sat.–Thurs. 9–5, Fri. 9–9* ⓉScience Park. All Ages

FRUGAL FUN. Take a cue from locals and sign up for one of the Boston Park Rangers' programs. Top picks include a visit to the city stables to meet the Mounties and their horses, regularly scheduled readings of Robert McCloskey's *Make Way for Ducklings* in Boston's Public Garden, and city scavenger hunts geared for families. Contact Boston Parks and Recreation (☎ 617/635–7487 ⊕www.cityofboston.gov/parks).

❶ **TD Banknorth Garden.** Diehards still moan about the loss of the old Boston Garden. A decade after it opened as the FleetCenter, the home of the Celtics (basketball) and Bruins

HIGH-TECH HIDE & SEEK

Geocaching—finding hidden caches using GPS coordinates posted on the Web—is a fun way to explore a neighborhood, and it turns out that Boston is full of buried treasure with more than 3,900 caches hidden throughout the area.

What's in a cache? There's always a logbook with information from the cache's founder, and notes from fellow discoverers. Often the cache contains a small treasure, anything from maps, books, jewelry, games, and more. We know one lucky cache discoverer who found a gift certificate to one of the finest restaurants in Boston. Get coordinates for Boston caches at www.geocaching.com.

(hockey) is once again known as the Garden. Okay, so it's got the name of a bank attached now, but to locals it's once again just the good old "Gah-den." The original is fondly remembered as the playing grounds for the likes of Larry Bird and Bobby Orr. The Garden occasionally offers public skating sessions in the winter months; call ahead for hours and prices. The fifth and sixth levels of the TD Banknorth Garden house the **Sports Museum of New England** (✉*Use west premium seating entrance* ☎*617/624–1234* ⊕*www. sportsmuseum.org*), where displays of memorabilia and photographs showcase the history and the legends behind Boston's obsession with sports. Take a behind-the-scenes tour of locker and interview rooms in the off-season, or test your sports knowledge with interactive games. You can even see how you stand up to life-size statues of sports heroes Carl Yastrzemski and Larry Bird. The museum is open daily 11–5, with admission allowed only on the hour. Last entrance is at 3 PM on most days, 2 PM on game days; admission is $6. The sports museum is closed on rare matinee-game days. Come early on the day of a night game (around 10:30 AM) and you may spot teams conducting their practice shoot- or skate-arounds. ✉*Causeway St. at Canal St., Old West End* ☎*617/624–1000* ⊕*www.tdbank northgarden.com* Ⓣ*North Station.* 9 + up

TOP GOVERNMENT CENTER EXPERIENCES

Faneuil Hall. The two-story venue practically echoes with past voices of Revolutionary War leaders.

Haymarket. It's smelly, it's chaotic and totally nutty. And, that's exactly why you should stick around with the kids and watch the spectacle.

Quincy Marketplace. Stroll through the food with chowda, zuppa, and everything in between. The aromas alone are worth the visit. Be sure to take in a street show between Faneuil Hall and Quincy Market. Sure, it looks like a day-long audition for America's Got Talent. But, once you stop and watch, you'll realize why everybody's smiling.

GOVERNMENT CENTER

Government Center contains some of the bleakest architecture since the advent of poured concrete. But the expanse is enlivened by feisty political rallies, free summer concerts, and the occasional festival. Kids will at least get a kick out of the local landmark Steaming Kettle, a gilded kettle cast in 1873 that once boiled around the clock. (It now marks a Starbucks.) But the big draw is just a little farther on: 18th-century Faneuil Hall and the frenzied Quincy Market where you can shop, eat, and be entertained to your heart's content.

Numbers correspond to the Government Center & the North End map.

WHAT TO SEE

★ ❶ **Faneuil Hall.** The single building facing Congress Street is the real Faneuil Hall, though locals often give that name to all five buildings in this shopping complex. Bostonians pronounce it *Fan*-yoo'uhl or *Fan*-yuhl. Like other Boston landmarks, Faneuil Hall has evolved over many years. It was erected in 1742, the gift of wealthy merchant Peter Faneuil, who wanted the hall to serve as both a place for town meetings and a public market. It burned in 1761 and was immediately reconstructed according to the original plan of its designer.

In 1772 Samuel Adams stood here and first suggested that Massachusetts and the other colonies organize a Committee of Correspondence against a hardening British repression. Faneuil Hall was substantially enlarged and remodeled

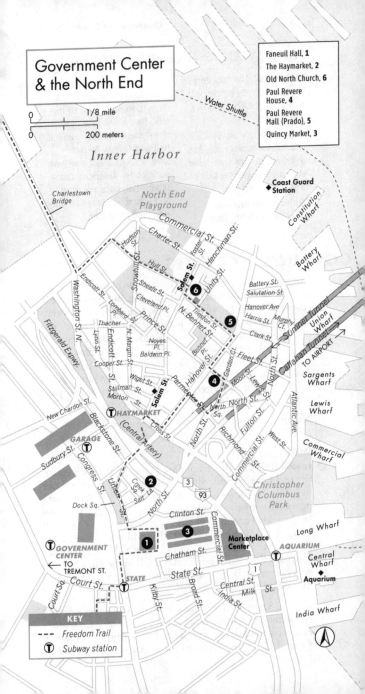

Government Center & the North End

Faneuil Hall, 1
The Haymarket, 2
Old North Church, 6
Paul Revere House, 4
Paul Revere Mall (Prado), 5
Quincy Market, 3

Inner Harbor

Water Shuttle

Charlestown Bridge

Coast Guard Station

North End Playground

Constitution Wharf

Commercial St.

Battery Wharf

Charter St.

Hudson St.

Hull St.

Snowhill St.

Foster St.

Henchman St.

Salem St.

Unity St.

6

Sheafe St.

Cleveland Pl.

Prince St.

N. Bennet St.

Tileston St.

Battery St.
Salutation St.

Murphy Ct.

Hanover Ave

Harris St.

5

Clark St.

Sumner Tunnel

Union Wharf

Callahan Tunnel

TO AIRPORT

Endicott St.

Lombard St.

Thacher St.

Lynn St.

N. Margin St.

Endicott St.

Cooper St.

Noyes Pl.

Baldwin Pl.

Bennet Pl.

Fleet St.

Garden Ct.

Moon St.

North St.

Lewis St.

Sargents Wharf

Wiget St.

Stillman St.

Morton St.

Salem St.

Parmenter St.

Hanover St.

4

North Sq.

Fulton St.

Atlantic Ave.

Lewis Wharf

Commercial Wharf

Washington St. N.

Fitzgerald Expwy.

New Chardon St.

Blackstone St.

GARAGE

Sudbury St.

Congress St.

HAYMARKET (Central Artery)

Cross St.

North St.

North St.

Richmond St.

Commercial St.

West St.

Christopher Columbus Park

Union St.

2

Creek Sq.

Salt La.

North St.

3

93

Clinton St.

Commercial St.

Long Wharf

Dock Sq.

1

3

Marketplace Center

AQUARIUM

Chatham St.

State St.

Central Wharf

GOVERNMENT CENTER

TO TREMONT ST.

STATE

Court Sq.

Court St.

Kilby St.

Broad St.

Central St.

India St.

Milk St.

1

Aquarium

India Wharf

KEY
- - - Freedom Trail
Ⓣ Subway station

0 ——— 1/8 mile
0 ——— 200 meters

THE STORY BEHIND THE GRASSHOPPER

Why is the gold-plated weather vane atop Faneuil Hall's cupola in the shape of a grasshopper? One apocryphal story has it that Sir Thomas Gresham—founder of London's Royal Exchange—was discovered in a field in 1519 as a babe by children chasing grasshoppers. He later placed a gilded metal version of the insect over the Exchange to commemorate his salvation. Years later Peter Faneuil admired the critter (a symbol of good luck) and had a model of it mounted over Faneuil Hall. The 8-pound, 52-inch-long grasshopper is the only unmodified part of the original structure.

in 1805. Park rangers give informational talks about the history and importance of the structure on the hour and half hour. The rangers are a good resource, as interpretive plaques are few. On the building's top floors are the headquarters and museum of the **Ancient & Honorable Artillery Company of Massachusetts** (☎617/227–1638), the oldest militia in the Western Hemisphere, and the third oldest in the world. The shops at ground level sell New England bric-a-brac. When visiting with kids, it might be tempting to skip the trip upstairs to the Hall and go straight to the shopping and eating downstairs and next door. But, the great hall is one of those historic gems that breathes its past. Even the kids will get it. Definitely worth the time. Be advised, however, that the Hall is used for myriad purposes and is occasionally closed for special events. ⊠*Faneuil Hall Sq., Government Center* ☎617/242–5690 ⊕*www.cityof boston.gov/freedomtrail/faneuilhall.asp* ⊡*Free* ⊙*Great Hall daily 9–5; informational talks every ½ hr. Shops Mon.–Sat. 10–9, Sun. noon–6.* ⊤*Government Center, Aquarium, State.* 9 + up

❷ **The Haymarket.** Loud, self-promoting vendors pack this exuberant maze of a marketplace at Marshall and Blackstone streets on Friday and Saturday from 7 AM until midafternoon (all vendors will likely be gone by 5 at the latest). Pushcart vendors hawk fruits and vegetables against a backdrop of fish, meat, and cheese shops. The accumulation of debris left every evening has been celebrated in a whimsical 1976 public-arts project—Mags Harries's *Asaroton,* a Greek word meaning "unswept floors"—consisting of bronze fruit peels and other detritus smashed into the pavement. Another Harries piece, a bronze depiction of a gathering of stray gloves, tumbles down between the escalators in the Porter Square T station in Cambridge.

At Creek Square, near the Haymarket, is the **Boston Stone.** Set into the brick wall of the gift shop of the same name, this was a marker long used as milepost zero in measuring distances from Boston. It's not your traditional tourist attraction, but Haymarket is a local oddity that's a kick to see (and smell). Just keep a close eye on kids as the place is definitely chaotic. ✉*Marshall and Blackstone Sts., Government Center* ☉*Fri. and Sat. 7 AM–mid-afternoon.* 9 + up

❸ **Quincy Market.** Not everyone likes Quincy Market. Some people prefer grit to polish. But there's no denying that this pioneer effort has brought tremendous vitality to a once-tired corner of Boston. The market consists of three block-long annexes: **Quincy Market, North Market,** and **South Market,** each 535 feet long and across a plaza from Faneuil Hall. The central structure has kept its traditional market-stall layout, but the stalls now purvey international and specialty foods: sushi, frozen yogurt, bagels, calzones, sausage-on-a-stick, Chinese noodles, barbecue, and baklava, plus all the boutique chocolate-chip cookies your heart desires. This is perhaps Boston's best locale for grazing; the hardest part is choosing what to sample.

Along the arcades on either side of the Central Market are vendors selling sweatshirts, photographs of Boston, and arts and crafts—some schlocky, some not—along with a couple of patioed bars and restaurants. The North and South markets house a mixture of chain stores and specialty boutiques. Quintessential Boston remains here only in Durgin Park, opened in 1826 and known for its plain interior, brassy waitresses, and large portions of traditional New England fare.

At Christmastime, trees along the cobblestone walks are strung with thousands of sparkling lights. In summer, up to 50,000 people a day descend on the market; the outdoor cafés are an excellent spot to watch the hordes if you can find a seat. Year-round the pedestrian walkways draw street performers, and rings of strollers form around magicians and musicians. With roughly 40 acts, there's bound to be performers here on any summer day. Special events take place for St. Patrick's Day and during the winter holidays. You can get a schedule of events and street performers by calling the Faneuil Hall Events Line (☎617/523–1300). Twenty-minute horse-and-carriage tours (for hire at North and Clinton streets) are another old-fashioned, albeit pricey ($35) diversion. On Congress Street, look for the graceful Holocaust Memorial. ⊠*Bordered by Clinton, Commercial, and Chatham Sts., Government Center* ☎*617/523–1300* ⊕*www.faneuilhallmarketplace.com* ⊙*Mon.–Sat. 10–9, Sun. noon–6. Restaurants and bars generally open daily 11 AM–2 AM; food stalls open earlier* ⊤*Government Center, Aquarium, State.* All ages

THE NORTH END

The warren of small streets on the northeast side of Government Center is the North End, Boston's Little Italy. In the 17th century the North End *was* Boston, as much of the rest of the peninsula was still under water or had yet to be cleared. It's now a charming neighborhood—and oh, the aromas! Strolling along the thoroughfares dotted with intimate eateries and outdoor courtyards, it's a challenge to choose between fresh pastas, delicious cannoli and ice-cold gelato.

This is Boston's haven not only for Italian restaurants but also for Italian groceries, bakeries, boccie courts, churches, social clubs, cafés, and street-corner debates over home-team soccer games. ■TIP→ **July and August are highlighted by a series of street festivals, or feste, honoring various saints, and by local community events that draw people from all over the city.** A statue of St. Agrippina di Mineo—which is covered with money when it's paraded through the streets—is a crowd favorite.

Although hordes of tourists follow the redbrick ribbon of the Freedom Trail through the North End, the jumbled streets retain a neighborhood feeling, from the grandmothers gossiping on fire escapes to the laundry strung on back porches. Linger for a moment along Salem or Hanover streets, and you can still hear people speaking with Abruzzese accents.

PLANNING YOUR TIME

Allow two hours for a walk through the North End. This part of town is made for strolling, day or night. Many people like to spend part of a day at nearby Quincy Market, then head over to the North End for dinner—the district has an impressive selection of traditional and contemporary Italian restaurants. Families should note that on Saturday afternoons from May through October the Paul Revere

LET FREEBIES RING

Freedom may not be free, but Boston's Freedom Trail is—and so are 13 of the 16 attractions that lie along its path, including Faneuil Hall, the USS *Constitution,* and the State House. Better yet, there are free 90-minute tours for visitors who'd like a guided walk, plus free MP3 tours (downloadable at ⊕ *www.boston.com/travel/ boston*) for those preferring to go it alone.

Additional theme routes—most notably the Black Heritage Trail, the Irish Heritage Trail, and HarborWalk—can also be enjoyed at no charge. Ditto for outdoor attractions like the city's major monuments, memorials, parks, and public gardens. Boston's to-die-for cemeteries (such as the Granary Burying Ground, a preferred resting place for patriots) also have no price tag attached.

Frugal souls can even take complimentary tours of the Boston Athenaeum, the Boston Public Library, and Trinity Church (one of the country's "architectural gems"). October through May, Symphony Hall offers guided tours, too: Boston Pops tickets can be pretty pricey, but every Wednesday afternoon you can see inside their sublime home base without spending a cent.

Other major sites waive admission at set times: among them, the Institute of Contemporary Art (Thursday evening); the Museum of Fine Arts (Wednesday evening); and the Harvard art museums (Saturday morning and every day after 4:30). The Isabella Stewart Gardner Museum, meanwhile, is always free for art lovers under 18—as well as for anyone who happens to be named Isabella!

House schedules some of the most delightful events for children in the city. And on Sunday, try to catch the ringing of the bells of the Old North Church after the 11 AM service; Paul Revere rang them on Sabbath mornings as a boy.

Numbers correspond to the Government Center & the North End map.

WHAT TO SEE

❻ **Old North Church.** Standing at one end of the **Paul Revere Mall** is a church famous not only for being the oldest one in Boston (built in 1723) but for housing the two lanterns that glimmered from its steeple on the night of April 18, 1775. This is where Paul Revere and the young sexton Robert Newman managed to signal the departure by water of the British regulars to Lexington and Concord. Newman, carrying the lanterns, ascended the steeple (the original tower blew down in 1804 and was replaced; the present one was put up in 1954 after the replacement was destroyed in a hurricane) while Revere began his clandestine trip by boat across the Charles.

Guests are welcome year-round, but the best time to visit is June to October, when the Behind the Scenes program is running. Tour guides lead you down to the church crypts, where more than 1,000 people—mostly original church members—are interred. Then you travel two flights up to the bell tower, where those famous lanterns were hung. Mr. Revere himself appears in the family-friendly "Paul Revere Tonight," a one-hour nighttime show performed Friday nights at 8 from July through October. Sunday, ask about watching the ringing of the bells, the oldest peal in North America. ✉193 Salem St., North End ☎617/523–6676 ⊕www.oldnorth.com ☉Daily 9–5. Sun. services at 9 and 11 AM Ⓣ Haymarket, North Station. 9 + up

❹ Paul Revere House. It's an interesting coincidence that the oldest house standing in downtown Boston should also have been the home of Paul Revere, as many homes of famous Bostonians have burned or been demolished over the years. Revere owned it from 1770 until 1800, although he lived there for only 10 years and rented it out for the next two decades. Special events are scheduled throughout the year, many designed with children in mind. During the first weekend in December, the staff dresses in period costume and serves apple-cider cake and other Colonial-era goodies. From May through October, you might encounter a silver-smith practicing his trade, a dulcimer player entertaining a crowd, or a military-reenactment group in full period regalia. And if you go to the house on Patriots' Day, chances are you'll bump into a fife-and-drum corps. Family-friendly activities take place most Saturdays throughout the year, as well as during many school-vacation weeks. Be sure to ask about the house's stock of period clothes. On quieter days, staff are often able to take out the authentically reproduced duds—britches and shifts—and allow kids to try them on. ✉19 North Sq., North End ☎617/523–2338 ⊕www.paulreverehouse.org ☜$3 adults, $1 children 5–17 ☉Jan.–Mar., Tues.–Sun. 9:30–4:15; Nov. and Dec., and 1st 2 wks of Apr., daily 9:30–4:15; mid-Apr.–Oct., daily 9:30–5:15 Ⓣ Haymarket, Aquarium, Government Center. 9 + up

A STICKY SUBJECT

Boston has had its share of grim historic events, from massacres to stranglers, but on the sheer weirdness scale, nothing beats the Great Molasses Flood. In 1919, a steel container of molasses exploded on the Boston Harbor waterfront, killing 21 people and 20 horses. More than 2.3 million gallons of goo oozed onto the unsuspecting citizenry, a veritable tsunami of sweet stuff. Some say you can still smell molasses on the waterfront during steamy weather; smells to us like urban myth!

WHERE CAN I FIND . . . IN NORTH END?

A Quick Meal

Tutto Italiano	20 Fleet Street	An Italian grocer and a place to get fresh-baked focaccia and sandwiches to go.
Bova's Bakery	134 Salem Street	A neighborhood institution. Takeaway Italian breads, calzones, and pastries, 24 hours a day.
Mike's Pastry	300 Hanover Street	Great cappuccino for you; a variety of gelato, cookies, and cakes for the kids.

A Good Grocery Store

Fresh Cheese Shop	81 Endicott Street	Authentic Italian spot, right down to its fresh mozzarella.

Good Coffee

Mike's Pastry	300 Hanover Street	The cappuccino's one reason to come. The cases of cookies, cannoli, you name it, is the other.
Polcari's	105 Salem Street	A local haunt with every kind of coffee and every kind of gadget to go with it.

A Fun Store

Prima Donna	30 Prince Street	Fun stuff here includes cannoli for your dog, plus gifts for kids, moms, and dads.

A Good Playground

Eliot School Playground	16 Charter Street	It's part of a public school, so hours are limited to after school and weekends.

❺ Paul Revere Mall (*Prado*). This makes a perfect time-out spot from the Freedom Trail. Bookended by two landmark churches—Old North and St. Stephen's—the mall is flanked by brick walls lined with bronze plaques bearing the stories of famous North Enders as well as the equestrian **statue of Paul Revere.** The quiet ambience borders on reverence, but it's an awfully nice place to grab a seat and nosh on a cannoli. Older kids could spend hours roaming around reading the placards. Younger kids will notice the playground off to one side; it's a public school to which there's no direct entry. You'll have to travel outside the Mall to access it via Charter Street. ⊠*Bordered by Tileston, Hanover, and Unity Sts., North End* Ⓣ*Haymarket, Aquarium, Government Center.* All ages

Salem Street. This ancient and constricted thoroughfare, one of the two main North End streets, cuts through the heart of the neighborhood and runs parallel to and one block west of Hanover. Between Cross and Prince streets, Salem Street contains numerous restaurants and shops. One of the best is Shake the Tree, one of the North End's trendiest boutiques, selling stylish clothing, gifts, and jewelry. The rest of Salem Street is mostly residential, but makes a nice walk to the Copp's Hill Burying Ground.

CHARLESTOWN

Half the fun of this historic plot of land is getting here. You could use foot power over the Charlestown Bridge, or the 93 Bus from Haymarket. For kids, the only way to go is via MBTA water shuttle, a regular service from downtown Boston's Long Wharf (it runs about every 15 or 30 minutes) that makes the whole adventure seem like part of a theme park. Charlestown itself is its own historical wonderland, a place marked by two of the most visible monuments in Boston: the Bunker Hill Monument, which commemorates the grisly battle that became a symbol of patriotic resistance against the British, and the USS *Constitution*, whose masts continue to tower over the waterfront where she was built more than 200 years ago.

PLANNING YOUR TIME

Give yourself two to three hours for a Charlestown walk; the lengthy Charlestown Bridge calls for endurance in cold weather. You may want to save Charlestown's stretch of the Freedom Trail, which adds considerably to its length, for a second-day outing. You can always avoid retracing

TOP CHARLESTOWN EXPERIENCES

Bunker Hill Monument. Hiking up the 294 stairs to the top is great exercise, and you'll get a little Revolutionary War insight as to why this plot of land was so valuable. In summer stick around for a musket-firing demonstration.

USS *Constitution.* When your kids go below deck and see just how small the space is that up to 200 men shared for 12 months, they may gain a new appreciation for their rooms. At the museum you'll get the lowdown on exactly how these ships prepared for and fought in battles.

your steps on the historic route by taking the MBTA water shuttle, which ferries back and forth between Charlestown's Navy Yard and downtown Boston's Long Wharf.

Numbers correspond to the Charlestown map.

WHAT TO SEE

★ Fodor'sChoice **Bunker Hill Monument.** The Battle of Bunker Hill
④ was actually fought on Breed's Hill, which is where the monument sits today. (The real Bunker Hill is about ½ mi to the north of the monument; it's slightly taller than Breed's Hill.) Bunker was the original planned locale for the battle, and for that reason its name stuck.

In 1823 the committee formed to construct a monument on the site of the battle chose the form of a 221-foot-tall granite obelisk, a tremendous feat of engineering for its day. The monument's zenith is reached by a flight of 294 steps. There's no elevator, but the views from the observatory are worth the effort of the arduous climb. A statue of Colonel Prescott stands guard at the base. In the Bunker Hill Museum across the street, artifacts and exhibits tell the story of the battle, while a detailed diorama shows the action in miniature. Children under 14 need to be accompanied up the stairs by an adult. National Park Service rangers often give talks (roughly 15 minutes each) on the historic encounter and are always available to answer questions. June through August, ask about the schedule of musket-firing demonstrations. ✉43 *Monument Sq., Charlestown* ☎617/242–5641 ⊕*www.nps.gov/bost/historyculture/bhm. htm.* ☞*Free* ☉*Museum daily 9–5, monument daily 9–4:30* Ⓣ*Community College.* 9 + up

① **Charlestown Navy Yard.** A National Park Service Historic Site since it was decommissioned in 1974, the Charlestown

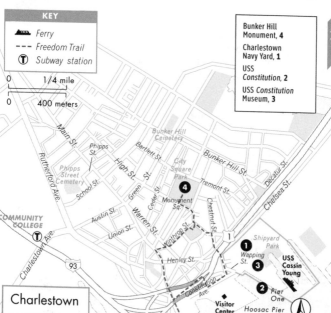

KEY

🚢 Ferry
--- Freedom Trail
Ⓣ Subway station

Bunker Hill
Monument, **4**
Charlestown
Navy Yard, **1**
USS
Constitution, **2**
USS *Constitution*
Museum, **3**

Charlestown

Navy Yard was one of six established to build warships.
Here are early 19th-century barracks, workshops, and
officers' quarters; a ropewalk (an elongated building for
making rope, not open to the public) used by the navy to
turn out cordage for more than 125 years; and one of the
oldest operational naval dry docks in the United States. The
USS *Constitution* was the first to use this dry dock, in 1833.
In addition to the ship itself, check out the *Constitution*
Museum, the collections of the Boston Marine Society, and
the USS *Cassin Young*, a World War II destroyer typical
of the ships built here during that era. ⊠ *55 Constitution
Rd., Charlestown* ☎ *617/242–5601* ⊕ *www.nps.gov/bost/
historyculture/cny.htm* 🎫 *Free* ⊙ *Visitors Information Center daily 9–5* Ⓣ *North Station; MBTA Bus 92 to Charlestown City Sq. or Bus 93 to Chelsea St. from Haymarket;
or Boston Harbor Cruise water shuttle from Long Wharf
to Pier 4.* 5 + up

USS *Cassin Young*. Built long after the *Constitution*, this
destroyer saw action in Asian waters during World War II.
She served the navy until 1960. ⊠ *Charlestown Navy Yard,
55 Constitution Rd., Charlestown* ☎ *617/242–5601 www.*

A GOOD WALK

If you choose to hoof it to Charlestown, follow Hull Street from Copp's Hill Burying Ground to Commercial Street; turn left on Commercial and, two blocks later, right onto the bridge. The entrance to the **Charlestown Navy Yard** ❶ is on your right after crossing the bridge.

Just ahead is the Charlestown Navy Yard Visitors Information Center; inside the park gate is the **USS** *Constitution* ❷ and the associated **USS** *Constitution* **Museum** ❸. From here, the red line of the Freedom Trail takes you to the **Bunker Hill Monument** ❹.

nps.gov/bost/historyculture/usscassinyoung.htm 🖃 *Free* ⊙ *Daily 10–5; tours at 11, 2, and 3* Ⓣ *North Station; MBTA Bus 92 to Charlestown City Sq. or Bus 93 to Chelsea St. from Haymarket; or Boston Harbor Cruise water shuttle from Long Wharf to Pier 4.* 5 + up

WHERE CAN I FIND . . . IN CHARLESTOWN?

A Quick Meal

Hot off the Press Cafe	39 1st Avenue	Locals swear by this little eatery, which has some of the best sandwiches in town.

Good Coffee

Sorelle Bakery & Café	1 Monument Avenue	Charlestonians come here to get good coffee, muffins, scones, and sandwiches.

A Fun Store

The Joy of Old	85 Warren Street	Mostly open on weekends, this emporium of crafts and local goodies is a delight.

Public Bathrooms

USS Constitution Museum	Charlestown Navy Yard	Restrooms with changing tables are on the first floor.
Bunker Hill Monument	Monument Square	The restrooms are downstairs in the museum.

★ **Fodor's**Choice **USS** *Constitution.* Better known as "Old Ironsides," the USS *Constitution* rides proudly at anchor in her berth at the Charlestown Navy Yard. The oldest commissioned ship in the U.S. fleet is a battlewagon of the old school, of the days of "wooden ships and iron men"—when she and her crew of 200 succeeded at the perilous task of asserting the sovereignty of an improbable new nation. Every July 4 and on certain other occasions she's towed out for a turnabout in Boston Harbor, the very place her keel was laid in 1797.

The nickname "Old Ironsides" was acquired during the War of 1812, when shots from the British warship *Guerrière* appeared to bounce off her tough oaken hull. The men and women who look after the *Constitution*, regular navy personnel, maintain a 24-hour watch. Sailors show visitors around the ship, guiding them to her top, or spar, deck, and the gun deck below. Another treat when visiting the ship is the spectacular view of Boston across Boston Harbor.

■TIP→ **Instead of taking the T, you can get closer to the ship by taking MBTA Bus 92 to Charlestown City Square or Bus 93 to Chelsea Street from Haymarket. Or you can take the Boston Harbor Cruise water shuttle from Long Wharf to Pier 4.** Be sure to ask tour guides about the Powder Monkeys. These quick and agile crewmen—some as young as age 8 but mostly young teens—carried gunpowder during battles, running from the ship's bottom (where the powder was stored) up several decks to the guns. ⊠*Charlestown Navy Yard, 55 Constitution Rd., Charlestown* ☎*617/242–5670* ⊕*www. ussconstitution.navy.mil* ☞ *Free* ⊙*Apr. 1–Oct., Tues.–Sun. 10–5:50; Nov.–Mar. 31, Thurs.–Sun. 10–3:50; last tour at 3:30* Ⓣ*North Station. 5 + up*

❸ **USS *Constitution* Museum.** Artifacts and hands-on exhibits pertaining to the USS *Constitution* are on display—firearms, logs, and instruments. One section takes you step-by-step through the ship's most important battles. Old meets new in a video-game battle "fought" at the helm of a ship. Kid-friendly highlights include some interactive devices through which 19th-century sailing gets a 21st-century twist. Virtual ammunition can be fired from the barrel of a real cannon. Kids can also raise a sail, or swing in a hammock. Anyone who has wondered how they get ships into those little bottles can visit the model makers' studios and maybe try a hand at fashioning a model themselves (check with the front desk on your way in for studio times). ⊠*Adjacent to USS Constitution, Charlestown Navy Yard, Charlestown* ☎*617/426–1812* ⊕*www.ussconstitutionmuseum. org* ☞*Free* ⊙ *May–Oct., daily 9–6; Nov.–Apr., daily 10–5* Ⓣ*North Station; MBTA Bus 92 to Charlestown City Sq. or*

Bus 93 to Chelsea St. from Haymarket; or Boston Harbor Cruise water shuttle from Long Wharf to Pier 4. 5 + up

NEED A BREAK? Take a breather at **Sorelle** (✉ *100 City Sq., Charlestown* ☎ *617/242–2125*), a hot little bakery with two locations, delicious sandwiches, and refreshing iced coffees.

DOWNTOWN BOSTON

"Downtown" in Boston is a concentrated maze of streets that seem to have been laid out with little logic; they are, after all, long-ago cart paths that happen to be lined today with modern 40-story office towers. Just as the Great Fire of 1872 cleared the old Financial District, the Downtown construction in more recent times has obliterated many of the buildings where 19th-century Boston businessmen sat in front of their rolltop desks. Yet many historic sites remain tucked among the skyscrapers; a number of them have been linked together to make up a fascinating section of the Freedom Trail.

Weekdays, this smallish section of metropolis is characteristically busy, with business folks heading to their towers, while weekends, the streets practically echo with emptiness. As is the case with much of Boston, Downtown closely overlaps with myriad other areas, and even families who stay in the Financial District on a quiet Saturday will be plenty close to the bustling action of, say, the Waterfront or Faneuil Hall.

PLANNING YOUR TIME

This section of Boston has a generous share of attractions, so it's wise to save a full day, spending the bulk of it at either the New England Aquarium or the Children's Museum. There are optimum times to catch some sights. For example, the only tours to the top of the U.S. Custom House are at 10 and 4 on sunny days. No need to visit the aquarium at a special hour to catch feeding time—there are five of them throughout the day.

Numbers correspond to the Downtown Boston map.

WHAT TO SEE

❷ Boston Massacre Site. Directly in front of the **Old State House** a circle of cobblestones (on a traffic island) marks the site of the Boston Massacre. It was on the snowy evening of March 5, 1770, that nine British regular soldiers fired in panic upon a taunting mob of more than 75 Bostonians. Five

TOP DOWNTOWN EXPERIENCES

Boston Massacre Site. Play dead and get your picture taken here (outside the Old State House, 206 Washington Street). It's a rite of passage.

The Children's Museum of Boston. Grownups who were raised here recall this place as a highlight of youth (even if they miss the ramshackle climbing sculpture of yore). Today's kids will find it equally memorable.

Christopher Columbus Park. Go for a walk along the park and ogle all the beautiful boats. Make a stop at the playground where the kids can romp around while mom and dad enjoy the view.

New England Aquarium. Scout for whales on an Aquarium-led whale watch (Central Wharf). It's a bit bumpy out there, but there is nothing like coming upon these enormous critters in the wild.

townsmen died. All but two of the nine regulars charged were acquitted; the others were branded on the hand for the crime of manslaughter. Paul Revere lost little time in capturing the "massacre" in a dramatic engraving that soon became one of the Revolution's most potent images of propaganda. "Traffic island" doesn't really explain it—the site is on a tiny plot in the middle of the street. That won't stop adventurous kids from wanting their de rigueur photo snapped, lying on the stones as if just done in by the British regulars. Just make sure you get them safely across traffic first. On March 5 each year, the anniversary of the Boston Massacre is commemorated with a reenactment. ⊠*Congress and Court Sts., Downtown* Ⓣ*State.* 9 + up

❻ **Boston Tea Party Ships & Museum.** After a lengthy renovation, the museum is, as of this writing, scheduled to reopen in summer 2009 (though the opening date has been extended more than once). The *Beaver II*, a reproduction of one of the ships forcibly boarded and unloaded the night Boston Harbor became a teapot, is supposed to return to the Fort Point Channel at the Congress Street Bridge and be joined by two tall ships, the *Dartmouth* and the *Eleanor*. Visitors are promised a chance to explore the ships and museum exhibits, meet reenactors, or drink a cup of tea in a new Tea Room. ⊠*Fort Point Channel at Congress St. Bridge, Downtown* ⊕*www.bostonteapartyship.com* ☉*Check Web site for updated information* Ⓣ*South Station.* All ages

★ Fodor'sChoice **Children's Museum.** Most children have so much
❼ fun here, they don't realize they're actually learning something. Creative hands-on exhibits demonstrate scientific
laws, cultural diversity, and problem solving. After com-
pleting a massive 23,000-square-foot expansion in 2007,
the museum has updated a lot of its old exhibitions and
added new ones, like the aptly named "Adventure Zone."
Some of the most popular stops are also the simplest: bub-
ble-making machinery, the two-story climbing maze, and
"Boats Afloat," where children can float wooden objects
down a 28-foot-long model of the Fort Point Channel.
The key word is "interactive," and just about everything
is meant to be pushed, pulled, or otherwise dallied with in
some way. The littlest visitors get their own special haven
in PlaySpace, a quiet, cozy spot with soft blocks, books,
train sets, and craft projects. For everybody, the new Kid-
Stage offers daily family performances that, at 15 to 30
minutes, are perfect for any attention span. Friday nights,
admission is only $1. Check if at-home museum member-
ships offer privileges here. ⊠ *300 Congress St., Downtown*
☎ *617/426–6500, 617/426–8855 recorded information*
⊕ *www.bostonkids.org* ⊠ *$10 ages 16 and up, $8 children 2–15, $2 children 1–2* ☉ *Sat.–Thurs. 10–5, Fri. 10–9*
Ⓣ *South Station.* All ages

Chinatown. Boston's Chinatown may seem small, but it's said
to be the third largest in the United States, after those in
San Francisco and Manhattan. As in most other American
Chinatowns, the restaurants are a big draw; on Sunday,
many Bostonians head to Chinatown for dim sum. Today
the many Chinese establishments—most found along Beach
and Tyler streets and Harrison Avenue—are interspersed
with Vietnamese, Korean, Japanese, Thai, and Malaysian
eateries. A three-story pagoda-style arch at the end of Beach
Street welcomes you to the district. Kids get big-eyed at
some of the interesting displays, such as a shop selling live
poultry. Colorful vendors along the main thoroughfares are
always a kick, especially for parents looking for bargains
on souvenir items, and kids seeking bric-a-brac like small
figurines, and cute silk-jacket key chains. The area has
most definitely improved over the years, and during the
day, it's an absolute pleasure to be out and about. Though
some of the restaurants are open into the wee hours, it still
seems prudent to avoid the area late at night. ⊠ *Bounded
(roughly) by Essex, Washington, Marginal, and Hudson*
Ⓣ *Chinatown.* All ages

❸ Christopher Columbus Park (*Waterfront Park*). It's a short stroll from the Financial District to a view of Boston Harbor. Once a national symbol of rampant pollution, the harbor is making a gradual comeback. This green space bordering the harbor and several of Boston's restored wharves is a pleasant oasis with benches and an arborlike shelter. In September, the park is home to the Boston Arts Festival. On weekends, the fully enclosed Christopher Columbus Park playground is a hotspot for parents and kids. It has the benefit of being a stellar place for wee ones, while offering spectacular waterfront scenery for mom and dad. ⊠*Bordered by Atlantic Ave., Commercial Wharf, and Long Wharf, Downtown* Ⓣ*Aquarium*. All ages

★ Fodor'sChoice **New England Aquarium.** This aquarium chal-
❹ lenges you to really imagine life under and around the sea. Seals bark outside the West Wing, while inside you can see penguins, sea otters, sharks, and other exotic sea creatures—more than 2,000 species in all. Some make their home in the aquarium's four-story, 200,000-gallon ocean-reef tank, one of the largest of its kind in the world. Ramps winding around the tank lead to the top level and allow you to view the inhabitants from many vantage points. Don't miss the five-times-a-day feedings; each lasts nearly an hour and takes divers 24 feet into the tank. "The Curious George Discovery Corner" is a fun spot for younger kids. Whale-watch cruises leave from the aquarium's dock from April to October, and cost $35.95. Across the plaza is the aquarium's Education Center, which has changing exhibits. The 6½-story-high IMAX theater takes you on virtual journeys from the bottom of the sea to the depths of outer space with its 3-D films. Crowds make the dark, narrow confines of the aquarium tough to navigate, particularly if you're trying to keep your eye on small, roving children. Good visiting times are Sunday before noon and after 1 PM during the week. Avoid Saturday completely if you can. Aqua Kids Family Day, with activities for families with tots, is offered the first and third Monday of every month, excluding holidays. ⊠*Central Wharf between Central and Milk Sts., Downtown* ☎*617/973–5200* ⊕*www.neaq.org* ⊒*$19.95 ages 12 and up, $11.95 children 3–11* ☉*July–early Sept., weekdays 9–6, weekends 9–7; early Sept.–June, weekdays 9–5, weekends 9–6* Ⓣ*Aquarium, State.* All ages

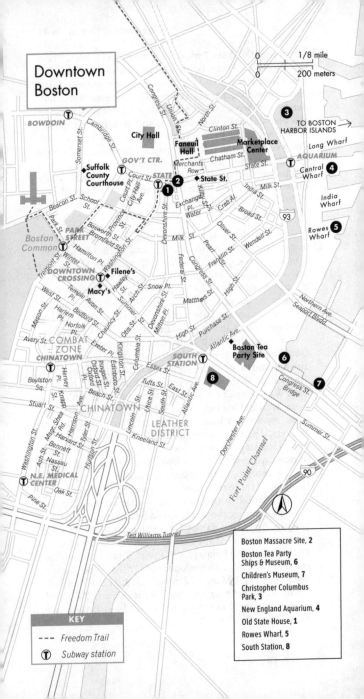

Downtown Boston

BOWDOIN Ⓣ

City Hall

Somerset St.
Cambridge St.

Faneuil Hall

Union St.
Congress St.
North St.
Clinton St.

Marketplace Center

Ⓣ ❸ TO BOSTON
HARBOR ISLANDS

Chatham St.
State St.
Merchants Row
Milk St.

AQUARIUM Ⓣ

GOV'T CTR.

Suffolk County Courthouse ◆

STATE Ⓣ

Court St.
City Hall Ave.
Court Sq.

❷ Ⓣ
❶

◆ **State St.**

Exchange Pl.
Water St.

Central
Wharf ❹

Long Wharf

India
Wharf

Beacon St.
School St.

Province St.
Bosworth St.
Bromfield St.
Washington St.
Devonshire St.

Crab Al.
Broad St.
India St.

Oliver St.

Boston Common

PARK STREET Ⓣ

Hamilton Pl.
Winter St.

Tremont St.

DOWNTOWN CROSSING Ⓣ

◆ **Filene's**

Milk St.
Franklin St.
Pearl St.
High St.
Wendell St.

Rowes
Wharf ❺

93

Macy's ◆

Hawley St.
Arch St.
Snow Pl.
Devonshire St.
Milton Pl.

West St.
Temple Pl.
Avon St.
Bedford St.
Chauncy St.
Summer St.

Mason St.
Harlem Pl.
Norfolk Pl.
Otis St.

Matthews

Congress St.
Federal St.
Purchase St.
Atlantic Ave.

Northern Ave.
Seaport Blvd.

Avery St.
COMBAT ZONE

High St.

Essex St.

SOUTH STATION Ⓣ

◆ **Boston Tea Party Site** ❻

CHINATOWN

Boylston St.
Stuart St.

Kingston St.
Edinboro St.
Columbia St.
Lincoln St.
South St.

Tufts St.
East St.
Utica St.
Atlantic Ave.

❽

Congress St. Bridge ❼

Hersey Pl.
Knapp St.
Harrison Ave.
Tyler St.

Ping On St.
Oxford St.
Oxford Pl.
Beach St.

❾

Mason St.
Exeter Pl.

CHINATOWN

LEATHER DISTRICT

Kneeland St.

Summer St.

Dorchester Ave.

Washington St.
Oak St.
Pine St.

Mgr. Shea Rd.
Ash St.
Bennett St.
Nassau St.

Hudson St.

Kneeland St.

Fort Point Channel

N.E. MEDICAL CENTER Ⓣ

90

Ted Williams Tunnel

0 — 1/8 mile
0 — 200 meters

KEY

‑ ‑ ‑ Freedom Trail

Ⓣ Subway station

Boston Massacre Site, **2**

Boston Tea Party
Ships & Museum, **6**

Children's Museum, **7**

Christopher Columbus
Park, **3**

New England Aquarium, **4**

Old State House, **1**

Rowes Wharf, **5**

South Station, **8**

WHERE CAN I FIND . . . IN DOWNTOWN BOSTON?

1

A Quick Meal

Eldo Cake House	36-38 Harrison Avenue	Never considered bean paste for dessert or eaten a Chinese-style pork bun? Expand your horizons at this eatery in Chinatown.

Good Coffee

Starbucks	63-65 Court Street	Great location. Drink your java under the world's largest teapot built in the 19th century.

A Playground

Christopher Columbus Park	Bordered by Atlantic Avenue, Commercial Wharf, and Long Wharf	No swings, but the playground is fully enclosed and this is the place to be with tots on weekends.

A Public Bathroom

Visitor Center	15 State Street	Changing facilities and bathrooms downstairs next to the Old State House.
Marriott Long Wharf	296 State Street	Clean, dependable, fully equipped restrooms right near Christopher Columbus Park.

❶ **Old State House.** This colonial-era landmark has one of the most recognizable facades in Boston, with its State Street gable adorned by a brightly gilded lion and unicorn, symbols of British imperial power. The original figures were pulled down in 1776. For proof that bygones are bygones, consider not only the restoration of the sculptures in 1880 but also that Queen Elizabeth II was greeted by cheering crowds on July 4, 1976, when she stood on the Old State House balcony (from which the Declaration of Independence was first read in public in Boston and which overlooks the site of the Boston Massacre).

Immediately outside the Old State House, at 15 State Street, is a **visitor center** run by the National Park Service; it offers free brochures and has restrooms. Ask about a special handout that allows kids to explore the museum scavenger-hunt style. Details inside include audio dramatizations of significant events, John Hancock's coat, and tea from the Boston Tea Party. Visiting this stately structure will take about 40 minutes to an hour, with the most captivated audience being kids who are studying this period in history. Though John Hancock's groovy duds may momentarily impress some little ones (grade 1 or lower), most of the historic value will be lost on them. ✉*206 Washington St., at State St., Downtown* ☎*617/720–3290* ⊕*www.boston history.org* ✑*$5 adults, $1 children 6–17* ☉*Daily 9–5* Ⓣ*State.* 9 + up

❺ **Rowes Wharf.** Take a Beacon Hill redbrick town house, blow it up to the *n*th power, and you get this 15-story extravaganza, one of the more welcome additions to the Boston Harbor skyline. From under the complex's gateway six-story arch, you can get great views of Boston Harbor and the yachts docked at the marina. Water shuttles pull up here from Logan Airport—the most intriguing way to enter the city. A windswept stroll along the HarborWalk waterfront promenade at dusk makes for an unforgettable sunset on clear days. One of the best ways to appreciate the hotel is via the Rowes Wharf Hotel's Intrigue Café, which has outdoor seating along the HarborWalk and a children's menu. On many spring and summer days, you're likely to see a wedding party go by (many are photographed in the gazebo). The length of the HarborWalk from the hotel to the Institute of Contemporary Art is lovely sunny-day walk for adults, kids, and the stroller set. ✉*Atlantic Ave. south of India Wharf* Ⓣ*Aquarium.* All ages

❽ **South Station.** The colonnaded granite structure is the terminal for all Amtrak trains in and out of Boston. Next door on Atlantic Avenue is the terminal for Greyhound, Peter Pan, and other bus lines. Behind the station's grand 1900s facade, a major renovation project has created an airy, modern transit center. Thanks to its eateries, coffee bars, newsstand, flower stand, and other shops, waiting for a train here can actually be a pleasant experience. Apart from the myriad eateries in the food court (everything from pizza to sandwiches), South Station is where you'll find Jupiter, or more specifically, one of the interplanetary stops along the Community Solar System Trail. The trail begins with Mercury and Venus at the Museum of Science. Check out *www.mos.org* for details. ✉*Atlantic Ave. and Summer St., Downtown* Ⓣ*South Station.* All ages

THE BACK BAY

Kids may be impressed at the Back Bay's storied architectural history. The place was once upon a time a swamp (okay, a bay) that was filled in during the 19th century to create the tony commercial and residential district it is today. The area retains its posh spirit, but now locals and tourists alike flock to the thoroughfares of Boylston and Newbury to shop at boutiques, galleries, and the usual mall stores. Many of the bars and restaurants have patio seating and bay windows, making the area the perfect spot to see and be seen while indulging in ethnic delicacies or an invigorating coffee. The Boston Public Library, Symphony Hall, and numerous churches ensure that high culture is not lost amid the frenzy of consumerism.

■TIP→ **One of the main thoroughfares, Huntington Avenue, which stretches from Copley Square past the Museum of Fine Arts, has technically been renamed the Avenue of the Arts. However, old habits die hard, particularly with Bostonians; everyone still calls it Huntington.**

Numbers correspond to the Back Bay, the South End & the Fens map.

WHAT TO SEE

★ Fodor'sChoice **Boston Duck Tours.** Boston Duck Tours is something of an overnight success story. Founded in 1994, the company and its colorful "duck" vehicles are already Boston fixtures, taking more than half a million people a year on unique, amphibious tours of the city: Boylston Street, Tremont Street, and the River Charles, all in one 80-minute trip. Tours depart from the Prudential Center and the Museum of Science, and run seven days a week, rain or shine, from late March to late November (all ducks are heated). Kids might be interested to know that they're sitting in the Duck seats of sports greatness. These are the same vehicles used to transport Patriots and Red Sox during victory parades. Ducks are heated, with plastic canopies that provide some, albeit not perfect, shelter during inclement weather. Tickets are available up to five days ahead. Summer tours often sell out by noon. Tours depart from the Huntington side of the Prudential Center and from the Museum of Science. ⊠ *3 Copley Pl., Suite 310, Back Bay* ☎ *617/723–DUCK* ⊕ *www.bostonducktours.com* ⊠ *$29, $19 children 3–11, $5 3 and under.* All ages

TOP BACK BAY EXPERIENCES

Copley Place and the **Prudential Center**. Shop 'til you drop.

Newbury Street. Sit at an outdoor café. The shopping mecca is loaded with sidewalk bistro tables where you can sip that latte (or chocolate milk).

Public Garden. Ride a swan boat. It's a short ride, but the experience is vintage Boston. While you're here, make sure to stop by the Make Way for Ducklings sculptures, ode to the famous story of the same name.

Prudential Skywalk. On a clear day, the vista is as far as the eye can see. Make sure to look for the "salt and pepper shaker" ornaments on the Longfellow Bridge.

Ride a Duck. It's hokey and silly and a ton of fun. A great, quick way to get the lay of the land.

Boston Public Garden. Although the Boston Public Garden is often lumped together with Boston Common, the two are separate entities. The Common has been public land since Boston was founded in 1630, whereas the Public Garden belongs to a newer Boston, occupying what had been salt marshes on the edge of the Common. The central feature is its irregularly shaped pond, intended to appear much larger than its nearly 4 acres. The pond has been famous since 1877 for its foot-pedal-powered (by a captain) **Swan Boats** (⊕*www.swanboats.com* ✆ *$2* ☉ *Mid-Apr.–June 20, daily 10–4; June 21–Labor Day, daily 10–5; day after Labor Day–mid-Sept., weekdays noon–4, weekends 10–4*), which make leisurely cruises during warm months. For the modest price of a few boat rides you can amuse children here for an hour or more. The dominant work among the park's statuary is Thomas Ball's equestrian **George Washington** (1869), which faces the head of Commonwealth Avenue at the Arlington Street gate. The park contains a special delight for the young at heart; follow the children quack-quacking along the pathway between the pond and the park entrance at Charles and Beacon streets to the *Make Way for Ducklings* bronzes sculpted by Nancy Schön, a tribute to the 1941 classic children's story by Robert McCloskey. The manicured garden is decidedly more of a keep-off-the-grass kind of place (don't even think about bringing the Frisbee). But, the nation's first botanical garden has its own charms, and kids are often delighted by the thousands of colorful in-season blooms. Feel free to climb on those duck sculptures, just don't take them home. Despite having their webbed feet sunk in cement, the quackers have been the occasional victims of duck nappers. ⊠*Bounded by Arlington, Boylston, Charles, and Beacon Sts., Back Bay* ☎*617/522–1966* Ⓣ*Arlington.* All ages

WHERE CAN I FIND . . . IN BACK BAY?

A Quick Meal		
Parish Café	361 Boylston Street	For about $10, you can get a sandwich designed by one of the top culinary minds in Boston.
A Good Grocery Store		
Shaw's Prudential	53 Huntington Avenue	It's mammoth; you won't leave empty handed.
Good Coffee		
Espresso Royale Caffe	286 Newbury Street	Come with the computer, or the kids, to this basement spot with solid coffee and espresso drinks, snacks, and Wi-Fi access.
A Fun Store		
Sugar Heaven	218 Newbury Street	Go ahead, reward yourself and the kids with one of about 3,500 different kinds of junk.
A Fun Playground		
Clarendon Street Playground	Clarendon at Commonwealth	Shady, enclosed with lots of stuff to play with/climb on/run around in.
A Public Bathroom		
Boston Public Library	700 Boylston Street	An always dependable bet is downstairs during library hours.

★ ❸ **Boston Public Library.** This venerable institution is a handsome temple to literature and a valuable research library. Enter the older part of the library from the Dartmouth Street side, passing under the motto *"Omni lux civium"* (Light of all citizens) through the enormous bronze doors by Daniel Chester French, the sculptor of the Lincoln Memorial. Or walk around Boylston Street to enter through the addition. The corridor leading from the annex opens onto the Renaissance-style **courtyard**—an exact copy of the one in Rome's Palazzo della Cancelleria—around which the original library is built. A covered arcade furnished with chairs rings a fountain; bring books or lunch into the courtyard, which is open all the hours the library is open, and escape the bustle of the city. Apart from the Rey Children's Room, the library hosts myriad summer activities including author talks and read-aloud book clubs. There is also a long list of activities for teens. Check the Web site for details. ✉*700 Boylston St., at Copley Sq., Back Bay* ☎*617/536–5400* ⊕*www.bpl.org* ☯*Mon.–Thurs. 9–9, Fri. and Sat. 9–5; Oct.–May, also Sun. 1–5. Free guided art and architecture tours Mon. at 2:30, Tues. and Thurs. at 6, Fri. and Sat. at 11, Sun. (Oct.–May) at 2* Ⓣ*Copley. All ages*

Boylston Street. Less posh than Newbury Street, this broad thoroughfare is the southern commercial spine of the Back Bay, lined with interesting restaurants and shops.

❹ **Copley Place.** Two bold intruders dominate Copley Square— the **John Hancock Tower** off the southeast corner, and the even more assertive Copley Place skyscraper on the southwest. An upscale, glass-and-brass urban mall built between 1980 and 1984, Copley Place includes two major hotels: the high-rise Westin and the Marriott Copley Place. Dozens of shops, restaurants, and offices are attractively grouped on several levels, surrounding bright, open indoor spaces. During the long winter months, locals use the mall to escape the elements and take a shortcut between Back Bay Station and points west. ✉*100 Huntington Ave., Back Bay* ☎*617/369–5000* ⊕*www.shopcopleyplace.com* ☯*Shopping galleries Mon.–Sat. 10–9, Sun. 11–6* Ⓣ*Copley. All ages*

Copley Square. Every April thousands find a glimpse of Copley Square the most wonderful sight in the world: this is where the runners of the Boston Marathon end their 26-mi race. A square now favored by skateboarders (much to the chagrin of city officials), the space is defined by three monumental older buildings: **Fairmont Copley Plaza Hotel,** Trinity Church, and the Boston Public Library. The John Hancock Tower looms in the background. To honor the runners who stagger over the marathon's finish line, bronze statues of the Tortoise and the Hare engaged in their mythical race were cast by Nancy Schön, who also did the much-loved *Make Way for Ducklings* group in the Boston Public Garden. ✉*Bounded by Dartmouth, Boylston, and Clarendon Sts. and St. James Ave., Back Bay* Ⓣ*Copley. All ages*

❷ **Esplanade.** Near the corner of Beacon and Arlington streets, the Arthur Fiedler Footbridge crosses Storrow Drive to the Esplanade and the **Hatch Memorial Shell.** The free concerts here in summer include the Boston Pops' immensely popular televised July 4 performance. For shows like this, Bostonians haul lawn chairs and blankets to the lawn in front of the shell; bring a take-out lunch from a nearby restaurant, find an empty spot—no mean feat, so come early—and you'll feel right at home. An impressive stone bust of the late maestro Arthur Fiedler watches over the walkers, joggers, picnickers, and sunbathers who fill the Esplanade's paths on pleasant days.

❻ Mary Baker Eddy Library for the Betterment of Humanity. One of the largest single collections by and about an American woman is housed at this library within Christian Science Plaza. The library is home to the fascinating **Mapparium,** a huge stained-glass globe whose 30-foot interior can be traversed on a footbridge. You can experience a sound-and-light show in the Mapparium and learn about the production of the *Christian Science Monitor* in the Monitor Gallery. The place is a great whispering gallery, as well as a perfect echo chamber. Single strollers are welcome, but side-by-side double strollers will not fit on the bridge. Kids will enjoy the rest of the library's exhibits, including interactive computer kiosks, the Monitor Gallery where you can learn what it takes to put out a newspaper, and the Hall of Ideas with a fountain that "rains" famous quotations. ✉ *200 Massachusetts Ave., Back Bay* ☎ *888/222–3711* ⊕ *www.marybakereddylibrary.org* ⊠ *Hall of Ideas and 3rd-fl. library free, exhibits $6 adults, $4 children 6–17* ☉ *Tues.–Sun. 10–4* Ⓣ *Hynes/ICA, Symphony.* All ages

Newbury Street. Eight-block-long Newbury Street has been compared to New York's 5th Avenue, and certainly this is the city's poshest shopping area, with branches of Chanel, Brooks Brothers, Armani, Burberry, and other top names in fashion. But here the pricey boutiques are more intimate than grand, and people live above the trendy restaurants and hair salons, giving the place a neighborhood feel. Toward the Mass Ave. end, cafés proliferate and the stores get funkier, ending with Newbury Comics, Urban Outfitters, and now, in a nod to the times, Best Buy. Ⓣ *Hynes/ ICA, Copley, Arlington.*

❺ Prudential Center. The only rival to the John Hancock's claim on Boston's upper skyline is the 52-story Prudential Tower. Its enclosed shopping mall is connected by a glass bridge to the more upscale Copley Place. There's also a branch of the Greater Boston Visitors Bureau here, in the center court of the mall. **Prudential Center Skywalk,** a 50th-floor

The Back Bay, the South End & the Fens

Charles River

Memorial Dr.

Harvard Bridge

Storrow Drive

Fairfield St.

Gloucester St.

Hereford St.

Massachusetts Ave.

Beacon St.

Newbury St.

Hynes Convention Center

Bay State Rd.
Raleigh St.
Deerfield St.

10 Ⓣ KENMORE

Brookline Ave.

Mass. Tpk.

Ipswich St.

Dalton St.

Lansdowne St.

HYNES CONVENTION CENTER/
ICA (AUDITORIUM)

Belvidere St.

Yawkey Way

11

Ipswich St.

Van Ness St.

Norway St.

St. Germain St.

Clearway St.

6

Boylston St.

Park Dr.

Hemenway St.

Burbank St.

Peterborough St.

Westland Ave.

Jersey St.

Fenway

Queensberry St.

Agassiz Rd.

Symphony Rd.

7 Ⓣ SYMPHONY

Gainsborough St.

of the Arts

Park Dr.

Back Bay
Fens Park

Ⓣ

St.-Stephen St.

Avenue

Ⓣ

MASSACHUSETTS
AVE.

Forsyth St.

Opera Pl.

 ⓉNORTHEASTERN

Fenway

Forsyth Way

9

Louis Prang St.

Museum Rd.

Ⓣ MUSEUM

Huntington Ave.

8

0		1/8 mile
0		200 meters

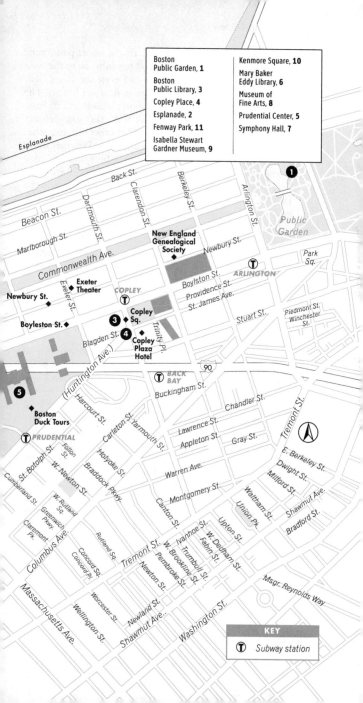

Boston Public Garden, **1**	Kenmore Square, **10**
Boston Public Library, **3**	Mary Baker Eddy Library, **6**
Copley Place, **4**	Museum of Fine Arts, **8**
Esplanade, **2**	Prudential Center, **5**
Fenway Park, **11**	Symphony Hall, **7**
Isabella Stewart Gardner Museum, **9**	

Esplanade

Back St.

Berkeley St.

Clarendon St.

Arlington St.

Public Garden

Beacon St.

Marlborough St.

Dartmouth St.

New England Genealogical Society

Newbury St.

Park Sq.

Commonwealth Ave.

Exeter St.

Exeter Theater

COPLEY

ⓣ ARLINGTON

Boylston St.

Providence St.

St. James St.

Newbury St.

ⓣ

Copley Sq.

Stuart St.

Piedmont St.
Winchester St.

Boylston St.

3

4

Blagden St.

Trinity Pl.

Copley Plaza Hotel

(Huntington Ave.)

ⓣ BACK BAY

90

5

Buckingham St.

Chandler St.

Tremont St.

Boston Duck Tours

Harcourt St.

Carleton St.

Yarmouth St.

Lawrence St.

ⓣ PRUDENTIAL

Hotyoke St.

Appleton St.

Gray St.

E. Berkeley St.

St. Botolph St.

Fallon St.

W. Newton St.

Braddock Pkwy.

Dwight St.

Milford St.

Warren Ave.

Shawmut Ave.

Cumberland St.

W. Rutland Sq.

Greenwich Pkwy.

Rutland Sq.

Canton St.

Montgomery St.

Waltham St.

Union Pk.

Bradford St.

Claremont Pk.

Columbus Ave.

Concord Sq.

Concord Pl.

Tremont St.

W. Brookline St.

Ivanhoe St.

W. Dedham St.

Fabin St.

Upton St.

Trumbull St.

Massachusetts Ave.

Worcester St.

Newton St.

Pembroke St.

Newland St.

Wellington St.

Shawmut Ave.

Washington St.

Msgr. Reynolds Way

KEY	
ⓣ	Subway station

observatory atop the Prudential Tower, offers panoramic vistas of Boston, Cambridge, and the suburbs to the west and south—on clear days, you can even see Cape Cod. There are also interactive exhibits on Boston's history. The Skywalk is one of the attractions on the Boston CityPass. Two films—one on immigration from the now-defunct "Dreams of Freedom" museum, and another offering aerial views of the city—play throughout the day. Personal audio tours, one for children and one for adults, are included in the price of admission. School-age children are most likely to enjoy the history, but toddlers often enjoy the view. Tickets can be purchased in the Prudential arcade kiosk from 10 to 6; after 6, purchase tickets at the observatory entrance on the 50th floor. The last elevator goes up a half-hour before closing. ⊠*800 Boylston St., Back Bay* ☎*617/236–3100, 617/859–0648 for Skywalk* ⊕*www.prudentialcenter.com* ⊠*Skywalk $11 adults, $7.50 children 11 and under* ⊙*Mon.–Sat. 10–9, Sun. 11–6; Skywalk Nov.–Feb., daily 10–8, Mar.–Oct., daily 10–10* Ⓣ*Hynes/ICA.* 3 + up

❼ **Symphony Hall.** With commerce and religion accounted for in the Back Bay by such monuments as the Prudential Center and the Christian Science headquarters, the neighborhood still has room for a temple to music: Symphony Hall, home of the Boston Symphony Orchestra and the Boston Pops, and frequent host to guest performers. Hour-long behind-the-scenes tours might appeal to musically inclined kids. Stops include dressing rooms, warm-up spaces, and an up-close look at the giant, four-story pipe organ, plus you'll get trivia, such as the story of the diminutive harpist who used her instrument case as a dressing room. Youth and Family concerts are designed for shorter attention spans and are held several times during the year. Saturday Family Concerts generally include special tours and the popular instrument petting zoo. Check the regular concert schedule for other kid-friendly shows, such as John Williams conducting his movie music, including the Harry Potter theme. ⊠*301 Massachusetts Ave., Back Bay* ☎*888/266–1200 box office, 617/638–9392 tours* ⊕*www.bso.org* ⊙*Free walk-up tours Oct.–May, Wed. at 4:30 and 1st Sat. of month at 1:30* Ⓣ*Symphony.* 9 + up

THE FENWAY & KENMORE SQUARE

Red Sox fans may be surprised to know that the neighborhood surrounding Fenway Park was not named for the home of the home team. Actually, it's the reverse. The marshland known as the Back Bay Fens gave this section of Boston its name but it's the park (and that love-it-or-hate-it Citgo sign) that gives it its character, with baseball-capped fans streaming in on game days to see their fabled heroes, who at last reversed the curse in 2004. You don't have to be a sports fan to love it here, as the area is also home to two of Boston's most famous art institutions, the Museum of Fine Arts (MFA) and the Isabella Stewart Gardner Museum.

The Fens also marks the beginning of Boston's Emerald Necklace, a loosely connected chain of parks designed by Olmsted that extends along the Fenway, Riverway, and Jamaicaway to Jamaica Pond, the Arnold Arboretum, and Franklin Park. Farther off, at the Boston–Milton line, the Blue Hills Reservation offers some of the Boston area's best hiking, scenic views, and even a ski lift.

Numbers correspond to the Back Bay, the South End & the Fens map.

PLANNING YOUR TIME

Although this area can be walked through in a couple of hours, art lovers could spend a week here, thanks to the glories of the MFA and the Isabella Stewart Gardner Museum. (If you want to do a museum blowout, avoid Monday, when the Gardner is closed.) To cap off a day of culture, plan for an area dinner, then a concert at nearby Symphony Hall. Another option, if you're visiting between spring and early fall, is to take a tour of Fenway Park—or better yet, catch a game. This district is most easily traveled via branches of the MBTA's Green Line; trains operate aboveground on Commonwealth and Huntington avenues.

■ TIP → **Avoid walking inside the Fens at night, when the marshy areas are poorly lighted.**

WHAT TO SEE

★ Fodor'sChoice **Fenway Park.** For 86 years, the Boston Red Sox
⑪ suffered a World Series dry spell, a streak of bad luck that fans attributed to the "Curse of the Bambino," which, stories have it, struck the team in 1920 when they sold Babe Ruth (the "Bambino") to the New York Yankees. All that changed in 2004, when a maverick squad broke the curse

TOP FENWAY & KENMORE EXPERIENCES

Fenway Park: Boston's shrine to baseball is where the devoted go to root, cheer and occasionally weep. Go to a game, or get to know the history via behind-the-bleachers tour.

Museum of Fine Arts: The cavernous institution is home to nearly a half-million works of art, and a perfectly lovely place to introduce the tykes to a little culture.

Tomb: Historic Boston gets history of an entirely different sort, via this high-tech trip through a mummy's tomb. Thrilling enough to make it fun, but not so scary to completely spook the kids.

in a thrilling seven-game series against the team's nemesis in the Series semifinals followed by a four-game sweep of St. Louis in the finals. Boston, and its citizens' ingrained sense of pessimism, hasn't been the same since. The repeat World Series win in 2007 has just cemented Bostonians' sense that the universe is finally working correctly. Fenway may be one of the smallest parks in the major leagues (capacity almost 39,000), but it's one of the most beloved, despite its oddball dimensions and the looming left-field wall, otherwise known as the Green Monster. Parking is expensive and the seats are a bit cramped, but the air is thick with legend. Tours of the park are a big hit with young baseball fans, who learn Sox lore, plus get to see the Green Monster up close, check out the press level and, on some days, gander at the bases from field level (available only on some tours). On game days, the last tour of the day is an abbreviated 40 minutes; the upside, though, is you might get to see some batting practice. ⊠ *4 Yawkey Way, between Van Ness and Lansdowne Sts., The Fenway* ☎ *617/267–1700 box office, 617/226–6666 tours* ⊕ *www.boston.redsox.mlb.com* ⊟ *Tours $12 adults, $10 children 2–15* ⊗ *Tours Mon.–Sat. 9–4, Sun. 9–3; on game days, last tour is 3½ hrs before game time.* 5 + up

★ Fodor'sChoice **Isabella Stewart Gardner Museum.** A spirited young
❾ society woman, Isabella Stewart came in 1860 from New York—where ladies were more commonly seen *and* heard than in Boston—to marry John Lowell Gardner, one of Boston's leading citizens. Through her flamboyance and energetic acquisition of art, "Mrs. Jack" promptly set about becoming the most un-Bostonian of the Proper Bostonians. When it came time finally to settle down with the old master paintings and Medici treasures she and her husband

A GOOD WALK

Boston's two major art museums are on this itinerary. From the intersection of Massachusetts and Huntington avenues, with the front entrance of Symphony Hall on your right, walk down Huntington Avenue. On your left is the New England Conservatory of Music and, on Gainsborough Street, its recital center, Jordan Hall. Between Huntington Avenue and the Fenway is the **Museum of Fine Arts (MFA)** 8 and, just around the corner, the **Isabella Stewart Gardner Museum** 9. If you prefer to pay homage to the Red Sox, from Symphony Hall, go north on Mass Ave., turn left on Commonwealth Avenue, and continue until you reach **Kenmore Square** 10; from here it's a 10-minute walk down Brookline Avenue to Yawkey Way and **Fenway Park** 11.

had acquired in Europe she decided to build the Venetian palazzo of her dreams.

At one time Gardner lived on the fourth floor of Fenway Court. When she died, the terms of her will stipulated that the building remain exactly as she left it—paintings, furniture, everything, down to the smallest object in a hall cabinet. An intimate restaurant overlooks the garden, and in spring and summer tables and chairs spill outside. A first-floor gallery has revolving exhibits of historic and contemporary art. ■TIP➔ **If you've visited the MFA in the past two days, there's a $2 discount to the admission fee. Also note that a charming quirk of the museum's admission policy waives entrance fees to anyone named Isabella, forever.** The Gardner museum prefers to incorporate children into the general visiting experience, rather than cater specifically to them. The palatial and lovely building alone appeals to some kids. There are family guides, available free of charge at the information desk near the courtyard. Strollers are allowed, but side-by-side doubles and joggers will not fit in the galleries. Front-carrier snuglis are allowed, but baby backpacks are not. ⊠ *280 The Fenway, The Fenway* ☎ *617/566–1401, 617/566–1088 café* ⊕ *www.gardnermuseum.org* ✉ *$12 adults, free for children 17 and under* ☉ *Museum Tues.–Sun. 11–5, open some holidays; café Tues.–Fri. 11:30–4, weekends 11–4. Weekend concerts at 1:30* Ⓣ *Museum.* All ages

🔟 **Kenmore Square.** Two blocks north of Fenway Park is Kenmore Square, where you'll find fast-food joints, record stores, and an enormous sign advertising Citgo gasoline. The red, white, and blue neon sign from 1965 is so thoroughly identified with the area that historic preservationists fought, successfully, to save it—proof that Bostonians are an open-minded lot who don't insist that their landmarks be identified with the American Revolution. ✉ *Convergence of Beacon St., Commonwealth Ave., and Brookline Ave.* Ⓣ *Kenmore.* All ages

★ Fodor'sChoice **Museum of Fine Arts.** The MFA's collection of
❽ approximately 350,000 objects was built from a core of paintings and sculpture from the Boston Athenaeum, the city of Boston, and donations by area universities. Today, the museum's holdings of American art surpass those of all but two or three U.S. museums.

American decorative arts are also liberally represented, particularly those of New England in the years before the Civil War. The museum also owns one of the world's most extensive collections of Asian art under one roof. The Egyptian rooms display statuary, furniture, and exquisite gold jewelry; a special funerary-arts gallery exhibits coffins, mummies, and burial treasures. French impressionists abound and are perhaps more comprehensively displayed here than at any other new-world museum outside the Art Institute of Chicago. Three important galleries explore the art of Africa, Oceania, and the Ancient Americas. The museum has strong collections of textiles, costumes, and prints dating from the 15th century.

The **West Wing,** an airy, well-lighted space, is used primarily to mount special exhibitions. Kids can keep busy with workshops (Tuesday–Sunday) and special programs.

In 2005, the museum broke ground on a massive construction project that the trustees hope will keep it in America's cultural vanguard for the next 100 years. Two-age "Paper Guides" available at the Sharf Information Desk detail particular exhibits and proffer scavenger-hunt-type explorations. High-tech-minded kids might prefer getting to know the museum via audio guide. Headsets are available at the ticket desk for $6 ($5 for members) or $4 for children. Older kids who are really into art might like the daily docent-guided tours, free with admission. Because of the museum's size, experts suggest focusing on one gallery and avoiding weekends. Also, check out the gift shop which has

1

some exceptional kid-oriented art books. ✉*465 Huntington Ave., The Fenway* ☎*617/267–9300* ⊕*www.mfa.org* ✒*$15 adults; $6.50 children 7–17, children free weekdays after 3 and all day on weekends* ⊙*Sat.–Tues. 10–4:45, Wed.–Fri. 10–9:45. 1-hr tours daily; call for scheduled times* Ⓣ*Museum.* All ages

Tomb. Unlike the historic attractions located elsewhere around town, this one is purely for fun, a theme park-y kind of thing that conjures up mild scares as you venture through an Egyptian tomb. Only the littlest kids, for whom the realism may be too much, will be scared. Tweens and teens will have a blast. The attraction gets quite warm, so leave outerwear in the coatroom. The cooperative style makes the experience most fun if you visit with a group or with the whole family. ✉*186 Brookline Ave., The Fenway* ☎*617/375–9487* ⊕*www.5-wits.com* ✒*$20 adults, $16 children 12 and under* ⊙*Mon. and Tues. 10–7, Wed. and Thurs. 10–10, Fri. and Sat. 10–11, Sun. 10–7.* Ⓣ*Kenmore.* 9 + up

THE "STREETCAR SUBURBS"

The landfill project that became South Boston—known as "Southie" and not to be confused with the South End—isn't a true streetcar suburb; its expansion predates the era of commuting. Some of the brick bowfront residences along East Broadway in City Point date from the 1840s and 1850s, but the neighborhood really came into its own with the influx of Irish around 1900, and Irish-Americans still hold sway here. Southie is a Celtic enclave, as the raucous annual St. Patrick's Day parade attests.

Among the other streetcar suburbs are Dorchester and Jamaica Plain—rural retreats barely more than a century ago that are now thick with Boston's distinctive three- and six-family triple-decker apartment houses. Dorchester is almost exclusively residential, tricky to navigate by car, and accessible by the T only if you know exactly where you're going. Jamaica Plain is a hip, young neighborhood with a strong lesbian and ecofriendly population; brunch and a wander through the neighborhood's quirky stores or through the Arnold Arboretum makes for a relaxing weekend excursion. Both towns border Franklin Park, an Olmsted creation of more than 500 acres, noted for its zoo. Farther west, Brookline is composed of a mixture of the affluent and students.

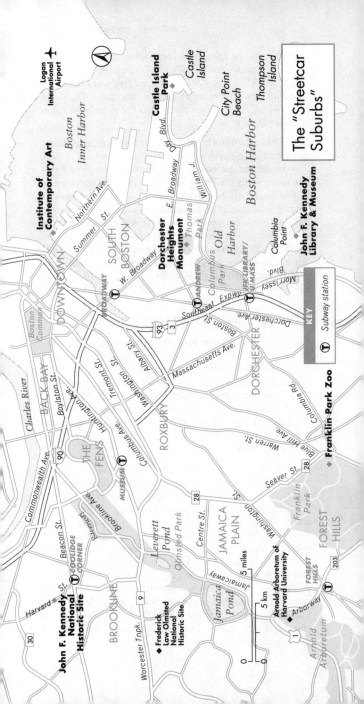

The "Streetcar" Suburbs

1

TOP STREETCAR SUBURBS EXPERIENCES

Institute of Contemporary Art. The outdoor patio juts out right over the water. It's quiet and peaceful and on a sunny day, there's just no better place in Boston to be.

The Franklin Park Zoo. Walk on Boston's wild side right in the middle of the city.

Puppet Showplace. Brookline is a lovely suburb to visit in its own right, and the puppet shows for little ones are a staple bit of the area's entertainment.

SOUTH BOSTON

WHAT TO SEE

Castle Island Park. South Boston projects farther into the harbor than any other part of Boston except Logan Airport, and the views of the Harbor Islands from along Day Boulevard or Castle Island are expansive. At L Street and Day Boulevard is the L Street Beach, where an intrepid group called the L Street Brownies swims year-round, including a celebratory dip in the icy Atlantic every New Year's Day. Castle Island Park is no longer on an island, but **Fort Independence,** when it was built here in 1801, was separated from the mainland by water. The circular walk from the fort around Pleasure Bay, delightful on a warm summer day, also has a stunning view of the city's skyline by night (South Boston is considered one of the city's safest neighborhoods). Paved paths around the bay accommodate different types of wheels—stroller, roller, or bike. A playground and fishing pier are perfect outdoor diversions. There are bathrooms, but they're only open April through October. Fort Independence can only be accessed Memorial Day through Columbus Day. Hours vary. For a trick-or-treat, take the park's annual Halloween tour through the ghoulishly decked-out grounds. ✉*Off William J. Day Blvd., South Boston* ☎*617/268–5744* ⊕*www.mass.gov/ dcr/parks/metroboston/castle.htm* ⊗*Tours Memorial Day– Labor Day, call for specific tour times.* All ages

Franklin Park Zoo. Lion and tiger habitats, the Giraffe Savannah, and a 4-acre mixed-species area called the Serengeti Crossing that showcases zebras, ostriches, ibex, and wildebeests keep this zoo roaring. The Tropical Forest, with its renovated Western Lowland Gorilla environment, is a big draw, and wallabies, emus, and kangaroos populate the Australian Outback Trail. From May to September, butterflies flit and flutter at Butterfly Landing, where docents are on hand to answer questions and give advice on attracting the colorful insects to your own garden. The Children's Zoo entices with sheep, goats, and other petable beasts. In winter, call in advance to find out which animals are braving the cold. Acres of wide, flat paths make the zoo a particular favorite for families with young children who need a little time out of the city to run around. ⊠*1 Franklin Park Rd., Dorchester* ☎*617/541–5466* ⊕*www.zoonewengland.com* ✎ *$12 adults, $7 children 2–12* ⊙*Oct.–Mar., daily 10–4; Apr.–Sept., weekdays 10–5, weekends 10–6.* All ages

★ Fodor'sChoice **Institute of Contemporary Art.** Housed in a breathtaking cantilevered edifice that juts out over the Boston waterfront, the ICA moved to this site in 2006 as part of a massive reinvention that's seeing the museum grow into one of Boston's most exciting attractions. The performing arts get their due in the museum's new theater, and the Water Café features cuisine from Wolfgang Puck. The location alone is worth a visit, and a great place to start a stroll on the Harbor Walk. Free "Our Building" booklets are available at the admissions desk, and offer ideas for tailoring a visit for kids. Pencil sketching is allowed in the galleries (for obvious reasons, no markers or crayons) and the building has an additional space for drawing. Look for family activities at museum Play Dates, held the last Saturday of each month. ⊠*100 Northern Ave., South Boston* ☎*617/478–3100* ⊕*www.icaboston.org* ✎*$12 adults, free for children 17 and under* ⊙*Tues. and Wed. 10–5, Thurs. and Fri. 10–9, weekends 10–5. Tours on select weekends at 2 and select Thurs. at 6* Ⓣ*Courthouse.* All ages

★ **John F. Kennedy Library & Museum.** Chronicling a time now passing from memory to history, the library-museum is a focus for Boston's nostalgia for her native son, displaying a trove of Kennedy memorabilia, including re-creations of his desk in the Oval Office and of the television studio in which he debated Richard M. Nixon in the 1960 election. At the entrance, high and dry during the summer months, is the president's 26-foot sailboat; inside, two theaters show a film about his life. There's also a permanent display on the late Jacqueline Kennedy Onassis, including some samples of her distinctive wardrobe. A re-creation of the office Robert Kennedy occupied as attorney general from 1961 to 1964 complements "legacy" videos of John's idealistic younger brother. As a somber note in an otherwise gung-ho museum, continuous videos of the first news bulletin of the assassination and the funeral are shown in a darkened hall. The library is best for school kids familiar with this period in history. If you're bringing younger children, pick up the "Treasures of the Kennedy Library" guide, outlining a scavenger hunt of sorts through the museum. Don't miss a visit to the Situation Theater where videos replay anxious moments from the Cuban Missile Crisis. Also, make time to appreciate the stellar views of the city across the water. ⊠*Columbia Point, Dorchester* ☎*617/514–1600* ⊕*www. jfklibrary.org* ✉*$10 adults, $7 children 13–17, free for children 12 and under* ☉*Daily 9–5* Ⓣ*JFK/UMass, then free shuttle bus every 20 mins.* 9 + up

Exploring
Cambridge

WORD OF MOUTH

"I felt like a 6 year old girl when I went to the Harvard Museum of Natural History and saw "world famous" glass flower specimens (3000 on display). The museum also features weird taxidermy animals including species which no longer exist, in part because the hunting of them for museum specimens rendered them extinct."

–Kailani

Updated
by Lisa
Oppen-
heimer

FAMILIES IN SEARCH OF A more quirky venue head across the Charles River. The überliberal enclave is punctuated at one end by the funky technoids of MIT (Massachusetts Institute of Technology), and at the other by the intelligentsia of Harvard. Civic life combines the two camps into an urban hodgepodge of 100,000 diverse residents who work at every kind of job from tenured professor to taxi driver and are passionate about living on this side of the river. Visitors in search of ethnic food or music will find it here, a place where the local high school educates students who speak more than 40 different languages.

All of which makes Cambridge a free-spirited counterpoint to buttoned-up Boston and an especially interesting place for families to explore. No place is this more true than Harvard Square, the area's hub—the place to see how the ultra-educated live, perhaps by an "unofficial" Harvard tour led by a cheeky undergrad. Farther along Massachusetts Avenue is Central Square, an ethnic melting pot of residents and restaurants. Ten minutes more brings you to the seemingly futuristic fantasyland of MIT. Notorious pranksters from MIT give kids an additional point of interest, namely the Mass Ave. Bridge where the span from Cambridge to Boston is measured in "Smoots" (⇨*see "Campus Pranksters" under Massachusetts Institute of Technology*).

GETTING YOUR BEARINGS

Just minutes from Boston, Cambridge is easily reached by taking the Red Line train (otherwise known as the "T") outbound to any stop past Charles Street. In Cambridge any commercial area where three or more streets meet in a jumble of traffic and noise is dubbed a "square." Harvard Square draws the most visitors, with its funky collection of shops, restaurants, and cafés of the independent and chain varieties. Other neighborhoods—Porter, Inman, and Central squares, to name a few—exude their own charms.

Harvard Square is the best place to begin any visit to Cambridge. The area is notorious for aggressive drivers, lack of parking, and floods of pedestrians. Do yourself a favor and take the T. If you must drive, avoid endlessly circling the block by pulling into a garage. Two good ones: the Harvard Square garage at JFK and Eliot streets, and the University Place garage behind the Charles Hotel, on University Road at Bennett Street. Some offer validation from specific retailers—ask about it when you park. There's also a small

TOP CAMBRIDGE EXPERIENCES

■ Do the Harvard Museum circuit: The Sackler for art; the Semitic Museum; the Peabody and the Natural History Museum for artifacts and culture.

■ Visit MIT to wander the halls, visit its museum, and see Frank Gehry's Seuss-like Stata Center.

■ Breathe the rarefied air of Harvard on an official tour,

then return to real life with an ice-cream cone from Herrell's or a burger from Mr. Bartley's Burger Cottage.

■ Amble down Brattle Street, visiting the 1700s era homes of Tory Row (Washington really did sleep here.), and have a treat at Hi-Rise bakery .

public lot on Church Street between Brattle Street and Mass Ave. Those who like to gamble for meters can find a large concentration of the coin-operated gizmos underneath the Harvard Square Hotel on Mt. Auburn Street. Take note, though: even if you're lucky enough to snag one, the one-hour limits will probably impede your visit.

HARVARD SQUARE

In Cambridge, all streets point toward Harvard Square. On a warm day, street musicians coax exotic tones from their Andean pan flutes and Chinese erhus, while cranks and local pessimists pass out pamphlets warning against various end-of-the-world scenarios. Everyone is on a cell phone, speaking in dozens of languages. In the small plaza atop the main entrance to the Harvard T station known as "the Pit," skaters and punks strut and pose while fresh-faced students impress each other and/or their dates, and quiet clusters study the moves and strategy of the chess players seated outside Au Bon Pain.

A good place to start is the **Cambridge Visitor Information Booth.** Volunteers at this kiosk outside the MBTA station entrance hand out free maps, brochures, and guides about the city. Material available includes a walking tour of historic places, an excellent list of bookstores in the area, and a guide to seasonal events. If you plan ahead you can check the organization's Web site for a walking tour available for download to your iPod. The tours are currently free, but may in the future charge a fee. The booth is supervised by the Cambridge Tourism office at 4 Brattle Street. ✉0

A GOOD WALK

Begin your tour at the **Cambridge Visitor Information Booth** in **Harvard Square ❶** near the MBTA station entrance, for maps, a guide to local bookstores, and brochures that cover walking tours of old Cambridge and seasonal events. Take some time to appreciate the area itself. Many kids are wowed by the funky shops (alas, many chains now) and the remarkable collection of worldwide periodicals at Out of Town News. Enter the dignified hush of the Yard at **Harvard University ❷**. Stick your nose into **Widener Library**; it houses one of the largest collections of books, historical materials, and journals in the academic world. Then circle back through the yard, crossing Mass Ave. to view the **First Parish in Cambridge and the Old Burying Ground ❸** on the corner of Church Street. The Cambridge Common, across Garden Street, has a terrific playground, and is a good spot to take a rest.

Retrace your steps along Mass Ave. and cross the street near the First Parish Church. Cut through Harvard Yard, bearing to your left, pass the modern Science Center. If you want to understand what makes Harvard a cultural epicenter, a visit to its museums is advised. It's not just that Harvard has everything, it has the best of everything—from Picassos to Pollocks to Egyptian mummies. Just past Memorial Hall, at the intersection of Quincy and Kirkland streets, turn right onto Kirkland Street and then take a quick left onto Divinity Avenue. At 6 Divinity Avenue is Harvard's **Semitic Museum.** At 11 Divinity Avenue is the entrance to the extensive **Peabody Museum of Archaeology & Ethnology** and the **Harvard Museum of Natural History ❹** (in the same building). When you've had your fill of culture, head back to one of the Harvard Square cafés for a snack and serious people-watching.

TIMING

Harvard Square is worth an afternoon, at least—more if you plan to explore Harvard's natural-history or art museums.

Harvard Sq. ☎*617/497–1630* ⊕*www.cambridge-usa.org* ⊙*Weekdays 9–5, Sat. 10–3, Sun. 1–5* Ⓣ*Harvard.* All ages

Numbers in the margin correspond to numbers on the Harvard Square map.

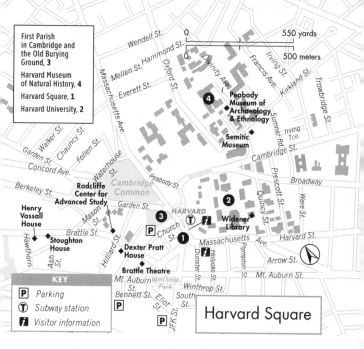

KEY

P Parking

T Subway station

i Visitor information

Harvard Square

WHAT TO SEE

★ FodorśChoice **Harvard Museum of Natural History.** Many muse-
④ ums promise something for every member of the family;
the vast Harvard Museum complex actually delivers. The
Museum of Comparative Zoology traces the evolution of
animals and humans. You literally can't miss the 42-foot-
long skeleton of the underwater *Kronosaurus*. Dinosaur
fossils and a zoo of stuffed exotic animals can occupy
young minds for hours. The museum is also the right size
for kids—not jazzy and busy, a good place to ask and
answer quiet questions.

Oversize garnets and crystals sparkle at the **Mineralogical
and Geological Museum,** founded in 1784. The museum
also contains an extensive collection of meteorites.

Perhaps the most famous exhibits of the museum complex
are the glass flowers in the **Botanical Museum,** created as
teaching tools that would never wither and die. This unique
collection holds 3,000 models, each one a masterpiece,
meticulously created in glass by a father and son in Dres-
den, Germany. Ultracool exhibits make this a kid favor-

ite. Dino lovers will want to explore prehistoric leftovers from the Triassic period. The collection of taxidermic animals is extraordinary, but will either thrill or horrify kids, depending on their disposition about such things. Look for events for families with middle schoolers, held Sunday at 2 PM. ⊠*26 Oxford St.* ☎*617/495-3045* ⊕*www.hmnh. harvard.edu* ☎*$9, includes admission to Peabody Museum of Archaeology & Ethnology, Massachusetts residents free,* $6 children 3–18 ⊙*Daily 9–5* Ⓣ*Harvard.* 3 + up

NEED A BREAK? The **Broadway Marketplace** (⊠ *468 Broadway* ☎ *617/547-2334*) is just around the corner from the now-defunct Fogg Art Museum. Besides the excellent fresh produce, there's a selection of sandwiches and prepared meals; choose one to be heated up and then grab a seat for a quick bite.

WHERE CAN I FIND . . . IN HARVARD SQUARE?

A Quick Meal		
Au Bon Pain	1360 Mass Avenue	Dependable chain, great for quick eats to go, and a prime spot to grab an outdoor table and people-watch.
A Grocery Store		
Market in the Square	60 Church Street	The new spot is a place to get a few grocery staples. The sushi, buffet, and deli have made it a local favorite.
Good Coffee		
Crema Cafe	27 Brattle Street	A lovely little old-school shop with coffee, tea, sandwiches, pastries—all the good stuff.
A Fun Store		
Curious George Goes to Wordsworth	1 JFK Street	It's part of a chain now, but you'd never know it. The local favorite has maintained its indy charm with games and books and ultrafriendly staff.
A Good Playground		
Cambridge Common Playground	Garden and Waterhouse streets	Climbing and sliding—the perfect place to take a break.
A Public Bathroom		
Holyoke Center	75 Mt. Auburn Street	The Harvard building has a restaurant and bookstore and most importantly, a bathroom for all to use.

★ **Fodor**s**Choice** **Harvard Square.** Tides of students, tourists, polit-
❶ ical-cause proponents, and bizarre street creatures are all
part of the nonstop pedestrian flow at this most celebrated
of Cambridge crossroads.

On an average afternoon, you'll hear earnest conversations
in dozens of foreign languages; see every kind of youthful
uniform from Goth to impeccable prep; wander by street
musicians playing Andean flutes, singing opera, and doing
excellent Stevie Wonder or Edith Piaf imitations; and lean
in on a tense outdoor game of pickup chess between a
street-tough kid and an older gent wearing a beard and a
beret, while you slurp a cappuccino or an ice-cream cone
(the two major food groups here). An afternoon in the
square is people-watching raised to a high art; the parade
of quirkiness never quits.

Across Garden Street is **Cambridge Common**, decreed a
public pasture in 1631. It's said that under a large tree that
once stood in this meadow George Washington took com-
mand of the Continental Army on July 3, 1775. A stone
memorial now marks the site of the "Washington Elm."
⊕*www.harvardsquare.com* Ⓣ*Harvard.*

NEED A BREAK? **Herrell's Ice Cream** (⊠*15 Dunster St., Harvard Sq.*
☎*617/497–2179*) is a Harvard Square institution. Mix-ins (those
yummy bits of candy and cookie that make ice cream a full-
fledged decadence) were born here. Add the hand-rolled cones
and nine flavors of chocolate, and you've got a don't-miss deli-
cacy. The friendly scoopers are young, punk Cambridge-ites—
their tattoos and body piercings make odd counterpoints to the
sweet sundaes.

❷ **Harvard University.** The tree-studded, shady, and redbrick
expanse of **Harvard Yard**—the very center of Harvard University—has weathered the footsteps of Harvard students
for more than 300 years. Named in 1639 for John Harvard,
a young Charlestown clergyman who died in 1638 and left
the college his entire library and half his estate, local wags
refer to Harvard as WGU—World's Greatest University—
and it's certainly the oldest and most famous American
university. The oldest buildings in Harvard Yard are of the
18th century; together the buildings chronicle American
architecture from the colonial era to the present. Many of
Harvard's cultural and scholarly facilities are important
sights in themselves, including the **Harvard Museum of**

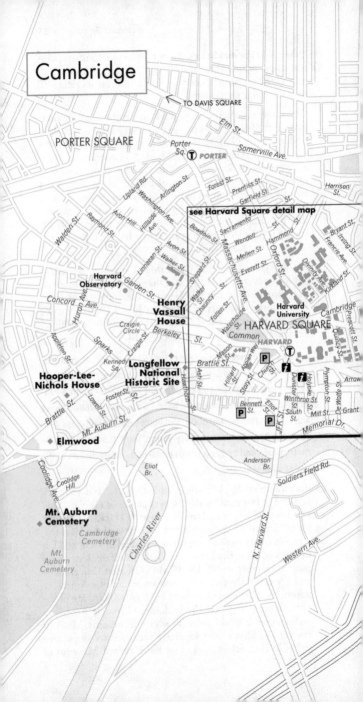

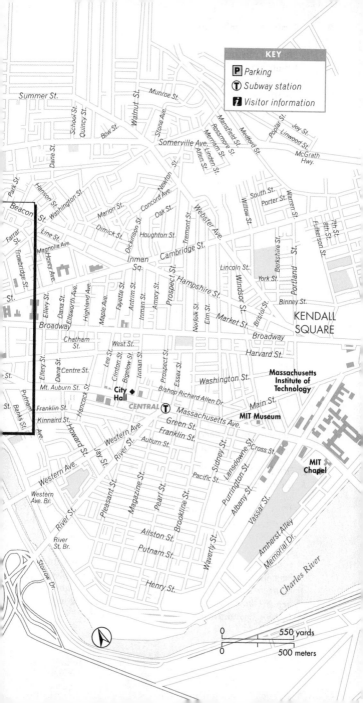

Natural History, the **Peabody Museum of Archaeology &
Ethnology**, and the **Widener Library**. Be aware that most
campus buildings, other than museums and concert halls,
are off-limits to the general public.

Harvard University Events & Information Center (⊠*Holyoke
Center, 1350 Massachusetts Ave.* ☎*617/495–1573* ⊕*www.
harvard.edu*), run by students, includes a small library, a
video-viewing area, computer terminals, and an exhibit
space. It also distributes maps of the university area and has
free student-led tours of Harvard Yard. The tour doesn't
include visits to museums, and it doesn't take you into
campus buildings, but it provides a fine orientation. The
information center is open year-round (except for during
spring recess and other semester breaks), Monday through
Saturday 9–5. Tours are offered September–June, weekdays at 10 and 2 and Saturday at 2. In July and August,
guides offer four tours: Monday–Saturday, 10, 11:15, 2,
and 3:15. Groups of 20 or more can schedule their tours
ahead. Kids who have ivy-league dreams might appreciate the academic tour. There's also a cheekier, unofficial
version with a higher humor quotient offered daily by
Unofficial Tours (☎*617/848–8576*). ⊠*Bounded by Massachusetts Ave., Mt. Auburn St., Holyoke St., and Dunster St.*
☎*617/495–1573 for Harvard directory assistance* ⊕*www.
harvard.edu* Ⓣ*Harvard.* 12 + up

DID YOU KNOW? One perk of being a University Professor (holding
an endowed chair)—a title awarded to about a dozen preeminent
members of the Harvard faculty—is the official right to graze
cattle in Harvard Yard. Not surprisingly, few, if any, ever do.

❸ **First Parish in Cambridge and the Old Burying Ground.** Next to
★ the imposing church on the corner of Church Street and
Mass Ave., a spooky-looking colonial graveyard houses
17th- and 18th-century tombstones of ministers, early
Harvard presidents, and Revolutionary War soldiers. The
wooden Gothic Revival church, known locally as "First
Church" or "First Parish," was built in 1833 by Isaiah Rogers. The congregation dates to two centuries earlier, and has
been linked to Harvard since the founding of the college. ⊠*3
Church St.* ☎*617/876–7772* ⊕*www.firstparishcambridge.
org* ⊙*Church weekdays 8–4, Sun. 8–1, service at 10:30.
Burying ground daily dawn–dusk* Ⓣ*Harvard.* 9 + up

BRATTLE STREET/TORY ROW

On a nice day, even kids will enjoy the lovely walk along Brattle Street, one of New England's most elegant thoroughfares. Parents will get to appreciate the elaborate mansions lining both sides from where it meets JFK Street to Fresh Pond Parkway. Brattle Street was once dubbed Tory Row because during the 1770s its seven mansions were owned by staunch supporters of King George. Many of the historic houses are marked with blue signs, but only two (the Hooper-Lee-Nichols House and the Longfellow National Historic Site) are open to the public. Less than 2 mi down Brattle Street from Harvard Square stretches Mt. Auburn Cemetery, an exquisitely landscaped garden cemetery.

NEED A BREAK? The **Hi-Rise Bread Company in the Blacksmith House** (☎*617/492–3003*), on the first floor of the Dexter Pratt House, is the perfect stop for a pick-me-up coffee and fresh-baked treat or fantastic sandwich on their homemade bread. Snag a table at the outdoor café; it's a choice spot for people-watching. Chocolate lovers may be seduced by the aromas emanating from **L. A. Burdick Chocolates** (✉*52 Brattle St.* ☎*617/491–4340* ⊕*www.burdickchocolate.com*); rich confections or elegant hot cocoa may be just the things to restore flagging spirits.

KENDALL SQUARE/MIT

Harvard Square may be the center of the "People's Republic of Cambridge," but the Kendall Square neighborhood is the city's hard-driving capitalist core. This is MIT-land, the heart of the computer age, and the place techno-loving kids may already be envisioning for their futures. Although the MIT campus may lack the ivied elegance of Harvard Yard, major modern architects created signature buildings here. To reach MIT, take the Red Line T to Kendall station; if you're headed for the MIT Museum on the western edge of the campus, the Central Square station is more convenient.

WHAT TO SEE

List Visual Arts Center. Local Boston-area artists and art students consider the List Gallery to be the most interesting gallery in town. Founded by Albert and Vera List, pioneer collectors of modern art, this MIT center has three galleries showcasing exhibitions of cutting-edge art and mixed media. Works from the center's collection of contemporary art, such as Thomas Hart Benton's painting *Fluid Catalytic Crackers* and Harry Bertoia's altarpiece for the MIT Chapel, are on view here and around campus. The center's Web site includes a map indicating the locations of more than 25 of these works. ⊠ *Wiesner Bldg., 20 Ames St., off Main St.* ☎ *617/253–4680* ⊕ *web.mit.edu/lvac* ☞ *Free* ⊘ *Sept.–July, Tues.–Thurs. noon–6, Fri. noon–8, weekends noon–6* Ⓣ *Kendall/MIT.* 12 + up

WHERE CAN I FIND ... IN KENDALL SQUARE/MIT?

Quick Meals

Emma's Pizza	40 Hampshire Street	Locals know this small, brick-front chain for its homemade and delicious pizza.
La Luna Caffe	403 Massachusetts Avenue	A local gem with everything from grilled cheese to gourmet sandwiches on Rosemary focaccia. For dessert: try the chocolate cake!

A Grocery Store

7-Eleven	589 Massachusetts Avenue	For staples and a Slurpee 24 hours a day.

Good Coffee

Toscani's Ice Cream	899 Main Street	A well-loved local spot, with many creative flavors, a good place for coffee, and on weekends, you can get breakfast, too.

A Fun Store

Buckaroo's Mercantile	5 Brookline Street	A hodgepodge of retro (and humorously off-color) stuff will appeal to teens, even while occasionally making mom and dad blush.

A Public Bathroom

MIT Information Center	77 Massachusetts Avenue	

Massachusetts Institute of Technology. Celebrated for both its brains and its cerebral sense of humor, this once-tidy engineering school at right angles to the Charles River is growing like a sprawling adolescent, consuming old industrial buildings and city blocks with every passing year. Once dissed as "the factory," MIT mints graduates that are the sharp blades on the edge of the information revolution.

CAMPUS PRANKSTERS

A popular recurring exhibit at the MIT Museum is the "Hall of Hacks," a look at the pranks MIT students have played over the years. Most notable here is a rare photo of Oliver Reed Smoot Jr., a 1958 MIT Lambda Chi Alpha pledge. Smoot's future fraternity brothers used the diminutive freshman to measure the distance of the nearby Harvard Bridge. Every 5 feet and 6 inches became "one Smoot." The markings on the bridge are repainted by the frat every two years, and Boston police actually use them to indicate location when filing accident reports. All told, the bridge is "364.4 Smoots plus 1 ear" long.

Founded in 1861, MIT moved to Cambridge from Copley Square in the Back Bay in 1916. It has long since fulfilled the predictions of its founder that it would surpass "the universities of the land in the accuracy and the extent of its teachings in all branches of positive science."

Architecture is important at MIT. Although the original buildings were obviously designed by and for scientists, many represent pioneering designs of their times.

East Campus's **Great Dome,** which looms over neoclassical Killian Court, has often been the target of student "hacks," and has at various times supported a telephone booth with a ringing phone and a campus police cruiser. Nearby, the domed **Rogers Building** has a series of hallways and tunnels dubbed "the infinite corridor." Twice each winter, the sun's path lines up perfectly with the corridor's axis, and at dusk students line the third-floor hallway to watch the sun set through the westernmost window. The phenomenon is known as "MIT-henge."

MIT maintains an information center in the Rogers Building and offers free tours of the campus weekdays at 11 and 3. Check holiday schedule as the tours are often suspended during school holidays. General hours for the information center are weekdays 9–5. Tours can be taken either with a guide—weekdays 11 to 3; meet in Lobby 7 in the main building at 77 Massachusetts Avenue—or on your own with one of the self-guided maps available at the information center. Kids who aspire to an MIT education will thoroughly enjoy the opportunity to get to know the campus, and pick up that all-important logo sweatshirt.

✉ *77 Massachusetts Ave.* ☎ *617/253–4795* ⊕ *web.mit.edu*
Ⓣ *Kendall/MIT.* 10 + up

MIT Museum. A place where art and science meet, the MIT Museum displays photos, paintings, and scientific instruments and memorabilia in a dynamic, hands-on setting. The world's largest collection of holograms is downright eye-popping, though young kids may prefer the moving gestural sculptures of Arthur Ganson. The robot room shows off inventions of MIT's renowned robotics lab and an extensive exhibit on artificial intelligence. The museum is small, but decidedly appealing to kids, especially kids who'd categorize an MIT robot as the coolest creation ever. Look for programs geared specially toward middle- and high-schoolers. Kids who are really into the museum will want to spend a couple of hours. There's no food on premises, but plenty of restaurants in the surrounding area. ✉ *265 Massachusetts Ave.* ☎ *617/253–4444* ⊕ *web.mit.edu/ museum* ✑ *$7.50 adults, $3 children 5–18* ☉ *Daily 10–5* Ⓣ *Kendall/MIT.* 8 + up

Where to Eat

3

WORD OF MOUTH

"You must have dinner in the North End for Italian. I also like Neptune Oyster in North End for fried clams and board-walk-style French fries and oysters, lobster rolls, or their more refined fish dishes. If you're in Harvard Square, go for a casual burger at Mr. Bartley's Burger Cottage. It is a landmark and great burgers. Make sure to order the onion rings and a lime rickey."

—gyppielou

Updated by Lisa Oppen- heimer

WHEN IT COMES TO FOOD in Boston, the Revolution never ended. Bostonians have proudly clung to their traditional eats (chowders, baked beans, and cream pies can still be found) and local chefs still respect the power of the staples—the bread and butter, so to speak. But, Boston and Cambridge have also become home to the kind of restaurant overseen by a creative mastermind, often locally born, concocting inspired food served in human surroundings without excessive formality. Such casual gourmets mean families are often welcome anywhere, from quaint bistros to multistar palaces that tend to young palates with specific children's menus (more common than one might think) or via a congenial chef willing to adjust sauces or create half-plate servings. Not that it's an entirely open field. Some establishments will charge heartily for the kids' fare, while in others, you may have to withstand withering stares from the upscale locals who've left junior at home with the nanny. Bottom line: it pays to inquire, "Do people actually dine there with children?" rather than the more general, "Do you allow tots?"

WHAT IT COSTS

Entrée prices fluctuate with the state of the economy. Top-tier restaurants remain impervious to market changes, but more restaurants are accommodating every price range with small or half portions at a lower price. Credit cards are widely accepted, but many restaurants (particularly smaller ones Downtown) accept only cash. Our restaurant reviews indicate which credit cards are accepted (if any) at each establishment, but it's a good idea to double-check.

WHAT IT COSTS				
¢	$	$$	$$$	$$$$
AT DINNER				
under $8	$8–$14	$15–$24	$25–$32	over $32

Prices are per person for a main course at dinner. Some restaurants are marked with a price range ($$–$$$, for example). This indicates one of two things: Either the average cost straddles two categories, or if you order strategically, you can get out for less than most diners spend.

BOSTON DINING PLANNER

WHAT TO WEAR

Boston is a notch or two more reserved in its fashion than New York or Los Angeles. Its dining dress code normally hovers at the level of casual chic. Few of the city's most formal restaurants require jackets and even at some of the most expensive places jeans are acceptable as long as they're paired with a dressy top and posh shoes. Shorts are appropriate only in the most casual spots. When in doubt, call and ask.

MEALTIMES

Boston's restaurants close relatively early; most shut their doors by 10 or 11 PM. Restaurants that serve breakfast often do so until 11 AM or noon, at which point they start serving lunch.

RESERVATIONS

Reservations generally need to be made at least a few nights in advance, but this is easily done by your concierge or online at www.opentable. com. Tables can be hard to come by if you want to dine between 7 and 9, or on Friday or Saturday night. But most restaurants will get you in if you show up and are willing to wait.

EATING OUT STRATEGY

To find the best around Boston follow the roads that radiate out from Downtown like the spokes of a giant wheel. Smack inside the hub are the huge, and hugely famous, waterfront seafood restaurants—but go north, west, or south and you're suddenly in the neighborhoods, home to numerous smaller restaurants on the way up.

TIPPING

Never tip the maître d'. In most restaurants, tip the waiter at least 15%–20%. (To figure the amount quickly, just double the 8.625% tax on the bill and, if you like, add a little more.) Bills for parties of six or more sometimes include service. Tip at least $1 per drink at the bar, and $1 for each coat checked.

SMOKING

Smoking is prohibited in all enclosed public spaces in Boston and Cambridge, including restaurants and bars.

BOSTON

BACK BAY/BEACON HILL

Enticing restaurants of every ilk are on Newbury Street, where kids nosh chicken nuggets at a chain restaurant while hipsters sip chardonnay at the bistro next door. Parents in a pinch will find plenty of fast-food eateries on Boylston, or over in the Copley/Prudential complexes where there's a food court plus dependable table-service chains.

$$$$ ✕**Abe & Louie's.** *American.* Go ahead: live the fantasy of the robber baron feasting among cavernous fireplaces and deep-textured, plush mahogany booths. Abe & Louie's may be a tad Disney-esque in its decor, but its menu lives up to the promise with gorgeous, two-tiered raw platters and juicy rib-eye steaks under velvety hollandaise. Even the linen napkins have little buttonholes for the perfect collar hold. **Family Matters:** You won't find a kids' menu or crayons. But, you will find high chairs and booster seats, and a kitchen willing to adapt dishes to your kids' needs. There's plenty to choose from (signature dessert: hot fudge sundae!), and the atmosphere isn't the kind to make a parent with kids uncomfortable. Your best bet is lunch. For dinner, especially weekends, make a reservation. ✉*793 Boylston St., Back Bay* ☏*617/536–6300* ▭*AE, D, DC, MC, V* Ⓣ*Copley.*

$$–$$$ ✕**Bouchee.** *French.* With its sunken patio and two-story dining room, Bouchee is a warm, noisy, and lovable neighborhood bistro. There's a wide variety of brasserie-style French cuisine such as raw bar items, salad Niçoise, cassoulet, and steak frites, plus easy-to-eat flatbread pizzas. Shiny tiles and brass fixtures gleam in the first-floor bar while the second floor is more spacious and filled with well-to-do Back Bay residents. **Family Matters:** Don't let the hipness be intimidating. Children are frequent guests here. A full scan of the menu shows a good ole burger next to that duck confit, and kitchen staff will happily customize the former to suit junior's appetite. Macaroni is also available, as are high chairs and booster seats. ✉ *159 Newbury St, Back Bay* ☏*617/450–4343* ⌂*Reservations essential* ▭*AE, D, DC, MC, V* Ⓣ*Copley.*

$$$–$$$$ ✕**Bristol Lounge.** *Steak.* Off the lobby of the Four Seasons Hotel, this lovely spot across the street from the Public Garden is a perfect place to temporarily get away from it all. Soft music plays and diners cozy up in enormous cushy booths while enjoying tasty specialties like lemon sole or gourmet pastas. It's an elegant yet everything-goes kind of place, with folks coming to grab a bite in suit or tie, or even scrubs.**Family Matters:**Despite its upscaleness, describing this place as merely "Kid friendly" doesn't seem to do it justice. Little kids get their own colorful, plastic placemats

plus bibs, crayons, coloring book, and their own reasonably priced menu. Even teens are specially taken care of, with fare ranging from small portions of beef tenderloin to a juicy burger. ⊠*Four Seasons 200 Boylston St., Back Bay* ☎*617/351–2071* ⚐*Reservations essential* ▤*AE, D, DC, MC, V* ⓣ*Arlington*

$$ ╳**Charley's Saloon.** *American.* Saloons may be no place for kids, but this is no real saloon. The local chain doles out dependable if not earth-shattering American classics (grilled cheese, steaks, and apple pies) in a fun retro setting, where families will feel right at home. **Family Matters:** With a coloring menu and crayons provided, Charley's is a welcome respite for parents tooling around the upscale Newbury neighborhood. Booster seats and high chairs available. ⊠*284 Newbury St., Back Bay* ☎*617/266–3000* ▤*AE, D, DC, MC, V* ⓣ*Hynes/ICA.*

$–$$ ╳**Croma.** *Italian.* Of all the sidewalk patios on Newbury, Croma's has the best view. The easy pasta dishes and somewhat inventive pizzas make it an ideal refueling spot if you're trolling the street for deals. Grab a seat in the shade and order a glass of wine from the varied list before tucking into the fluffy dough balls and a Peking duck pizza. **Family Matters:** Croma is an "everybody's happy" kind of place—local flavor with lots of choices, from ahi tuna for mom, to cheese pizza for junior. There's a small kids' menu, but, with so many pastas and pizzas, you might not need it. Boosters and high chairs are available. There's plenty of seating, but the stroller set will find more room during the week. ⊠*269 Newbury St., Back Bay* ☎*617/247–3200* ▤*AE, MC, V* ⓣ*Copley.*

★ Fodor'sChoice ╳**Eastern Standard Kitchen and Drinks.** *American.*
$$ A vivid red awning beckons those entering this spacious brasserie-style restaurant. The bar area and red banquettes are filled most nights with Boston's power players (members of the Red Sox management are known to stop in), thirtysomethings, and students from the nearby universities all noshing on raw-bar specialties and comfort dishes such as veal schnitzel, rib eye, and burgers. **Family Matters:** It definitely doesn't scream "family restaurant," but kids are absolutely welcome, as evidenced by the crayons supplied for drawing on the paper table covers. Ask about "off-menu" items like chicken fingers. Game nights (at nearby Fenway), dinner starts at 4:30, and the place gets just chaotic enough for a family to feel right at home. High

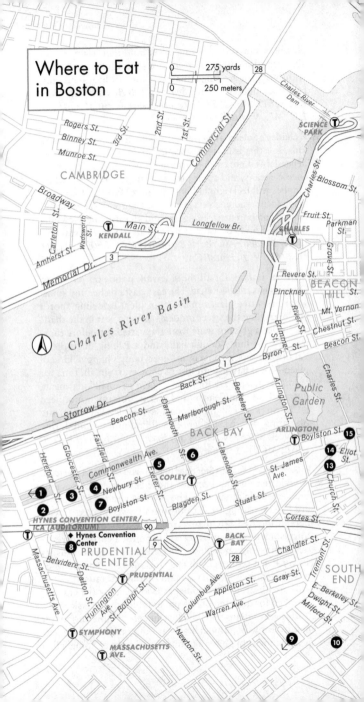

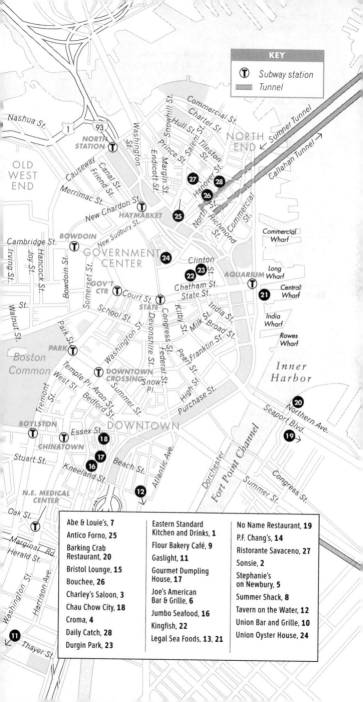

KEY

Ⓣ Subway station
▬ Tunnel

Nashua St.
93
1
NORTH STATION Ⓣ
OLD WEST END
Causeway
Merrimac St.
Canal St.
Friend St.
Washington St.
Endicott St.
New Chardon St.
Commercial St.
Charter St.
Hull St.
Salem St.
Tileston St.
Snowhill St.
Prince St.
Margin St.
Hanover St.
NORTH END
Sumner Tunnel
Callahan Tunnel →
HAYMARKET Ⓣ
New Sudbury St.
BOWDOIN
Cambridge St.
Hancock St.
Joy St.
Irving St.
Bowdoin St.
GOVERNMENT CENTER Ⓣ
GOV'T CTR Ⓣ
Somerset St.
Court St.
STATE Ⓣ
School St.
Washington St.
Devonshire St.
Congress St.
Kilby St.
Milk St.
Broad St.
India St.
Clinton
Chatham St.
State St.
AQUARIUM Ⓣ
Commercial Wharf
Long Wharf
Central Wharf
India Wharf
Rowes Wharf
Inner Harbor
North St.
Richmond St.
Commercial St.
PARK Ⓣ
Park St.
Tremont St.
West St.
Temple Pl.
Avon St.
DOWNTOWN CROSSING Ⓣ
Summer St.
Bedford St.
Snow Pl.
Franklin St.
Pearl St.
Federal St.
High St.
Purchase St.
DOWNTOWN
Northern Ave.
Seaport Blvd.
20
19 →
Boston Common
Walnut St.
Beacon St.
BOYLSTON Ⓣ
CHINATOWN Ⓣ
Stuart St.
Essex St.
Beach St.
Kneeland St.
Atlantic Ave.
Dorchester
Fort Point Channel
Summer St.
Congress St.
18
17
16
12
N.E. MEDICAL CENTER Ⓣ
Oak St.
Marginal Rd.
Herald St.
Washington St.
Harrison Ave.
Thayer St.
11

27
28
26
25
24
22
23
21

Abe & Louie's, **7**	Eastern Standard Kitchen and Drinks, **1**	No Name Restaurant, **19**
Antico Forno, **25**	Flour Bakery Café, **9**	P.F. Chang's, **14**
Barking Crab Restaurant, **20**	Gaslight, **11**	Ristorante Savaceno, **27**
Bristol Lounge, **15**	Gourmet Dumpling House, **17**	Sonsie, **2**
Bouchee, **26**	Joe's American Bar & Grille, **6**	Stephanie's on Newbury, **5**
Charley's Saloon, **3**	Jumbo Seafood, **16**	Summer Shack, **8**
Chau Chow City, **18**	Kingfish, **22**	Tavern on the Water, **12**
Croma, **4**	Legal Sea Foods, **13, 21**	Union Bar and Grille, **10**
Daily Catch, **28**		Union Oyster House, **24**
Durgin Park, **23**		

chairs and booster seats available. ✉*528 Commonwealth Ave., Kenmore Sq.* ☎*617/532–9100* ⊟*AE, D, DC, MC, V* Ⓣ*Kenmore.*

$$ ✕**Joe's American Bar & Grille.** *American.* So what if the restaurant looks as if it has been decorated by a raving mob at a July 4 parade? Next to an oversize burger and a slice of apple pie, the red, white, and blue overload is kind of fun. The clam chowder is almost always a hit with all generations. **Family Matters:** Food-wise, there are more exciting places, but if comfort is the goal, the Joe's chain is a good bet. It's got the all-important kids' menu, crayons, high chairs, booster seats, and completely kid-friendly environment right in the Newbury neighborhood. If you want scenery, too, check out Joe's on the waterfront. It occupies one of the choicest plots of land in town. ✉*279 Dartmouth St., Back Bay* ☎*617/536–4200* ⊟*AE, D, DC, MC, V* Ⓣ*Copley.*

$$–$$$ ✕**Legal Sea Foods.** *Seafood.* What began as a tiny restaurant upstairs over a Cambridge fish market has grown to important regional status, with more than 20 East Coast locations, plus a handful of national ones. The hallmark is the freshest possible seafood, whether you have it wood grilled, in New England chowder, or doused with an Asia-inspired sauce. The smoked-bluefish pâté is delectable, and the clam chowder is so good it has become a menu staple at presidential inaugurations. A preferred-seating list allows calls ahead, and this location has private dining inside its beautiful, bottle-lined wine cellar. **Family Matters:** Convenient after an afternoon running around the Common, Legal decidedly draws with seafood, but kids can opt for plenty of land specialties from the kids' menu that they can also color in. Even better, adventurous small palates can try out the specially prepared and priced kids' steamed lobster or fish special of the day. Oversized, comfy booths are great for families. Booster seats and high chairs are available. ✉*26 Park Sq., Theater District* ☎*617/426–4444* ⌖*Reservations not accepted* ⊟*AE, D, DC, MC, V* Ⓣ*Arlington.*

$$ ✕**P.F. Chang's China Bistro.** *Chinese.* Straightforward, Americanized, and inexpensive Chinese food makes the rounds in this theatrically decorated spot. Kids love the fake Imperial sculptures and screens; parents love the prices and the accommodating staff. **Family Matters:** There's no kids' menu, but little ones favor the lemon chicken and spare

ribs. In the theater district, the restaurant is perfect after a movie (the theme-park-like Loews complex is a five-minute walk) or a visit to the Common/Garden. Desserts include The Great Wall of Chocolate Cake, but there's also ice cream next door at the Coldstone Creamery. Booster seats and high chairs are available. ⊠ *8 Park Plaza, Back Bay* ☎*617/573–0821* ⊟*AE, D, DC, MC, V* Ⓣ*Arlington.*

$$–$$$ ╳**Sonsie.** *American.* Café society blossoms along Newbury Street, particularly at Sonsie, where a well-heeled crowd sips coffee up front or angles for places at the bar. Lunch and dinner dishes, such as charcoal duck breast and leg with brown rice and five-spice turnips, are basic bistro with an American twist. The restaurant is a terrific place for weekend brunch, when the light pours through the long windows, and is at its most vibrant in warm weather, when the open doors make for colorful people-watching. **Family Matters:** Older kids will like the location at the funky end of Newbury Street near Newbury Comics and Urban Outfitters. The restaurant is best for either babies (high chairs are available) or school age and up, as there are no booster seats. Toddlers might do better elsewhere. There's no specific menu for kids, but they'll be happy with plentiful burgers and pasta. ⊠ *327 Newbury St., Back Bay* ☎*617/351–2500* ⊟*AE, D, MC, V* Ⓣ*Hynes/ICA.*

$$ ╳**Stephanie's on Newbury.** *American.* Here's comfort food at its best—sophisticated enough for parents, simple enough for kids. The place is pretty but homey, and has plenty of booths for spreading out. **Family Matters:** Not a family restaurant per se, but a comfy place to get interesting grownup food, while tending to the kids, too. In the absence of a separate menu, pastas like macaroni and cheese and baked ziti satisfy young tastes. Look for high chairs, but no booster seats. ⊠ *190 Newbury St., Back Bay* ☎*617/236–0990* ⊟ *AE, D, DC, MC, V* Ⓣ*Copley.*

$$ ╳**Summer Shack.** *Seafood.* Boston überchef Jasper White has given New England seafood an urban tweak in his laid-back, loud, and fun spot next to the Prudential Center. The colors are bright, and the entire year-round experience (despite the name) is like one big indoor clambake. The giant lobster tank in the dining room makes an attention-getting centerpiece, although probably less so for kids when they find out what the lobsters are for. Reservations are strongly recommended as waits, particularly weekend nights, can be long. **Family Matters:** The kids' menu is

uncommonly huge and interesting, with seafood items like fish-and-chips, steamed lobster, and even calamari served in pint-size portions (and prices). There's standard kids' fare like corn dogs and pizza, too. High chairs and booster seats are available. ⊠*50 Dalton St., Back Bay* ☎*617/867–9955.*

CHARLESTOWN

This little neighborhood across Boston Harbor contains the Bunker Hill Monument, the USS *Constitution*, and one culinary landmark, Todd English's famous Olives. The latter might merit some curiosity from families, but with no more than a stray high chair, it seems aimed squarely at a grown-ups-only crowd.

$$$ ✕**Tavern on the Water.** *American.* It's a long way back to Boston from the end of the Freedom Trail, and the family is probably hungry. With the added bonus of the scenery implied by its name, Tavern's got good food year round, from broiled seafood to burgers, plus a large children's menu. **Family Matters:** In addition to dependable fare, the restaurant offers kids a stellar spot from which to watch the boats. Booster seats and high chairs are available. ⊠*1 8th St., Charlestown* ☎*617/242–8040* ⊟*AE, D, MC, V* Ⓣ*Community College.*

CHINATOWN

On the fringe of the theater district, Boston's Chinatown is the focal point for Asian cuisines of all types, from authentic Cantonese and Vietnamese to Malaysian, Japanese, and Mandarin. It's definitely worth the trek, especially for those adventurous enough for dim sum. On the other hand, though the eateries are open into the wee hours, lunch or early dinner is recommended for families, as the late-night neighborhood can feel a little sketchy.

$$–$$$ ✕**Chau Chow City.** *Chinese.* Spread across three floors, this is the largest, glitziest, and most versatile production yet of the Chau Chow dynasty, with dim sum by day and live-tank seafood by night. Overwhelmed? At lunch, head to the third floor for dim sum. Or sit on the main floor and order the clams in black-bean sauce, the sautéed pea-pod stems with garlic, or the honey-glazed shrimp with walnuts. **Family Matters:** Not the place for a quiet family night out, Chau is chaos with a capital "C." Tables are close together, the atmosphere is loud—but these are the very attributes

that make the restaurant so family friendly. The specialty is seafood, but look for a full menu of more traditional chicken and pork dishes that should please even the littlest ones in your group. High chairs and booster seats are available. ✉ *83 Essex St., Chinatown* ☎*617/338–8158* ⊟*AE, D, MC, V* Ⓣ*Chinatown.*

$$–$$$ ✕**Gourmet Dumpling House.** *Chinese.* This small, newish kid on the block developed a quick following among young folks looking for good, inexpensive fare. A counterpoint to the mammoth eateries in the area, the simple, intimate dining room is often full, calling to students and business people who enjoy the surprisingly vast menu of Northern and Southern Chinese cuisine.**Family Matters:** Kids will probably turn their noses up at some of the more unusual fare like pork bellies and pigs' feet. But, there's plenty of Americanized offerings like chicken with broccoli. High chairs are available. No booster seats. ✉ *52 Beach St., Chinatown* ☎*617/338–6222* ⊟*MC, V* Ⓣ*Chinatown.*

$$ ✕**Jumbo Seafood.** *Seafood.* Although this Cantonese/Hong Kong–style restaurant has much to be proud of, it's happily unpretentious. Have a whole sea bass with ginger and scallion to see what all the fuss is about. Nonoceanic offerings are equally outstanding—even such simple dishes as stir-fried sugar-snap-pea tendrils with white rice. The Hong Kong influence results in a lot of fried food; crispy fried calamari with salted pepper is a standout. The waiters are very patient with newcomers' questions, though some don't speak English fluently. **Family Matters:** The restaurant is one of the friendliest in the area, and you're bound to spot kids here any time you visit. High chairs and booster seats are both available and while there's no children's menu, as with many area restaurants, there's plenty to please young palates, including a characteristically long list of chicken, beef, and pork dishes. ✉ *7 Hudson St., Chinatown* ☎*617/542–2823* ⊟*AE, MC, V* Ⓣ*Chinatown.*

FANEUIL HALL

A perfect refueling stop before hitting the Freedom Trail, Faneuil Hall is a tourist magnet, packed with fast-food concessions as well as some more serious alternatives. If you're not on a schedule, and if you've seen enough of Faneuil Hall and want a change of scene, you shouldn't rule out a walk to the North End.

On the Menu

Not for nothing did Boston become known as the home of the bean and the cod: simple Yankee specialties—many of them of English origin—and traditional seafood abound.

Boston baked beans are a thick, syrupy mixture of navy beans, salt pork, and molasses that is cooked for hours. They were originally made by Puritan women on Saturday so that the leftovers could be eaten on Sunday without breaking the Sabbath by cooking.

You may also want to keep an eye out for Parker House rolls, yeast-bread dinner rolls first concocted at the Parker House Hotel in the 1870s.

Boston cream pie is an addictive simple yellow vanilla cake filled with a creamy custard and iced with chocolate frosting. Many traditional New England eateries (and some steak houses and hotel restaurants) serve a house version. Occasionally you'll find a modernized version, with some creative new element added at trendier restaurants.

¢–$$ ✕**Durgin Park Market Dining Room.** *American.* You should be hungry enough to cope with enormous portions, yet not so hungry you can't tolerate a long wait (or sharing a table with others). Durgin Park was serving its same hearty New England fare (Indian pudding, baked beans, corned beef and cabbage, and a prime rib that hangs over the edge of the plate) back when Faneuil Hall was a working market instead of a tourist attraction. **Family Matters:** Don't expect an especially warm welcome. Part of the restaurant's "charm" is the curtness, and families come here expressly for the brusque service that's just as it was when fishmongers and boat captains dined here (if anything, some folks lament the softening of the staff over the years). Look for niceties such as a kids' menu that starts at $7.95, and high chairs and booster seats. The kids will absolutely leave with a memory. ⊠*340 Faneuil Hall Market Pl., North Market Bldg., Government Center* ☎*617/227–2038* ⊟*AE, D, DC, MC, V* Ⓣ*Haymarket*

$$$ ✕**Kingfish Hall.** *American.* Families not quite ready for the Olives scene can partake of Todd English cuisine at this Faneuil Hall eatery. Seafood is the primary draw, with tasty dishes like scallops with truffle parsnip puree. Parents can also dig into the fresh raw bar while junior sups on clam chowder and watches the grill in the open kitchen. **Family Matters:** The Faneuil Hall Marketplace location makes

Kingfish a good place to take a rest between street shows and shopping, without the chaos of the food court. The kids' menu is pretty standard land fare (hot dogs, pasta, etc.), but youngsters willing to try something new can be accommodated with specially made fish dishes. High chairs are available. No booster seats. ⊠ *1 S. Market St., Downtown* ☎ *617/523–8862* ⊟ *AE, MC, V* Ⓣ *Haymarket.*

NORTH END

Kids and parents get instantly hungry here, with the aroma of garlic wafting through the streets like salt air at the seashore. The North End is Boston's oldest immigrant neighborhood, and the vibe still rings old-world, with grandmothers pushing past suburban foodies to get groceries, and locals perched outside neighborhood haunts shouting greetings to each other in Italian. Since the late 1990s, small storefront restaurants have been converting from red-sauce tourist traps to innovative trattorias. And some of Boston's most authentic old-country restaurants are still here (as you might guess, the smaller the place, the better the kitchen), along with charming cafés serving to-die-for espresso and cannoli. Many of the restaurants don't take credit cards or reservations, but because they're so close to each other, it's easy to scout among them for a table.

★ Fodor's Choice ✕ **Antico Forno.** *Italian.* Many of the menu choices
$–$$ come from the eponymous wood-burning brick oven, which turns out surprisingly delicate pizzas simply topped with tomato and fresh mozzarella. Don't overlook the hearty baked dishes and handmade pastas; the specialty, gnocchi, is rich and creamy but light. The room is cramped and noisy, but the hubbub is part of the fun. **Family Matters:** Here's the chance to introduce the kids to real pizza, instead of that droopy stuff that's delivered in 30 minutes or less. The warm, cozy, family vibe makes this a popular place, and it's one of a few North End eateries that takes reservations. Make one, lest your kids stand around hungry for the long wait for a table. The restaurant has all the essentials— high chairs, booster seats—and will adapt virtually any dish to fit the family's needs. ⊠ *93 Salem St., North End* ☎ *617/723–6733* ⊟ *MC, V* Ⓣ *Haymarket.*

$–$$ ✕ **Daily Catch.** *Seafood.* You've just got to love this place—for the noise, the intimacy, and, above all, the food. Shoulder-crowdingly small and always brightly lighted, the storefront restaurant specializes in calamari dishes, black squid-ink pastas, and linguine with clam sauce. There's something about a big skillet of linguine and calamari that would seem less perfect if served on fine white china. **Family Matters:** It's a pretty limited menu—seafood (including fish and chips) and pasta—so if your kids don't eat one of the two, it's best to go elsewhere. For fish-loving families, this is the place, although probably more for older kids since the restaurant is chaotic and there are no high chairs or booster seats. Twenty tables and no reservations mean long waits. On the other hand, for lunch on a rainy day, you can often walk right in. ⊠*323 Hanover St., North End* ☎*617/523–8567 or 617/734–5696* ⚠*Reservations not accepted* ⊟*No credit cards* Ⓣ*Haymarket.*

$$ ✕**Ristorante Saraceno.** *Italian.* It doesn't get as much press as some of its North End brethren, but this charming, long-time establishment has earned its longevity. Most nights, the proud owner greets you at the door, leading guests to a table in one of the two lovely and casual dining rooms. Fresh sauces turn dishes into cuisine worth coming back for. Try the linguine with seafood. You won't be disappointed. **Family Matters:** As with many North End eateries, Saraceno gets crowded, especially on weekends. Call ahead for a reservation. Make sure to ask for a table downstairs; the lovely lower-floor dining room is decked out like a Mediterranean villa, complete with scenery. Kids and parents will love it. The restaurant offers half portions for children, but no children's menu. High chairs are available. No booster seats. ⊠*286 Hanover St., North End* ☎*617/227–5888* ⊟*AE, DC, MC, V* Ⓣ*Haymarket.*

$$-$$$ ✕**Union Oyster House.** *Seafood.* Established in 1826, this is Boston's oldest continuing restaurant, and almost every tourist considers it a must-see. If you like, you can have what Daniel Webster had—oysters on the half shell at the ground-floor raw bar, which is the oldest part of the restaurant and still the best. The rooms at the top of the narrow staircase are dark and have low ceilings—very Ye Olde New England—and plenty of nonrestaurant history. The small tables and chairs (as well as the endless lines and kitschy nostalgia) are as much a part of the charm as the simple and decent (albeit pricey) food. One cautionary note: locals hardly ever eat here. There is valet parking after 5:30 PM. **Family Matters:** As befits a tourist haunt, the restaurant is entirely kid-friendly, offering the all-important high chairs, booster seats, coloring books, and crayons. If the "Oyster" in Oyster House doesn't appeal to them, they can

enjoy land fare like chicken fingers, spaghetti, and burgers from the kids' menu. ✉ *41 Union St., Government Center* ☎*617/227–2750* ▭*AE, D, DC, MC, V* Ⓣ*Haymarket.*

SOUTH END

Boston's South End is a highly diverse neighborhood, these days home to many of the city's gay professionals, hip straight couples, and young families. Barely a month seems to go by when a hot restaurant doesn't open—either at the restaurant row at the bend of Tremont Street or up and down the length of Washington Street.

¢–$ ✕**Flour Bakery Café.** *American.* When the neighbors need coffee, or a sandwich, or a muffin, or just a place to sit and chat, they come here. A communal table in the middle acts as a gathering spot around which diners enjoy classic sandwiches and a few specialties, like the grilled chicken with Brie and arugula or the BLT with applewood-smoked bacon. Takeout dinner is available in the form of Asian-inspired entrées. **Family Matters:** Counter service at this ultrafriendly spot is great for on-the-fly dining. Gourmet sandwiches are made to order, which means you'll have no trouble getting a turkey sandwich for the kids without all the grownup gourmet stuff. Pastries and cookies, like the raspberry crumb bar, are yummy. Good luck getting them to wait until dessert. High chairs and booster seats available. ✉ *1595 Washington St., South End* ☎*617/267–4300* ⌫*Reservations not accepted* ▭*MC, V* Ⓣ*Massachusetts Ave.*

$$$–$$$$ ✕**Gaslight.** *French.* The gaslights burning outside of the main entrance usher you into a cozy, darkly lit space that, despite its elegance, feels welcoming and warm. The menu is long and equally inviting, hearty French fare ranging from roasted sea scallops to braised pork to duck confit or a juicy steak. Do yourself a favor, and come for brunch. Even better, the parking is free all the time. **Family Matters:** Staff here take pride in their kid friendliness, noting that the restaurant is not a "hush, hush" kind of place. There's no children's menu, but the chefs are pros at creating great food on the fly, such as a recent order of house-made chicken fingers that appealed to grownups as well. High chairs are available. No booster seats. ✉ *560 Harrison Ave., South End* ☎*617/422–0224* ▭*AE, MC, V* ⊘*No lunch* Ⓣ*Back Bay/South End.*

$$–$$$$ ╳**Union Bar and Grille.** *American.* There's rarely a quiet night at Union, where the bar buzzes with the neighborhood's coolest residents and couples on dates fill the darkly lighted dining room's leather banquettes. Despite all the show, the menu keeps things relatively down-to-earth with tender-as-can-be burgers, spice-rubbed grilled steak, and thick, crispy fries. **Family Matters:** No doubt, it's primarily a grownups haunt. But hosts will not look askance at visitors toting a baby, particularly during the restaurant's popular Sunday brunch. There's no particular children's menu, but the kitchen will adapt to suit. High chairs are available. No booster seats. ⊠*1357 Washington St., South End* ☎*617/423–0555* ⊟*AE, MC, V* ⊘*No lunch* Ⓣ*Back Bay/South End.*

WATERFRONT

Tourists flock to Faneuil Hall and the Marketplace almost year-round, so tried-and-true cuisine tends to dominate there. However, some of Boston's most famous seafood restaurants are on the waterfront.

¢–$$ ╳**Barking Crab Restaurant.** *Seafood.* It is, believe it or not, a seaside clam shack plunked in the middle of Boston, with a stunning view of the downtown skyscrapers. An outdoor lobster tent in summer, in winter it retreats indoors to a warmhearted version of a waterfront dive, with chestnuts roasting on a cozy woodstove. Look for the classic New England clambake—chowder, lobster, steamed clams, corn on the cob—or the spicier crab boil. **Family Matters:** Around the corner from the Children's Museum, the restaurant is a nice place to recharge after an afternoon of interactive gizmos. High chairs and booster seats are available, as is a children's menu of fish and chips, grilled cheese, and mac and cheese. ⊠*88 Sleeper St., Northern Ave. Bridge, Waterfront* ☎*617/426–2722* ⊟*AE, DC, MC, V* Ⓣ*South Station.*

¢–$ ╳**No Name Restaurant.** *Seafood.* Famous for not being
★ famous, the No Name has been serving fresh seafood, simply broiled or fried, since 1917. Once you find it, tucked off New Northern Avenue (as opposed to Old Northern Avenue) between the World Trade Center and the Bank of America Pavilion, you can close your eyes and pretend you're in a little fishing village—it's not much of a stretch. **Family Matters:** No kids' menu, but the kitchen offers kids land specialties like fried chicken as well as fish. High

Family Fuel

If you're on the go, you might want to try a local chain restaurant where you can stop for a quick bite or get some takeout. The ones listed below are fairly priced and committed to quality, and use decent, fresh ingredients.

Au Bon Pain. The locally based chain whips up quick salads and sandwiches, fresh-daily croissants, and muffins, and has plenty of fruit and juices.

Bertucci's. Thin-crust pizzas fly fast from the brick ovens here, along with pastas and a decent tiramisu.

BoLoCo. For quick, cheap, healthful, and high-quality wraps and burritos, this is easily the city's most dependable (and also locally based) chain.

Finagle A Bagel. Find fresh, doughy bagels in flavors from jalapeño cheddar to triple chocolate, plus sandwiches and salads. Service is swift and efficient.

chairs are available. No booster seats. ✉*15½ Fish Pier, off New Northern Ave., Waterfront* 🕾*617/338–7539 or 617/423–2705* ▭*AE, D, MC, V* Ⓣ*Courthouse.*

CAMBRIDGE

Among other collegiate enthusiasms, Cambridge has a long-standing fascination with ethnic restaurants. A certain kind of great restaurant has also evolved here, mixing world-class cooking with a studied informality. Famous chefs, attired in flannel shirts, cook with wood fires and borrow flavors from every continent. For more posh tastes and the annual celebrations that come with college life (or the end of it), Cambridge also has its share of linen-cloth tables.

★ Fodor'sChoice ✕**All Star Sandwich Bar.** *American.* Chris Schle-
¢–$ singer has a strict definition of what makes a sandwich: no wraps. He's put together a list of classics, like crispy, over-stuffed Reubens and beef on weck, which are served quickly from an open kitchen. The only nonsandwich item on the board is a hot dog. The space has about a dozen tables that fill up at lunchtime. At dinner burgers are also served, along with a small selection of beer and wine. **Family Matters:** A dependable staple for families, the sandwich bar is one of those places you can't go wrong, sure to make mom and dad happy, while offering kids grilled cheese and hot dogs in addition to sandwiches. Opt for table service, or grab the food to go. High chairs and boosters are available. ✉*1245*

Baked Goods

Hi-Rise Bread Co. You practically walk right into the baking operation at this café and bread shop. Sample walnut, olive, and cheddar-pepper breads, or the house specialty, polka bread, a tough-crusted loaf marked with crosshatches. ⊠*208 Concord Ave., Cambridge* ☎*617/876–8766* Ⓣ*Harvard.*

Mike's Pastry. Mike's has been adopted by locals as *the* place for sweets. You are likely to see plenty of people on Hanover Street carrying Mike's butter cookies, tiramisu, cannoli, and biscotti. ⊠*300 Hanover St., North End* ☎*617/742–3050*

Ⓣ*Haymarket.*

Rosie's Bakery. Rosie's tempting cookies, pastries, and cakes give new meaning to the word rich—but it's the chocolate-chip cookies that make the place everyone's sweetheart. If you can't get enough, pick up the mouthwatering *Rosie's Bakery Chocolate-Packed, Jam-Filled, Butter-Rich, No-Holds-Barred Cookie Book.* ⊠*2 South Station, Downtown* ☎*617/439–4684* Ⓣ*South Station* ⊠*243 Hampshire St., Cambridge* ☎*617/491–9488* Ⓣ*Central.*

Cambridge St., Cambridge ☎*617/868–3065* ⌖*Reservations not accepted* ⊟*MC, V* Ⓣ*Central/Inmand.*

$–$$ ✕**Full Moon.** *American.* Here's a happy reminder that dinner with children doesn't have to mean hamburgers. Choices include child pleasers such as pasta as well as grown-up entrées that include herb-grilled pork chops with citrus salsa. **Family Matters:** Kids will delight in the play kitchen and dollhouse, and parents can cheer that they get to tuck into lovelies such as grilled salmon with bok choy. Youngsters can spread out with plenty of designated play space and juice-filled sippy cups while adults weigh the substantial menu and a well-paired wine list. ⊠*344 Huron Ave., Cambridge* ☎*617/354–6699* ⌖*Reservations not accepted* ⊟*MC, V* Ⓣ*Harvard.*

¢–$ ✕**Mr. Bartley's Burger Cottage.** *American.* It may be perfect cuisine for the student metabolism: a huge variety of variously garnished thick burgers, deliciously crispy French fries (regular and sweet potato), and onion rings. There's also a competent veggie burger. The nonalcoholic "raspberry lime rickey," made with fresh limes, raspberry juice, sweetener, and soda water, is the must-try classic drink. Tiny tables in a crowded space make eavesdropping unavoidable. **Family Matters:** Maybe it's the frappés (thick milk shakes), silly cartoons all over the walls, or just the fun, high-energy vibe. Whatever it is, Bartley's is a hit with kids. ✉ *1246 Massachusetts Ave., Cambridge* ☎ *617/354–6559* ⚖ *Reservations not accepted* 🖃 *No credit cards* ⊘ *Closed Sun.* Ⓣ *Harvard.*

$–$$ ✕ **S&S Restaurant.** *Deli.* Around for about the last hundred years, the S&S is always crowded and fortunately enormous. A sort of souped-up diner/Jewish Deli, the Inman Square eatery serves breakfast all day (as well as traditional lunch and dinner fare) off an enormous menu, shuttling folks in and out with the efficiency of a fine-oiled machine. The food is good. Really good. And, in the tradition of progenitor Jewish Grandmother Edelstein, nobody leaves hungry. **Family Matters:** There are small portions of everything from blintzes to chocolate-chip pancakes, making a kids' menu sort of redundant. Boosters and high chairs are available. One word of caution: the beloved Stella Bella toy store is next door. Be prepared for the inevitable begging. ✉ *1334 Cambridge St, Cambridge* ☎ *617/354–0777* ⚖ *Reservations not accepted* 🖃 *MC, V, AE* Ⓣ *Central Square.*

$$ ✕ **Sunset Café.** *Café.* The lively atmosphere here may make you feel as though you're attending a giant Portuguese wedding. Entire families come, and on a Friday or Saturday night (when the café has guitarists and singers), it's not unusual to see little girls in frilly dresses and boys in jackets and ties. Specialties include kale soup thickened with potatoes, *mariscada a chefe* (seafood casserole with fine spices), and *cabrito assado* (marinated, grilled goat meat). The bargain-price wines on the list include some of the best Dão reds available outside Portugal. **Family Matters:** If you're looking for something completely different, this might be the place. Weekdays can feel a little deserted here, but weekends, the place comes alive, with large crowds and live music. A modest kids' menu has all the kid-favorite greasy stuff like chicken fingers and pizza. High chairs and booster seats available. ✉ *851 Cambridge St., Cambridge* ☎ *617/547–2938* 🖃 *AE, D, DC, MC, V* Ⓣ *Central.*

BROOKLINE

Going to Brookline is a nice way to get out of the city without really leaving town. Although it's surrounded by Boston on three sides, Brookline has its own suburban flavor, seasoned with a multitude of historic—and expensive—

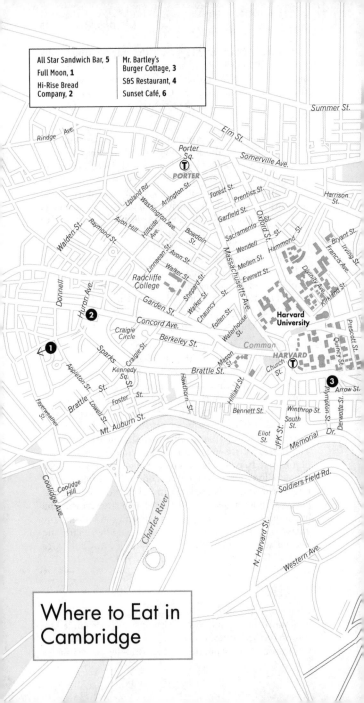

All Star Sandwich Bar, **5**

Full Moon, **1**

Hi-Rise Bread Company, **2**

Mr. Bartley's Burger Cottage, **3**

S&S Restaurant, **4**

Sunset Café, **6**

Where to Eat in Cambridge

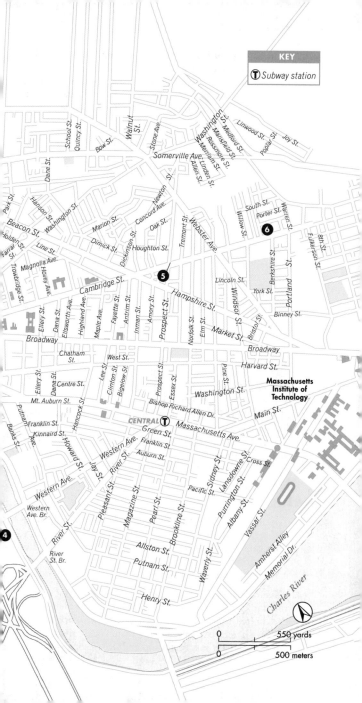

houses and garnished with a diverse ethnic population that supports a string of sushi bars and a small list of kosher restaurants. Most Brookline eateries are clustered in the town's commercial centers: Brookline Village, Washington Square, Longwood, and bustling Coolidge Corner.

$ ✕ **Rubin's.** *Deli* The last kosher Jewish delicatessen in the Boston area serves a hand-cut pastrami sandwich a New Yorker can respect. There are *kasha varnishkes* (buckwheat with bow-tie noodles), hot brisket, and many other high-cholesterol classics but, of course, no real cream for your coffee or dairy desserts. **Family Matters:** The fact that you can get your kids a bologna sandwich speaks volumes about this institution. It's an experience. There are plenty of other items on the children's menu, and high chairs and booster seats are available. ✉*500 Harvard St., Brookline* ☎*617/731–8787* ⊟*AE, DC, MC, V* ⊘*Closed Sat. No dinner Fri.* Ⓣ*Coolidge Corner.*

$$ ✕ **Village Smokehouse.** *American.* There's absolutely nothing pretentious about this establishment that has plastic checked covers on the tables and suggests patrons wear a bib. The giant open pit ensures that everyone goes home smelling like a barbecue. There are juicy burgers including the ominously named Death Burger. But, come for the barbecue ribs and chicken. Oh—and wear the bib. **Family Matters:** No reservations equals long waits. Come around 5 to be seated quickly. High chairs and booster seats are available, as is a kids' menu of chicken fingers, quarter chicken, pulled pork, and more. Be warned: the delicious cornbread that comes before the meal is an appetite buster. ✉*1 Harvard St., Brookline* ☎*617/566–3782* ♨*Reservations not accepted* ⊟*No credit cards* Ⓣ*Brookline Village.*

JAMAICA PLAIN

This neighborhood is a kind of mini-Cambridge: multiethnic and filled with cutting-edge artists, graduate students, political idealists, and yuppie families. Recently, the area, known for its affordable and unusual ethnic spots, has seen a swell of a more gentrified—but no less creative—sort.

$$ ✕ **Centre Street Café.** *American.* It's impossible not to love
★ this funky hangout, where neighborhood residents pack the limited number of tables and local artwork fills the walls. The eclectic menu veers from ethnic inspirations like spicy cream-sauced shrimp and rice to super-fresh sal-

CLOSE UP

I Scream for Ice Cream

Come snow, sleet, or horrendous humidity, Boston's appetite for ice cream remains undiminished. Flavors far exceed basic vanilla with burnt caramel, honey-anise, or cinnamon that could bring tears to your eyes (and not due to an "ice-cream headache").

Christina's (✉ *1255 Cambridge St., Cambridge* ☎ *617/492–7021*), Inman Square's dessert mecca, serves such creatively flavored scoops as Wild Turkey–walnut and an amazingly addictive chocolate mousse. Dieting meets decadence at **Emack & Bolio's** (✉ *290 Newbury St., Back Bay* ☎ *617/247–8772*), a pint-size parlor that's half juice bar, half ice-cream counter. You can lap up the delicious handiwork of ice-cream maestro Steve Herrell, pioneer of the "smoosh-in" (candy and nuts mixed into the cold stuff), at **Herrell's** (✉ *15 Dunster St., Cambridge* ☎ *617/497–2179*). Simple but sublime cones have addicted many a Bostonian to the fun and funky likes of **J.P. Licks** (✉ *659 Centre St., Jamaica Plain* ☎ *617/524–6740*). Don't miss J.P. Licks' ice-cream floats—equal parts cream and fizz. If you're looking for serious ice cream, look no farther than **Toscanini's** (✉ *899 Main St., Cambridge* ☎ *617/491–5877* ✉ *1310 Massachusetts Ave., Cambridge* ☎ *617/354–9350*). With such exotic flavors as cardamom and burnt caramel, and textures that range from refreshing to truly rich, Toscanini's has few (if any) equals. If it's quantity or a good cause that you're after, nothing beats the **Scooper Bowl** (☎ *800/525–4669* ⊕ *www.scooperbowl.org*), an annual all-you-can-eat extravaganza held in early June at City Hall Plaza. Organizers serve up 10 tons of brand-name ice-cream (including Baskin-Robbins, Ben & Jerry's, and Häagen-Dazs). Proceeds benefit the Dana-Farber Cancer Institute.

ads brimming with local produce. Lines snake around the block every Sunday for the spectacular (and spectacularly filling) brunch. **Family Matters:** For those willing to make the trip, it's a nice neighborhoody experience with tons of local flavor. Don't worry about the absence of a kids' menu. The kitchen will punt and create pasta or grilled cheese. High chairs and booster seats available. ✉ *669A Centre St., Jamaica Plain* ☎ *617/524–9217* ▭ *MC, V* Ⓣ *Green St.*

Where to Stay

WORD OF MOUTH

"We want a nice place to stay that we adults will really like, but also a hotel conveniently located to kid stuff. . . ."

—emcash

"I really like The Lenox for business or family reasons. The hotel is pretty small and has lovely rooms and excellent service. The T stop is just across the street; the Public Gardens are about five blocks away; Newbury Street Shopping is two blocks away; the Prudential Center Mall is three blocks away, and there are excellent restaurants very close to the hotel."

—Weadles

Lisa
Oppen-
heimer

BOSTON HOTELS ARE GOING UP faster than Sox slug-ger Jacoby Ellsbury can take third on a wild pitch. New names like Mandarin Oriental, InterContinental, Regent, and Renaissance have joined the old guard and upped the stakes for local hoteliers. To compete you've gotta have flat-screen TVs, MP3 decks, and Wi-Fi. Even hotels that haven't changed so much as a pair of drapes for decades ("old" equals "good" in Boston, yes?) suddenly took notice, and started collecting swatches of zebra-print leather.

But when you're traveling with your family, you have more pressing concerns such as "Will we like the neighborhood?" "Will my kids like it?" "Does the hotel like kids?" The search for familiarity—because really, adventurousness often takes a back seat when you're toting tots—leads parents to chains like Marriott and Hilton, of which there are plenty in Boston. A few small indy gems exist and are worth a look, although they might require sacrifices on space or upscale amenities. But, even the fanciest digs in this increasingly Cosmo metropolis aren't too hoity-toity to lay out the red carpet for tykes—at minimum offering kids' menus in the bistros (or the chef will adapt for you) and handing out crayons and goodies at check-in. Some, like the Ritz Carlton and Four Seasons go out of their way to court families, supplying everything from milk and cookies to diapers. Certain niceties are harder to secure, like connecting rooms, which can be requested, but often not guaranteed (hint: make friends with the front desk staff a few days before arrival). ■TIP→ **Be wary of your room lingo. "Connecting" implies a private door between two rooms; "Adjoining" just means, "next to each other."**

Be sure to check out promotional packages that can be far below standard "rack" rates and often include parking and breakfast to entice leisure travelers. The deals are out there if you're willing to spend some time sleuthing. And, the bazillion dollars many hotels spent on extreme make-overs this year shows; however, the dust hasn't completely settled yet. You may want to ask, "Are there any renova-tions underway?" lest your vacation be interrupted by the sound of jackhammers.

CHOOSING A NEIGHBORHOOD

Looking for a hotel in the heart of the city? An inn on a tree-lined street? Maybe you want the shopping found across the river in Cambridge? Here's a quick overview of Boston neighborhoods and what they offer.

Some of the most luxurious hotels are clustered near the Boston Common and Public Garden in **Beacon Hill, Back Bay**, and **Downtown**. The Seaport District will suit you if you're in town for a convention at the BCEC or the Seaport World Trade Center. Digs here include the **Seaport Hotel**, the **Westin**, and the new **Renaissance Boston Hotel**. Stay close to the theaters at the **Boston Park Plaza** or the **Radisson**, or near the water at the **Boston Harbor Hotel** or **Marriott Long Wharf**. The **Hyatt Regency** and the **Omni** give you easy access to the shops of Downtown Crossing and the seasonal perks of the Common. Boston proper is quite small, however, and, most areas, with the exception of the Seaport Hotel, are quite accessible from one another.

The **Kenmore Square** area has a distinct student vibe. Adjacent to Fenway Park is Lansdowne Street, a strip of college bars and nightclubs for young adults. The **Fenway** offers beautiful parks and community gardens. A short trolley ride east will bring you to the heart of Boston, and a short ride west will bring you to the suburbs of Brookline, Brighton, and Newton. Consider the **Hotel Commonwealth** in this area.

The suburb of **Brookline** is largely residential with lovely homes and parks, but there are still several bustling areas such as Coolidge Corner and Washington Square that give you plenty of shopping, dining, and recreation options. The subway offers quick access to downtown Boston.

BOOKING TIPS

With the wealth of colleges in Boston and Cambridge, commencement weekends in May and June book many months in advance. Sometimes prices are more than triple the off-season rate. Leaf-peepers arrive in early October during foliage season, and summer and fall conventions bring waves of business travelers. Many hotels in the Back Bay area receive a large portion of their business from conference attendees to the Hynes Convention Center. Check which events are happening before you reserve a room in the area. Other special events such as the Boston Marathon in April and the Head of the Charles in October are busy times for large hotels and small inns alike.

HOW TO SAVE

Business-oriented hotels will often lower their rates on weekends. Outlying areas often have some of the best deals. If you don't need to be right Downtown, look toward Cambridge, Brookline, and Dorchester, where rates are almost always lower and parking is easier. In winter the Back Bay is a good option when the large hotels attempt to lure leisure travelers with competitive packages and rates, especially on weekends. Many city hotels allow children under a certain age to stay in their parents' room at no extra charge. Request a "Kids Love Boston" brochure from the **Greater Boston Convention & Visitors Bureau** (☎*617/536–4100 or 888/733–2678* ⊕*www.bostonusa.com*). The Web site lists a variety of family-friendly packages that include such extras as complimentary use of strollers and discounts to city attractions.

WHAT IT COSTS				
¢	$	$$	$$$	$$$$
FOR TWO PEOPLE				
under $75	$75–$149	$150–$224	$225–$325	over $325

Prices are for two people in a standard double room in high season, excluding 12.45 % tax and service charges.

BOSTON

BACK BAY

$$$–$$$$ ★ **Colonnade Hotel.** A recent transformation from so-*over* '80s brass-and-mahogany to a clean, modern look with espresso, khaki, chocolate, and chrome has greatly improved Colonnade's design scheme. All this would be mere window dressing if it weren't for new, guest-friendly touches like flat-panel TVs, DVD players, and alarm clock/MP3 players, plus extendable reading lights and high-tech coffeemakers. Even the minibar goodies got an upgrade, with fresh shortbread cookies and the like. Floor-to-ceiling windows (these actually open) have been triple glazed to keep out the traffic noise of Huntington Avenue. In summer the roof deck pool is a huge draw. Open to hotel guests only, the pool area has great views of the neighborhood, and live music. **Pros:** Roof deck pool, T stop a few steps away, across the street from Prudential Center for shopping and restaurants. **Cons:** Prices have gone up since hotel was renovated. **Family Matters:** Rooms can accommodate a family of four, but it's a tight squeeze. For those who prefer more space, connecting rooms are available. Even better, the Colonnade is one of only a very few hotels that will actually promise that you'll get them (most will tell you they'll do their best). Certain packages offer admission into some local attractions and a Parisian breakfast. The on-site restaurant, Brasserie Jo, even has a kids' menu. Travel cribs are available upon request. ⊠*120 Huntington Ave., Back Bay* ☎*617/424–7000 or 800/962–3030* ⊕*www.colonnadehotel.com* ⤳*276 rooms, 9 suites* ⌖*In-room: safe, Wi-Fi. In-hotel: restaurant, room service, bar, pool, gym, laundry service, Wi-Fi, parking (fee), some pets allowed* ☐*AE, D, DC, MC, V* Ⓣ*Prudential Center.*

\$\$\$–\$\$\$\$ Ⓣ **Courtyard by Marriott Boston Copley Square.** Some call this the best Courtyard by Marriott they've ever seen, praising its modern, upscale, and large-for-Boston rooms. They don't mind that the lobby isn't grand, breakfast is a self-serve affair, and room service consists of a handful of menus to nearby eateries. The privations end, however, once you see your room, decked out in colorful, contemporary furnishings, and glammed up with cherry cabinets, granite countertops, and 37-inch flat-screen TVs. Small niceties include cookies and fruit in the lobby (4 PM) and make-up mirrors in the bathrooms. You can't beat the location: walk to Prudential Center and Copley Place shops and Back Bay restaurants, galleries, and boutiques, plus there's a big grocery store right around the corner. **Pros:** Good-size modern rooms, great location, free Internet. **Cons:** Restaurant is *just* serviceable, no room service. **Family Matters:** Families are welcome here, but you'll have to put in a little time up front to make it work. There are no connecting rooms and no space for cots, so ask for two double beds (as opposed to a king) if you're traveling with more than two people (unless one is an infant in a crib). On that note, porta-cribs are available upon request, but not guaranteed. If baby requires a bed, you're best advised to bring your own. ⊠*88 Exeter St., Back Bay* ☎*617/437–9300 or 800/321–2211* ☐*617/437–9330* ⊕*www.courtyardboston.com* ⤳*77 rooms, 4 suites* ⌖*In-room: refrigerator (some), Internet. In-hotel: restaurant, gym, laundry service, Wi-Fi, some pets allowed* ☐*AE, D, DC, MC, V* Ⓣ*Copley.*

★ FodorsChoice Ⓣ **Fairmont Copley Plaza.** Richly decorated, and
\$\$\$\$ very ornate—we're talking clouds on the ceiling here—this 1912 landmark favors romance and tradition over sleek and modern. Really love pampering? Stay on the Fairmont Gold floor, an ultradeluxe club level offering a dedicated staff, free breakfast, and tea-time snacks (mini crab cakes

and other delectables), and library. Shopping fanatics adore the close proximity to Newbury Street, the Prudential Center, and Copley Place. The Oak Room restaurant matches its mahogany-panel twin in New York's Plaza Hotel. If you're missing your dog, take Catie Copley, the in-house Labrador retriever, for a walk around the 'hood. (Paul Newman did when he stayed here.) **Pros:** Very elegant, great Copley Square location. **Cons:** Tiny bathrooms with scratchy towels, charge for Internet access (no charge on Fairmont Gold level), not much shelving or storage. **Family Matters:** There are no special family rooms/rates, but staff is ultrafriendly and the concierge happily helps with whatever you need. Eateries are equipped with kids' menus for all meals—in-restaurant or in-room. Cots are surprisingly popular in this swank hotel, but you might want to make your request in advance. Cots and cribs are provided at no extra charge. Prime location means you can walk out the door and push the stroller on to the Common, the Garden, or Newbury Street. ✉*138 St. James Ave., Back Bay* ☎*617/267–5300 or 800/441–1414* ✆*617/375–9648* ⊕*www.fairmont.com/copleyplaza* ⬧*366 rooms, 17 suites* ⬧*In-room: safe, refrigerator, Internet. In-hotel: restaurant, room service, bar, gym, laundry service, Wi-Fi, parking (fee), some pets allowed* ☐*AE, D, DC, MC, V* ⓣ*Copley, Back Bay/South End.*

$$$$ ⬚**Four Seasons.** Jeans-clad millionaires and assorted busi-
★ ness types cluster in the glossy lobby of the Four Seasons, while TV anchorfolk dis the competition over 'tinis and Bristol Burgers in the Bristol Lounge. (Visiting celebs are whisked to the 3,000-square-foot, $6,600-per-night Presidential Suite—no waiting in the lobby for them!) Thanks to a recent face-lift, the Four Seasons retains its perch as Boston's go-to hotel for luxury with a *soupçon* of hip. Luxury amenities include DVD players, 42-inch plasma TVs, and L'Occitane toiletries. (Celebrities stash the full-size soaps in their luggage, we're told.) Even if you spring for the basic city-view room, you can enjoy fab views of the Public Garden from the pool and whirlpool on the eighth floor, or from Aujourd'hui, the hotel's top-rated contemporary French restaurant, or the Bristol Lounge. ■TIP→**Check the Web for fantastic winter-weekend deals. Pros:** Great location, overlooking the Public Garden and a short walk to Newbury Street shops and the Theater District, Mercedes courtesy car makes drop-offs (within a 2-mi radius) around town, excellent gym. **Cons:** Front entrance can get busy

(valet parking service can be slow), restaurants are pricey. **Family Matters:** Four Seasons actually goes out of its way for children. Niceties include the usual cribs, plus milk and cookies, kid-size robes and toiletries, child-proofing gadgets, plus toys, games and baby equipment, and a little gift from the on-site store. Many amenities are gratis but subject to availability. If you absolutely must have that crib, ask ahead. Rooms themselves are roomy enough for a maximum of 3; more than that and you'll need connecting rooms. Ask about the hotel's Very Important Kids packages which, in addition to other perks, offer discounts on a second room, when available, plus gift packs of city guides, activities, treats, and more. ⊠ *200 Boylston St., Back Bay* 🕾 *617/338–4400 or 800/819–5053* ⊕ *www.fourseasons. com/boston* ⇗ *197 rooms, 76 suites* ⚊ *In-room: safe, refrigerator, Internet, Wi-Fi. In-hotel: 2 restaurants, room service, bar, pool, gym, laundry service, Wi-Fi, parking (fee), some pets allowed* ⊟ *AE, D, DC, MC, V* Ⓣ *Arlington.*

$$$ ▣ **Hilton Boston Back Bay.** The 26-story hotel occupies a corner pocket between the Prudential Center (shopping, restaurants) and the Christian Science Church complex. It's perfect if you like the anonymity of a large hotel and a location that's convenient to everything. You can't beat the oversize rooms, the big, comfy beds, and the availability of a pool and hot tub. Readers describe the guest rooms as "pleasant," and "fine," if a bit "old school." Wall-to-wall windows overlook the Back Bay and Fenway Park. (Views vary from room to room. You might have a great view of Boston's iconic neon Citgo sign! Bostonians would consider this a *good* thing, as the Citgo sign is a beloved—if odd—landmark.) Generally, rooms above the ninth floor have the best views. Bathrooms have oversize showers. Try one of the older rooms, which have windows that open (some even have balconies). **Pros:** Large rooms and bathrooms, nice views, good roof-level fitness center. **Cons:** Somewhat oddly situated, no VIP floor. **Family Matters:** Location, location, location is the reason to stay—right in the middle of Back Bay, walking distance to the Prudential Center and Newbury Street and a hop from the "T." This dependable staple is a sure in-the-city pick for families who want the security of knowing exactly what they're getting. Rooms are standard-issue. Cots are $20 per night (they'll fit, albeit snugly, in a double/double), fridges are $15 per stay, and cribs are free. ⊠ *40 Dalton St., Back Bay* 🕾 *617/236–1100 or 800/874–0663* ⊕ *www.hilton.com* ⇗ *385 rooms, 5 suites*

&In-room: refrigerator, Internet. In-hotel: restaurant, room service, bar, pool, gym, laundry service, Wi-Fi, parking (fee) ☐AE, D, DC, MC, V ‖©‖CP ⊤Hynes/ICA.

★ ☒Fodor'sChoice **Jurys Boston Hotel.** "Great staff." "Great bar."
$$$–$$$$ "Great vibe." See a pattern yet? Travelers rave about this hotel, one of the few in the city where you can nip into the bar for a beverage and actually chat with a friendly local or two. There's something about this place that thaws even the frostiest Bostonian—and it's not just the Irish coffee talking. Part of a Dublin-based hotel chain, Jurys may remind you more of Iceland than Ireland, design-wise. There's a fire-and-ice thing going on, from the bed of icy glass shards in the igloolike gas fireplace on the lower level to the puffs of steam coming from the staircase waterfall. Eye-catching blown-glass chandeliers add to the cool appeal. Rooms are decorated with warm taupes and golds, and Ireland-theme artwork adorns the walls. The hotel gets the small touches right, such as the Aveda products in the sleek, modern bathrooms; free bottled water in the fridge; toasty down comforters; and heated towel racks. **Pros:** Lively, friendly bar, great amenities like large-screen TVs, at a good price point, friendly staff. **Cons:** Not the prettiest location in the city, but close to the T (subway). **Family Matters:** Kids checking in get a police car (ode to the building's prior life as police headquarters) and a coloring book, and children's eats are on the menu. The place doesn't scream, "Family Friendly," but staff will go out of their way to accommodate. Double-queen rooms are plenty big for four (big bathrooms help a lot) and cots ($20) and cribs (free) can be brought in. ✉350 Stuart St., Back Bay ☎617/266–7200 ☎617/266–7203 ⊕www.jurysdoyle.com ⇔220 rooms, 3 suites &In-room: refrigerator, DVD, Wi-Fi. In-hotel: restaurant, room service, bar, laundry service, Wi-Fi, parking (fee) ☐AE, D, DC, MC, V ⊤Back Bay/South End.

★ Fodor'sChoice ☒**Lenox Hotel.** Family-owned and graced with
$$$–$$$$ period (circa 1901) details, this boutique-ish Back Bay property is a pleasing alternative to the nearby big-box hotels. The Copley Square location means you're steps away from a slew of restaurants and shops, and a T stop is right across the street. No car needed—a good thing, since overnight parking costs a bundle. (Skip the hotel's garage and use a city parking facility to save some cash.) This longtime Back Bay landmark won several awards for restoration work on its grand brick-and-granite facade. The smallish size of this hotel lends a feeling of personalized service, although

some say the staff can be chilly. Recently updated guest rooms have custom-made furnishings, marble baths, and flat-screen TVs (suites have mirror TVs in bathrooms). Of the 24 airily spacious corner rooms, 12 have working wood-burning fireplaces. ■TIP→ **Book your reservation from the hotel's Web site; they guarantee the best price.** Pros: Fantastic Copley Square location, historic/architectural charm. Cons: Bathrooms are small; no minibar/mini-refrigerator, safe, or coffeemaker (though available upon request). Family Matters: Children's menus in some of the restaurants, as well as in-room dining. Rooms with two double beds can easily accommodate a family of four, with children under 17 able to share at no extra charge. Cots can be rolled in for an extra charge of $25 per night; porta cribs, on the other hand, are free. Connecting rooms are also available, and, happily, will be guaranteed at reservation time. ⊠61 *Exeter St., Back Bay* ☎617/536–5300 *or* 800/225–7676 ☒617/267–1237 ⊕*www.lenoxhotel.com* ☞*187 rooms, 27 suites* ☐*In-room: Wi-Fi. In-hotel: 3 restaurants, room service, bars, gym, laundry service, Wi-Fi, parking (fee)* ☐*AE, D, DC, MC, V* Ⓣ*Copley.*

\$\$\$–\$\$\$\$ ☐**Marriott Hotel at Copley Place.** It's busy-busy, with throngs of tourists and their offspring, but you can't beat the location and the amenities of this 38-story "megahotel." To give you a sense of the size of this one, you can enter three ways: from the street-level lobby, a glass sky bridge from the Prudential Center–Hynes Auditorium complex, or the Copley Place shopping mall. (The Westin hotel also connects to Copley Place.) Rooms are smartly done up in shades of blue and gold with new flat-screen TVs; the best ones overlook the Charles River. Readers praise the spacious guest rooms as "above average for the price," and give the hotel high marks for its friendly staff, great sports bar, and awesome location, while others complain about long waits at the elevators and a sometimes kid-crowded swimming pool. One person's "lively buzz" is another one's "too crowded," something to keep in mind as you weigh the merits of this one against the Westin Copley Place (753 rooms) and others in the neighborhood. Pros: Exceptional service, plush beds, great location between two shopping malls. Cons: Crowded pool area, chaotic lobby, housekeeping not always up to par. Family Matters: The chaotic feel is actually a bonus for families who can count on feeling right at home. Even rooms with two double beds are spacious enough to accommodate a cot. Better still, rollaways, cribs, and refrigerators are available free of charge, but you'll need to ask for them when making a reservation, as the first-come, first-serve items often go fast. Connecting rooms are available, but not guaranteed. ✉ *110 Huntington Ave., Back Bay* ☎*617/236–5800 or 800/228–9290* ⊕*www. marriott.com* ⌖*1,100 rooms, 47 suites* ⚲*In-room: safe, refrigerator, Internet. In-hotel: 3 restaurants, room service, bars, gym, laundry service, Wi-Fi, parking (fee)* ▱*AE, D, DC, MC, V* Ⓣ*Copley, Back Bay/South End.*

$$–$$$ 🖫**Midtown Hotel.** With its white-brick exterior and circa 1960s signage, the Midtown Hotel is determinedly un-chic. Hustle quickly past the plain-Jane lobby, filled with clusters of tour groups, and you'll find clean, basic rooms with teal carpeting, bright crimson coverlets, and small but serviceable bathrooms. They're not selling style here, they're selling price. If you're coming to Boston by car, get ready for a shock: the parking here is cheap—$18 per day—and easy. (Most hotels charge around $40 a day.) The convenient location, near Prudential Center, Symphony Hall, and the Christian Science Center, and reasonable rates enable this motel-style property to hold its own against its large, expensive neighbors. High-speed Internet is available in each guest room for a small fee. The Midtown is owned by the Christian Science Church, whose visitors wouldn't think of staying anywhere else. **Pros:** Good value for the money, friendly staff, cheap parking. **Cons:** Uninviting pool area, no restaurant on-site. **Family Matters:** Lack of romance or much ambience at all make this a dependable family spot only for those who expect to spend little time in the room. Rollaways and cribs aren't free, but, at $10, they're a bargain next to the $20 and up charged at many places. The lack of on-site restaurant can be offset by renting a fridge for $5 a night. ✉ *220 Huntington Ave., Back Bay* ☎*617/262–1000* ⊕*www.midtownhotel.com* ⌖*159 rooms* ⚲*In-room: Wi-Fi. In-hotel: pool, laundry service, Wi-Fi, parking (fee), some pets allowed* ▱*AE, D, DC, MC, V* Ⓣ*Symphony.*

$–$$ 🖫**Newbury Guest House.** "Stay here—it's the center of the universe!" a reader raves about this elegant redbrick-and-brownstone 1882 row house. On Boston's most fashionable shopping street, the inn looks the part, with natural pine flooring, elegant reproduction Victorian furnishings, and prints from the Museum of Fine Arts. These days, it looks even better— a recent re-do has expanded and prettied-up the lobby. Also, guests can now order room service from the tiny French bistro, La Voile, located downstairs. Some rooms have bay windows; others have decorative fireplaces. Limited parking is available at $15 for 24 hours—a good deal for the area. **Pros:** Cozy, homey, great location. **Cons:** Some say that rooms don't look as nice as the Web site indicates, small bathrooms, small TVs. **Family Matters:** Newbury is one of the area's few small houses that welcome kids. Only two rooms have the desirable two-queen-bed setup (most rooms accommodate only two people; some that have a pullout sleep three) and there are no connecting rooms. No cribs or cots either. You'll have to reserve ahead for the $15 space for the family car as space is limited. ✉*261 Newbury St., Back Bay* ☎*617/670–6000 or 800/437–7668* 🖨*617/670–6100* ⊕*www.newburyguest house.com* ➘*32 rooms* ♿*In-room: Wi-Fi. In-hotel: no elevator, Wi-Fi, parking (fee)* ▭*AE, D, DC, MC, V* ⏹*BP* ⓣ*Hynes/ICA, Copley.*

$$$–$$$$ 🏨**Radisson Hotel Boston.** A bit drab from the outside, this circa-1970s high-rise hotel at the edge of the Theater District suits price-sensitive students and families just fine. The abundant oversize rooms with queen-size beds sleep four comfortably and get extra points for private balconies and luxurious beds with adjustable-firmness mattresses, goose-down quilts, and 250-thread-count sheets. **Pros:** Free Wi-Fi throughout the property, corner rooms, like 24 and 25, have great city views, indoor pool. **Cons:** No minibars, $20 fee to rent a refrigerator. **Family Matters:** Economy and location are the primary reason to stay here as there are no kid-specific amenities—although the pool is always nice to have. Rooms with two double beds can easily accommodate a cot or crib for which literature states there is a fee, but can sometimes be negotiated gratis. ✉*200 Stuart St., Back Bay* ☎*617/482–1800 or 800/333–3333* ⊕*www.radisson. com/bostonma* ➘*326 rooms, 30 suites* ♿*In-room: safe, Wi-Fi. In-hotel: 2 restaurants, room service, pool, gym, laundry service, Wi-Fi, parking (fee)* ▭*AE, D, DC, MC, V* ⓣ*Arlington, Boylston.*

$$$–$$$$ 🏨**Westin Copley Place Boston.** If your idea of bliss is sleeping in an upscale shopping mall, meet your new favorite hotel. The Westin has its own pod of retail shops, plus it's connected by a covered skywalk to Copley Place (high-end shopping) and the Hynes Convention Center—a real treat in the winter. The top-floor rooms of this contemporary 36-story hotel have some of the best views in Boston, most gorgeous when a-twinkle at night. No surprise that busi-

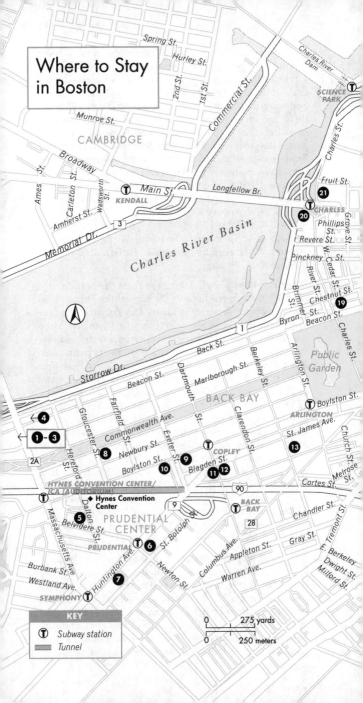

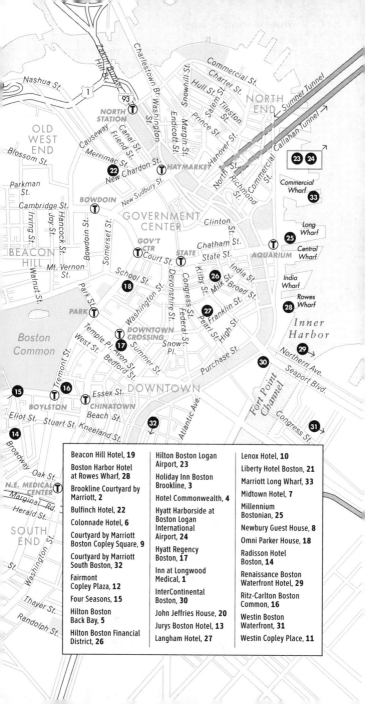

Beacon Hill Hotel, **19**

Boston Harbor Hotel at Rowes Wharf, **28**

Brookline Courtyard by Marriott, **2**

Bulfinch Hotel, **22**

Colonnade Hotel, **6**

Courtyard by Marriott Boston Copley Square, **9**

Courtyard by Marriott South Boston, **32**

Fairmont Copley Plaza, **12**

Four Seasons, **15**

Hilton Boston Back Bay, **5**

Hilton Boston Financial District, **26**

Hilton Boston Logan Airport, **23**

Holiday Inn Boston Brookline, **3**

Hotel Commonwealth, **4**

Hyatt Harborside at Boston Logan International Airport, **24**

Hyatt Regency Boston, **17**

Inn at Longwood Medical, **1**

InterContinental Boston, **30**

John Jeffries House, **20**

Jurys Boston Hotel, **13**

Langham Hotel, **27**

Lenox Hotel, **10**

Liberty Hotel Boston, **21**

Marriott Long Wharf, **33**

Midtown Hotel, **7**

Millennium Bostonian, **25**

Newbury Guest House, **8**

Omni Parker House, **18**

Radisson Hotel Boston, **14**

Renaissance Boston Waterfront Hotel, **29**

Ritz-Carlton Boston Common, **16**

Westin Boston Waterfront, **31**

Westin Copley Place, **11**

ness travelers and visiting families love this place, especially when you factor in the pool, fitness center, and the fabulous Copley Square location. Guest rooms have wildly comfortable beds and plush linens. For dining, you can't go wrong with a meal at Turner Fisheries Bar and Restaurant (don't miss the award-winning clam chowder). ■TIP➔**Check the Starwood Web site for promotional rates. Also, stay on July 4 and get amazing views of the fireworks over the Charles River.** Pros: Great location, great views, clean, spacious rooms. Cons: Big and busy-feeling, pool area is nothing special, some say it's overpriced. **Family Matters:** It goes without saying that teen girls will find heaven in the mall-side location. They'll also like teen-friendly room-service packages that include junk food and a teen magazine. For littler kids, ask for goody bags, one with a nightlight and ducky for tots, and colored pencils and activities for the school-age set. Cots and cribs are free, but they'll only fit in king rooms (not in double double setups) as maximum occupancy is four. A very limited number of connecting rooms can be requested, though not guaranteed. Minimize the food bill by requesting a fridge that the hotel will be happy to provide free of charge, if available. ✉*10 Huntington Ave., Back Bay* ☎*617/262–9600 or 800/937–8461* ⊕*www.westin.com/ copleyplace* ⤴*753 rooms, 50 suites* ♿*In-room: safe, refrigerator, Wi-Fi. In-hotel: 5 restaurants, room service, bar, pool, gym, spa, laundry service, Wi-Fi, some pets allowed* ▤*AE, D, DC, MC, V* Ⓣ*Copley, Back Bay/South End.*

BEACON HILL

$$$ Ⓦ**Beacon Hill Hotel & Bistro.** Two 19th-century town houses
★ have been meticulously renovated to house this intimate boutique hotel on Beacon Hill. You can't beat the location on Charles Street, one of the city's premier addresses, within walking distance of the Public Garden, Back Bay, and Government Center. Minimalist-style rooms are individually decorated with soft neutral colors and plush bed linens. Rooms have plenty of natural light filtering through the large windows overlooking city streets. There's a rooftop deck for lounging and a popular street-side bistro with fireplace and bar that's open for breakfast, lunch, and dinner. Pros: Beacon Hill location, with boutiques and restaurants within walking distance, parking available at nearby Boston Common garage. Cons: Rooms are small. **Family Matters:** The local charm and surprising family friendliness (and location a short walk from the Charles

River Reservation) make the hotel a priceless opportunity for some real Boston city living—and, everyone gets a free breakfast at the attached bistro. Still, you'll have to make some concessions. Small rooms make adding an extra bed (for $25/night) a tight squeeze, and even at maximum capacity, there's only room for three. The hotel's one suite, with its sitting area, can squeeze in 5, but again, it's a tight fit. If you're game, it's worth the extra effort. ✉*25 Charles St., Beacon Hill* ☎*617/723–7575 or 888/959–2442* ⊕*www. beaconhillhotel.com* ⤳*12 rooms, 1 suite* ⚲*In-room: Wi-Fi. In-hotel: restaurant, laundry service, Wi-Fi* ▱*AE, D, DC, MC, V* ⊙*BP* Ⓣ*Arlington, Charles/MGH.*

$$$$ Ⓣ**Liberty Hotel Boston**. Boston's most buzz-worthy hotel, bar none, is the new Liberty Hotel, set in the old (19th century) Charles Street Jail. The jail puns eventually wear thin—the bar is called "Alibi," a restaurant is "Clink," and so on—but you can't deny the cool factor of this unique luxury hotel. Jailhouse style includes the trademark windows, catwalks, and even jail cells. This circa 1851 National Historic Landmark building sits at the foot of Beacon Hill, close to boutiques and restaurants. A soaring lobby of exposed brick leads to 18 guest rooms (in the main building), while an adjacent 16-story tower houses 280 more rooms with expansive views of the city. Aside from the SOLITARY sign you hang from your door when you wish to be alone, there's nothing about the rooms that suggests confinement. Small but freshly modern, they provide luxe linens, flat-panel TVs and Wi-Fi. Don't expect a quiet getaway here—the Alibi bar (the former drunk tank) draws lines to get in. Check out the fried mac-and-cheese balls at Clink. **Pros:** Great lobby, lively nightlife, Beacon Hill location. **Cons:** Some say HVAC system is noisy, lively nightlife, service has a few bugs to work out. **Family Matters:** There are few kid-specific amenities as yet (except for cribs), but that may change. The place aims to please, with a concierge and front desk staff eager to help families plan their stays, and packages like the Sleepover Package that includes "BFF" stationery sets. A limited number of connecting rooms are available upon request. Cribs and cots are free of charge but often booked up, so ask ahead. Families of more than four will want to ask for the so-called Breathtaking Rooms, the only accommodations (outside of suites) that can sleep five—albeit snugly. ✉*215 Charles St., Beacon Hill* ☎*617/224–4000 or 860/507–5245* ⊕*www.libertyhotel.com* ⤳*298 rooms* ⚲*In-room: safe, DVD, Internet, Wi-Fi. In-hotel: 2 res-*

taurants, room service, bar, gym, laundry service, Wi-Fi, parking (fee), some pets allowed ⊟ AE, D, DC, MC, V ⊤Charles/MGH

DOWNTOWN

★ Fodor'sChoice ⊤**Boston Harbor Hotel at Rowes Wharf.** Red Sox
$$$$ owner John Henry parks his yacht here in summertime. The rest of us can arrive by boat in a less grand fashion—the water shuttle runs from Logan Airport to the back door of this deluxe waterfront hotel. The lobby is stunningly elegant, with marble arches, antique maps, and a huge tumble of fresh flowers. Guest rooms sport marble bathrooms, custom-made desks, Frette linens, high-end radio/ CD players, flat-panel TVs, and laptop-size safes. Amenities abound—there's even complimentary daily shoe shines. The older, well-heeled clientele appreciates these niceties, along with the fabulous views of the city and Boston harbor. **Pros:** Readers praise the impeccable service, beautiful rooms and views, easy walk to Faneuil Hall. **Cons:** Gym equipment somewhat outdated, spa gets booked, so may not have availability. **Family Matters:** Not outwardly a "family" establishment, Rowes Wharf will graciously accommodate family requests. The biggest bargain—relatively speaking— will be for one-infant broods that can make use of a standard, city-view room (queen bed) with an added crib (free of charge). A limited number of superior rooms have two doubles, making them suitable for a family of four, while deluxe rooms have a king bed, a queen sofabed, and just enough space to squeeze in a crib. Rollaways are available, but be warned: they run a whopping $75 a night. Ask at the front desk about games available for kids, and operating times for the pool which, in order to accommodate spa guests, limits hours for children. The HarborWalk, just outside, is a perfect place to push a stroller on a nice day. ⊠70 *Rowes Wharf, Downtown/Waterfront* ☎617/439–7000 *or 800/752–7077* ⊕*www.bhh.com* ⇆*206 rooms, 24 suites* ⚬*In-room: refrigerator, Wi-Fi. In-hotel: 2 restaurants, room service, bar, pool, gym, spa, laundry service, Wi-Fi, parking (fee), some pets allowed* ⊟*AE, D, DC, MC, V* ⊤*Aquarium, South Station.*

$$–$$$ ⊤**Bulfinch Hotel.** The clean, crisp, contemporary look of
★ this boutique hotel is simplicity at its best. Steps from TD Banknorth Garden (forever known as Boston Garden) and an easy walk to Government Center, Faneuil Hall, and the North End, this unique nine-floor flatiron (triangular) prop-

erty offers one of the best values in town, if you don't mind tiny digs. The immaculate, minimalist rooms have honey-hue walnut furnishings, gunmetal light fixtures, marble-tiled baths, and high-end mattresses, plus flat-screen TVs, CD players, and work desks. The neutral and white-on-white color scheme adds additional serenity—a welcome oasis from the maddening Garden crowds just outside the door. If you're looking for nightlife, you don't have to go far: the hotel's award-winning Flat Iron Tapas Bar and Lounge is one of the hippest nightspots in the city. **Pros:** Modern, spotless rooms, free Internet, lots of restaurants and bars nearby (including the on-site lounge), close to North Station commuter rail and the T. **Cons:** Small guest rooms and lobby, parking garage is across the street. **Family Matters:** With no cribs or cots, the Bulfinch is definitely a hotel for older kids who will probably be wowed by the funky building. Rooms are small (very small!), and four people staying in a two-double-bed setup will be cozy. A very few connecting rooms are available but can't be guaranteed. ✉ *107 Merrimac St., Downtown* ☎ *617/624–0202* ⊕ *www.bulfinchhotel. com* ⇄ *79 rooms* ⚇ *In-room: Internet. In-hotel: restaurant, bar, gym, laundry service, parking (fee), some pets allowed* ⊟ *AE, D, DC, MC, V* Ⓣ *North Station.*

$$$–$$$$ ▧ **Hilton Boston Financial District.** If you're looking for sleek,
★ comfortable, and quiet, you'll find it at this luxury hotel. And if you're looking for the old Wyndham hotel, this is it, now a Hilton property. The place has been freshened up some, with stylish teal and taupe carpeting and new linens. The lobby's mahogany paneling and soft gold lighting complement the restored bronze elevators and original letterbox. Comforting touches include terry robes, feather pillows, and nightly turndown service. Night owls can take advantage of the 24-hour health club and business center. Readers praise the comfort touches such as the warm cider available in the lobby on a cold day. **Pros:** Well-maintained, clean, and quiet; friendly, helpful staff. **Cons:** Poor-quality breakfast buffet (try the nearby Bean Leaf Café, instead), expensive food in general (lots of options in the neighborhood, though), daily fee for Wi-Fi, hard to find. **Family Matters:** The hotel is decidedly all business, but can be a great deal for families on weekends. High ceilings augment the already oversized rooms (especially those at the end of the halls). Some rooms with two queens will fit a cot, but you'll have to pay $30 a night for the privilege. Cribs are free. Kids' menus are available. Although the skyscraper

jungle of the Financial District may not be especially scenic, you're only a short walk to Faneuil Hall and other attractions. Generous Family Fun packages include a backpack for each child, breakfast, and an attraction admission for four, plus an in-room movie with popcorn and soda. ⊠*89 Broad St., Downtown* ☎*617/556–0006* ⊕*www.hilton.com* ⇨*362 rooms, 66 suites* ⮔*In-room: refrigerator, safe, Wi-Fi. In-hotel: restaurant, room service, bar, gym, laundry service, Wi-Fi, parking (fee)* ⊟*AE, D, DC, MC, V* ⓣ*State.*

$$–$$$$ ⛉**Hyatt Regency Boston.** Aromatherapy wafts through the halls of this 22-story Downtown Crossing hotel—perhaps an energizing citrus scent in the a.m. to get you going and a calming lavender essence to relax you upon your return. Business travelers who frequent this hotel might not notice, or care, but they do enjoy the high-end amenities that come standard in guest rooms, including Sony Dream Machines, pillow-top mattresses and featherbeds (with foam beds upon request), bathrobes, and bath products from Newbury Street's Portico. The hotel is a short walk from the Financial District, not to mention Boston Common and Chinatown, and the fitness center is open 24/7. Savvy vacationers find weekend bargains and good package deals with theater tickets and shopping discounts. Spacious guest rooms, set around four atriums, are decorated with mahogany furnishings, taupe linen walls, and soothing earth tones. We like the fact that this property is fairly green—among other things, they compost leftover food, and use energy-efficient lighting, including motion-detector light switches in guest rooms. **Pros:** High-end amenities in a moderately priced hotel, good package deals, saunas and whirlpools. **Cons:** Views of neighboring office buildings from guest rooms, few chairs around indoor pool, small gym. **Family Matters:** In-room Nintendo 64 is a sign of the hotel's desire to appeal to families. Most kids will find the console positively retro, but enjoy it nonetheless. Cribs and cots fit easily into most rooms and are free of charge, but refrigerators cost $25 per night. Connecting rooms are available. Ask about the Explorer Package that includes a bag full of city guides and activities for the whole family, plus two adult attraction admissions. The Downtown Crossing location may not appeal to everyone. To be sure, it's on the upswing, but still suffers from a questionable after-hours reputation. ⊠*1 Ave. de Lafayette, Chinatown* ☎*617/912–1234 or 800/233–1234* ⊕*www.bostonfinancial.hyatt.com* ⇨*474 rooms, 26 suites* ⮔*In-room: refrigerator, Internet, Wi-Fi.*

In-hotel: restaurant, room service, bar, pool, gym, laundry service, Wi-Fi, parking (fee), some pets allowed ⊟AE, D, DC, MC, V ⓣChinatown, Downtown Crossing.

★ Fodor'sChoice ⚏**InterContinental Boston.** Call it the anti-boutique
$$$$ hotel. Boston's 424-room InterContinental Hotel, facing the harbor and the grassy strip known as the Rose Kennedy Greenway—is housed in two opulent, 22-story towers wrapped in blue glass. Miel, the hotel's organic Provençal brasserie, is open 24/7. Hallways are lined with Texan limestone, and lobbies are gleaming with Italian marble and leather—there's not a red brick in the place. Guest rooms are oversize, wired with the latest technology, and have flat-screen TVs, and readers rave about the spalike bathrooms ("the best bathroom I have ever seen"), done in mosaic tile and granite, with separate tubs and showers. Another drawing card here is the 6,600-square-foot spa and health club, and a pool that overlooks Atlantic Avenue and the Rose Kennedy Greenway. Sushi-Teq, the hotel's sushi-tequila restaurant, draws crowds, while movers and shakers from local financial, real estate, and law firms of the Financial District make merry after work in the bars. **Pros:** Rooms have great views and great bathrooms, close to Financial District and South Station, brasserie open 24 hours. **Cons:** Huge function rooms mean lots of conventioneers, guests say that soundproofing could be better. **Family Matters:** Families will feel right at home here. Situated right on the Harbor Walk, the hotel provides an easy (and scenic) walk to the Children's Museum nearby. It's also a quick walk to South Station. Attention to children and families has been thoughtfully folded into about every area of hotel operations, from goodies at check-in, to junior spa services, to Shirley Temples at Sushi-Teq. The latter is a particularly pleasant surprise in summer, when outdoor entertainment (particularly Tuesday Salsa dancers) draws the stroller set, parents sipping gourmet margaritas while the kids play on the grass alongside. Roomy accommodations make the standard double/double seem decidedly airier. Kid equipment includes cribs (complimentary), cots ($35 per night, king rooms only) and fridges ($35 per stay). ✉510 Atlantic Ave., Downtown/Waterfront ☎617/747–1000 ⊕www.intercontinentalboston.com ⌖424 rooms, 38 suites ⌂In-room: safe, refrigerator, DVD, Wi-Fi. In-hotel: 2 restaurants, room service, bar, pool, gym, spa, laundry service, Wi-Fi, parking (fee) ⊟AE, D, DC, MC, V.

4

VERY IMPORTANT PETS

Some Boston hotels roll out the red carpet for their VIPs (Very Important Pets). It's Fido's birthday? **Hotel Marlowe** will order a special cake from Polka Dog Bakery. And, the pet ambassadors at the **Fairmont Copley** will be happy to take your pets out for a scenic stroll around the city. At the **Onyx Hotel**, Lassie can have her own bed, fleece blanket, and gourmet dog biscuits; fine felines get a scratching post, too. There are also pet-sitting and pet-walking services. The **Ritz-Carlton Boston Common** Pampered Pet package includes a welcome fruit-and-cheese platter, dog biscuits, a ceramic water bowl, custom-ized dog tag, and a purr-fect one-hour pampering session for you and your pet—one of you gets a massage and the other gets groomed.

$$$–$$$$ ⚅**Langham Hotel.** The red awnings of this 1922 Renaissance
★   Revival landmark (the former Federal Reserve Building) lead to a gleaming lobby of honeyed gold, deep red, and creamy marble, a stark contrast to the ubiquitous gray suits of Financial District types who gather here. It's a bit of a hike to Newbury Street and Boston's museums from here, but there are good reasons to stay put: Café Fleuri is the site of an all-chocolate buffet Saturday afternoon (September–June) and a wonderful jazz brunch on Sunday. The hotel recently added Chuan Body & Soul, a health club with a pool and spa services. **Pros:** Fabulous Sunday brunch, thick, fluffy towels and robes, good discounts on weekends. **Cons:** Extra charge for Internet use, a bit pricey, expensive valet parking. ■ TIP→ **Use a public parking lot, where rates are cheaper on weekends. Family Matters:** It's all business during the week, but families and couples drop in on weekends for the dramatically lower room rates. Specialty packages include the Very Important Baby package, with luxury baby bedding, unlimited disposable diapers, preordered baby food, and top-of-the-line baby bath products. For older groups, family-fun packages include deep discounts on second rooms, plus admission into several area attractions. On any day, enjoy free cribs and cots, children's menus, and a kids-eye-level check-in so little peepers don't miss a thing. ⊠*250 Franklin St., Downtown* ☎*617/451–1900 or 800/543–4300* ⊕ *www.langhamhotels.com/* ⤻*318 rooms, 17 suites* ⌂*In-room: safe, refrigerator, Wi-Fi. In-hotel: 2 restaurants, room service, bar, pool, gym, spa, laundry*

service, Wi-Fi, parking (fee), some pets allowed ☐AE, D, DC, MC, V ⊤South Station.

$$$–$$$$ ⊞**Marriott Long Wharf.** Jutting out into the bay, this airy, multi-tiered redbrick hotel resembles a ship. Most of the rooms, pleasantly decorated in cream and gold brocade with pillow-top mattresses, open onto a five-story atrium. Some rooms have views of the park or New England Aquarium. Clean-freak alert: Plush feather duvets on the beds are changed every night. There's no excuse to avoid the gym here—it's open 24 hours a day. **Pros:** Waterfront location, good weekend rates (check the Web for deals), convenience store close by. **Cons:** Restaurant is pricey. ▣TIP→ **Head to Quincy Market instead of eating on-site, even for breakfast. Family Matters:** The hotel is across a plaza from the New England Aquarium, and a hop from whale-watch tours, Quincy Market, and the North End, not to mention cute Christopher Columbus Park and playground. Standard guest rooms are small for families. Kids love the great swimming pool, overlooking the harbor and there's an itty-bitty game room. Got a big family? Ask for a corner room that can accommodate two double beds, plus a cot. Cots, cribs, and refrigerators, all available free of charge. ✉296 State St., Downtown/Waterfront ☎617/227–0800 or 800/228–9290 ⊕www.marriott.com/boslw ⇨397 rooms, 15 suites ♿In-room: refrigerator, Internet, Wi-Fi. In-hotel: 2 restaurants, room service, bar, pool, gym, laundry facilities, laundry service, parking (fee) ☐AE, D, DC, MC, V ⊤Aquarium.

$$–$$$$ ⊞**Millennium Bostonian Hotel.** Open for business, the Millennium hotel is in the final stages of a $23 million transformation. The circular front entrance now features stone floors, polished wood, and two fireplaces, plus a mini-waterfall. The old Seasons restaurant is no more, but the hotel is opening a new eatery, the Millennium Grille. The working fireplaces and balconies remain (hooray!) and guest rooms are punched up with stone entryways, wood paneling, crown moldings and earth-toned hues, accented with Boston-theme photography and artwork. Rooms are being updated with duvets and 300-thread-count sheets, flat-screen TVs, and safes large enough for laptops, and Wi-Fi is now available in public spaces. As part of the renovation, windows got extra soundproofing—a real plus in a busy area like Quincy Market. **Pros:** New look, located next to Faneuil Hall Marketplace. **Cons:** Renovation continues at this writing; contact hotel for updated informa-

tion. **Family Matters:** It's primarily a business hotel, so rooms with two double beds are few (reserve early!) and there really aren't any kid-specific features. The bonuses: you're as close as you can get to Faneuil Hall, and some of those doubles can even squeeze in a cot ($20/night) to accommodate a family of five. Cribs and fridges are free when available. For the best leisure deals, come weekdays in winter. ⊠*Faneuil Hall Marketplace, 26 North St., Downtown* ☎*617/523–3600 or 866/866–8086* ⊕*www. millenniumhotels.com* ⚲*187 rooms, 14 suites* ⚐*In-room: safe, Wi-Fi. In-hotel: restaurant, room service, bar, gym, laundry service, Wi-Fi, parking (fee)* ☐*AE, D, DC, MC, V* Ⓣ*Government Center, Haymarket.*

$$–$$$$ 🍴 **Omni Parker House.** America's oldest continuously operat-
★ ing hotel just got a $30 million facelift, so you can steep yourself in Boston history but still watch a flat-screen TV, work out with the latest equipment, and stash your stuff in a laptop-size safe. And, happily, you can still get Boston cream pie for breakfast, since they invented it here. If any hotel really says "Boston," it's this one, where you may well see a Dickens impersonator in the lobby, since history tours put the Parker House on their hit list. The downside: guests' rooms are small (furnishings were custom-built to fit). At least they're nicely turned out, with red-and-gold Roman shades, ivory wall coverings, and cushy mattress covers. Another plus: rooms are extremely quiet—a claim that can't be made by some of the Omni's newer neighbors. The hotel stands opposite old City Hall, on the Freedom Trail. **Pros:** Historic, quiet, near Downtown Crossing on Freedom Trail. **Cons:** Small rooms, some say that staff could be friendlier. **Family Matters:** Kids are welcomed with colorful backpacks stocked with a kazoo and other goodies. Look for milk and cookies at turndown, and board games available to borrow from the front desk. Cribs are available for free, but a rollaway bed (which just fits in some rooms) will cost $30 per night. Tiny rooms make connecting accommodations a particularly good idea. Ask about packages that include attraction admission. ⊠*60 School St., Downtown* ☎*617/227–8600 or 800/843–6664* ⊕*www. omniparkerhouse.com* ⚲*551 rooms, 21 suites* ⚐*In-room: Wi-Fi. In-hotel: 2 restaurants, room service, bars, gym, laundry service, Wi-Fi, parking (fee), some pets allowed* ☐*AE, D, DC, MC, V* Ⓣ*Government Center, Park St.*

$$$–$$$$ 🍴 **Renaissance Boston Hotel.** Set along the working wharves of Boston Harbor, near the BCEC and the Institute of Contemporary Art, the Renaissance plays to a watery theme that you'll notice the moment you enter the lobby. Glass orbs are filled with blue or green liquid, while a lighting fixture and staircase are spiral-shaped like a nautilus shell. The building is flooded with light, and nearly all guest rooms have water views. It all adds up to a clean, cool, modern ambience, completely different from the dark woods and comfy Colonial look you encounter at the city's older hotels. The pool is a lap pool, not designed for lingering. If it all feels a bit no-nonsense, that's just fine to the business folk who make up much of the hotel's clientele. The mood changes on weekends, when package deals lure weekenders and family travelers. **Pros:** Inviting lobby bar and lounge area, close proximity to Silver Line (take the T to the airport), restaurant is comfortable for solo guests. **Cons:** Some guest-room views of Boston Harbor are more industrial than scenic. **Family Matters:** Being off the beaten path means the family will either be married to public transportation, or walking a mile to pretty much anywhere. The tradeoff? Roomy accommodations, all of which comfortably fit a crib or cot (both available free of charge). The out-of-the-way location costs less, too. Room service stops between midnight and 5:30 AM, so ask for a fridge (free or charge) if little ones are prone to wee-hours cravings. ✉606 Congress St., Downtown/Seaport District ☎617/338–4111 ⓦwww. renaissancehotels.com/boswf ⟶471 rooms ⌂In-room: DVD, Internet, Wi-Fi. In-hotel: 2 restaurants, room service, bar, pool, gym, spa, laundry service, Wi-Fi, parking (fee)☰AE, D, DC MC, V ⓉSouth Station

$$$$ 🖵**Ritz-Carlton Boston Common.** While the hotel gets compared, ★ often unfavorably, to the late, lamented Ritz-Carlton Boston, it's only fair to judge it for what it is: a sleek, contemporary hotel that speaks more to rock stars than royalty. Warm wood walls and trim complement an extensive art collection in the lobby lounge, where furnishings are draped in velvet and silk and lamps are made of hand-blown Venetian glass. Recently upgraded guest rooms are dressed in apricot, yellow, and blue, with hardwood armoires, separate marble showers and deep tubs, and the all-important flat-screen HD TV. Some rooms have spectacular views of Boston Common. A short walk will get you to Downtown Crossing's shopping zone, the Theater District, and Newbury Street. Besides the fitness center, the hotel complex houses a movie theater. **Pros:** Killer gym, central location. **Cons:** Readers complain that guest rooms are too dark,

food service is "brutally expensive." (Lots of other options in Downtown Crossing, though.) **Family Matters:** Various room configurations and sizes meet any need. Children are tended to with Ritz Kids amenities like in-hotel scavenger hunts, kid-friendly (and healthy!) foods and snacks, plus a plethora of available equipment from strollers to high chairs. Teens 16 and up will want to get fit in LA Sports Club, the Ritz's mega fitness center, where the sweating body next to you could be a pop star or famous athlete. ⊠*10 Avery St., Downtown* ☎*617/574–7100 or 800/241–3333* ⊕*www.ritzcarlton.com* ⌸*150 rooms, 43 suites* &*In-room: safe, refrigerator, Internet, Wi-Fi. In-hotel: restaurant, room service, bar, pool, gym, laundry service, Wi-Fi, parking (fee)* ⊟*AE, D, DC, MC, V* ⓣ*Boylston St.*

$$$–$$$$ Ⓣ**Westin Boston Waterfront.** A modern, 17-story tower of gleaming glass and steel, this South Boston waterfront property is connected to the megasize Boston Convention & Exhibition Center, a magnet for those wearing suits and name tags. Rooms are handsome with a neutral palette of whites, tans, and pastels, punctuated with cherrywood furnishings. Most—some 85%—have water or skyline views. **Pros:** Lobby stations with wireless check-in, Silver Line from Logan takes you directly to hotel, the Westin's signature "heavenly" beds. **Cons:** Clusters of convention-eers and meeting goers crowd the place, too sterile for some tastes, South Boston waterfront neighborhood is still up-and-coming, rooms are pricey during top conventions. **Family Matters:** The November to January period is a family's best friend, when rates go down due to lack of conventioneers. On the other hand, that means you'll be taking the T everywhere as the long walk will probably not appeal to kids in cold weather. The upside: accommodations are a little roomier than Downtown, with double rooms that can fit a crib (cots will only fit in king rooms). Year-round, kids get automatic membership into the Westin Club that includes a goody-stuffed backpack at check-in. ⊠*425 Summer St., Downtown/Seaport District* ☎*617/532–4600* ⊕*www.starwood.com* ⌸*739 rooms, 32 suites* &*In-room: Wi-Fi. In-hotel: restaurant, room service, bar, pool, gym, laundry service, Wi-Fi, parking (fee)* ⊟*AE, D, DC, MC, V* ⓣ*South Station.*

KENMORE SQUARE

$$$$ ⊤**Hotel Commonwealth.** Luxury and service without pretence
★ make this hip hotel anything but common, blending old-world charm with modern conveniences for a sophisticated, boutiquey feel. Rich color schemes enhance the elegant rooms, and king- or queen-size beds are piled with down pillows and Italian linens. Choose rooms with views of bustling Commonwealth Avenue or Fenway Park. All rooms have marble baths and floor-to-ceiling windows, separate work areas (divided by a curtain) and flat-screen TVs. The bend-over-backward staff and car and driver available to guests are added bonuses. The much-acclaimed seafood restaurant, Great Bay (be sure to make reservations upon arrival) and the Eastern Standard Bar & Restaurant are also on-site. **Pros:** Luscious bedding and bath products, great service, Red Sox fans will love the views of Fenway Park from some of the rooms (request these when booking), on-site restaurant is one of the best in the city for fresh fish. **Cons:** Hotel and surroundings can be mobbed during a Red Sox game, small gym. **Family Matters:** Rooms here are big—even double queen rooms handily fit a cot. Young baseball fans will love the proximity to the Sox ballpark, and the Fenway rooms from which you can see the fabled Green Monster. Other rooms overlook either Commonwealth Avenue or Kenmore Square—but don't worry; while you can see the Citgo sign from some windows, the lights won't be a bother. Cribs, cots, and fridges are free when available. Not surprisingly, the cheapest time to visit is midweek when the Sox are away, and nearby Boston University is quiet. The Fenway package includes, among other things, two tickets to a game, while Explore Your School gives parent and prospective student tools to get to know the college scene. ⊠*500 Commonwealth Ave., Kenmore Sq.* ☎*617/933–5000 or 866/784–4000* ⊕*www.hotel commonwealth.com* ⤴*149 rooms, 1 suite* ⌂*In-room: safe, refrigerator, DVD, Internet, Wi-Fi. In-hotel: 2 restaurants, room service, bar, gym, laundry service, Wi-Fi, parking (fee)* ⊟*AE, D, DC, MC, V* ⊤*Kenmore.*

4

BOSTON OUTSKIRTS

BROOKLINE

$$$ ⊞**Brookline Courtyard by Marriott.** If you enjoy the anonymity and predictability of a chain hotel and don't mind an outside of Boston location, this is a decent choice. The hotel is popular with families of students at nearby colleges—there are about a dozen schools within 5 mi of here, including Boston University and Boston College—who like the fact that they can treat the kids to dinner at one of several funky Coolidge Corner eateries, then unwind in the indoor pool and hot tub or hit the small gym. The T is right outside the door, as are 15 or so restaurants. (An on-site eatery is open for breakfast only.) And in the Stuff You Won't Find Everywhere Department: rooms with Sabbath locks on the door for Jewish guests. **Pros:** Indoor pool, close to T station. **Cons:** Staff can be indifferent. **Family Matters:** Kids will get a big kick out of the extended king rooms that, for about $20 more than standard kings, include a Murphy bed. An additional cot fits in any of the spacious rooms, and both cots and cribs are free. Some rooms connect. Store sandwiches in the fridge (refrigerators are free, when available, upon request) and enjoy them in the courtyard outside. A nice playground is about a five-minute walk down Harvard Street. ⊠*40 Webster, Brookline* ☎*617/734–1393 or 866/296–2296* ⊕*www.brooklinecourtyard.com* ⇋*180 rooms, 8 suites* ♨*In-room: safe, Internet, Wi-Fi. In-hotel: restaurant, pool, gym, laundry facilities, Internet terminal, Wi-Fi, parking (fee)* ⊟*AE, D, DC, MC, V* ⊤*Beacon St.*

$$–$$$ ⊞**Holiday-Inn Boston-Brookline.** The utilitarian property is more or less a workhorse, with rooms catering to college visitors and those visiting the nearby medical facilities. Still, it's got its merits. The lovely residential Brookline neighborhood is just a short walk to the funky shops at Coolidge Corner, and a slightly longer walk to the more upscale Brookline Village. Even better, the Green Line is literally right outside your door, with Boston just a few stops away. Rooms are unremarkable—standard issue Holiday Inn (although a huge makeover is scheduled to be completed in January '09)—but big enough for a family of four, at a price significantly cheaper than Downtown. **Pros:** Safe neighborhood, T right out front. **Cons:** Tired decor, low on glamour, located outside the city proper. **Family Matters:** It's a nice neighborhood, but even so, some parents say that rooms on the second floor and up (in other words, off the ground floor) feel most secure. In the Holiday Inn tradition, kids under 12 eat free off the kids' menu when they're with a paying adult. That makes the economy good, but there are tastier options kids will love—such as Barbecue at the Village Smokehouse. One unhappy surprise: the hotel is one of the few that charges for both cots and cribs ($15 per night each). ⊠*1200 Beacon St., Brookline* ☏*617/277–1200 or 800/315–2621* ⊕*www.holidayinn.com* ➪*225 rooms, 25 suites* &*In-room: refrigerator, Wi-Fi. In-hotel: restaurant, bar, pool, gym, laundry facilities, Internet terminal, Wi-Fi, parking (fee)* ▭*AE, D, DC, MC, V* Ⓣ*Brookline.*

$$ ⊞ **Inn at Longwood Medical.** Within walking distance of Fenway Park and the Museum of Fine Arts, this modern Best Western affiliate is also near six hospitals. Many hotel guests are patients or relations of patients (there's a discount medical rate, even on the busiest weekends). In summer expect Sox fans to crowd the halls and lobby. Rooms are Best Western cookie-cutter, but nicely appointed with desks and updated linens and bed coverings. **Pros:** Friendly, helpful staff, medical rate packages are hard to beat, attached to Longwood Galleria Mall and food court. **Cons:** Many guests are here for medical treatments or visiting family members in nearby hospitals. **Family Matters:** Transportation is a snap, with two Green Line trains within a short walk, the D line to Fenway (to which you can also easily walk) and the E line to the Museum of Fine Arts and Prudential Center. The hotel includes the two-double-bed setup, but smallish rooms mean you can't add a cot. Families of more than four will have to either upgrade to a suite or get connecting rooms. Cots and fridges are available for $15 and $10, respectively; cribs are free. Ask about Red Sox packages that include hats, game admission, and discounts on hotel and dining. ⊠*342 Longwood Ave., Brookline* ☏*617/731–4700 or 800/468–2378* ⊕*www.innatlongwood. com* ➪*140 rooms, 15 suites* &*In-room: kitchen (some), Wi-Fi. In-hotel: restaurant, room service, bar, laundry service, Internet terminal, Wi-Fi, parking (fee)* ▭*AE, D, DC, MC, V* Ⓣ*Longwood.*

DORCHESTER

$$–$$$ ⊞ **Courtyard by Marriott South Boston.** Tucked behind the Fortress, a behemoth storage facility, this property is a higher-end option to the neighboring Holiday Inn Express. What this hotel has going for it will hit you in the face, figuratively speaking, as soon as you enter. Standing in front of the

crescent-shape cherry reception desk (topped by a big flat-screen TV), you can easily take it all in. There's the business center (with a neat two-sided fireplace), the lobby lounge, and the breakfast bar, all done up in coral and green, with leather chairs and cherry pillars. Guest rooms are pleasant enough, with two queen beds in a standard room. It's all brighter than the drab surroundings. The T station is two blocks away, and free shuttles will get you to Downtown, the airport, Faneuil Hall, and the convention center. Fun feature: the Beantown Trolley shows up every morning at 8:30 sharp; join 'em for a day of sightseeing 'round town. **Pros:** Free parking, city skyline views from some rooms, family-friendly with weekend package deals. **Cons:** Not much going on in this area. **Family Matters:** Great for families on a budget, the hotel is worth the "price" of being out of the way. A couple of chain restaurants are nearby, but to save further on food, stock up from the nearby grocery store (fridges are in all rooms) and heat and eat in the microwave that the hotel will provide gratis upon request (when available—ask at reservation time). Double-queen rooms are your most economical option for a family of four, as suites are the only rooms that accommodate a cot. On the other hand, weekend deals often make the two-room suites extremely economical. Cribs are available free of charge. ⊠*63R Boston St., Dorchester* 🕿*617/436–8200 or 800/642–0303* ⊕*www.marriott.com/property/propertypage/BOSSO* ⟿*161 rooms, 5 suites* ⚹*In-room: refrigerator, Internet. In-hotel: bar, pool, gym, laundry service, Internet terminal, parking (no fee), some pets allowed* ⊟*AE, D, DC, MC, V* ⦿*CP* 🕙*Andrew.*

LOGAN AIRPORT (EAST BOSTON)

$$-$$$ ⊠**Hilton Boston Logan Airport.** Quiet rooms, competitive prices, and an airport location make this modern Hilton a popular choice with in-and-out visitors to Boston. There's a skywalk to terminals A and E and a free shuttle bus to the airport. Rooms have been recently updated with granite countertops in the baths and desks with ergonomic chairs. There's an unremarkable restaurant and an Irish pub on the premises, and a health club with a steam room. **Pros:** Easy access to Logan Airport, competitive prices. **Cons:** Extras like Internet access and parking can add up. **Family Matters:** For kids, the coolest part of the hotel has to be the view; if you have a plane lover, request a room with an odd number, which looks out over the runways. (Don't worry parents: it's surprisingly quiet.) Staff will let you squeeze a cot into a double/double, but don't. It's a tight, tight fit. Otherwise, opt for connecting rooms (cots do, however, fit in king rooms). If you're planning to spend time in town, make sure the group doesn't mind a schlep. City-bound transportation currently requires a courtesy shuttle to the blue line and the subway in. But, it beats the cost of a cab and/or parking. Cots, cribs, fridges . . . they're all free. Ask about packages that include admission into attractions such as the Aquarium and Duck Tours. ⊠ *1 Hotel Dr., East Boston* ☎*617/568–6700* ⊕*www.hilton.com* ⋧*595 rooms, 4 suites* ⊘*In-room: refrigerator, Internet, Wi-Fi. In-hotel: restaurant, room service, bar, pool, gym, Internet terminal, Wi-Fi, parking (fee)* ⊟*AE, D, DC, MC, V* Ⓣ*Silver Line.*

$$$–$$$$ ⊤**Hyatt Harborside at Boston Logan International Airport.** A 15-story glass structure punctuates this luxury hotel, on a point of land separating the inner and outer sections of Boston Harbor. Half of the rooms have sweeping views of either the city skyline or the ocean; the others overlook planes taking off and landing at the airport. The Hyatt operates its own 24-hour shuttle to all Logan Airport terminals and the airport T stop, and you'll get a discount on the water shuttle that runs between the airport and Downtown. Rooms, all decorated in soothing taupes and beiges, are soundproof. **Pros:** Convenient base for early flights out of Boston, pool area has skyline views, competent, can-do staff. **Cons:** Overpriced restaurant (skip it), airport shuttle service can be frustratingly slow. **Family Matters:** Convenience—and the fact that, to kids, the water-taxi boats feel like a theme-park ride—is a big plus. But, at $17 round-trip per person (children 12 and under are free) those 7-minute trips add up. If you're feeling the pinch (especially if older kids mean you're paying 3-plus adult fares) take the free shuttle to the Blue Line, which will take you downtown for a max of $4 round-trip each. Kids like the even-numbered rooms looking over the runways. Flight delay? Call downstairs and have them send up a game of Cranium to play while you wait. Cots and cribs are free, but the former only fit in king rooms. Fridges cost $25 per night. ⊠*101 Harborside Dr., East Boston* ☎*617/568–1234 or 800/233–1234* ⊕*www. harborside.hyatt.com/hyatt/hotels/index.jsp* ⋧*273 rooms, 6 suites* ⊘*In-room: Internet, Wi-Fi. In-hotel: restaurant, room service, bar, pool, gym, spa, laundry service, Wi-Fi, parking (fee)* ⊟*AE, D, DC, MC, V* Ⓣ*Airport.*

4

CAMBRIDGE

$$$–$$$$ ⊞ **Boston Marriott Cambridge.** Businesspeople and vacationing families like the sleek, modern look and efficiency of this 26-story, high-rise hotel in Kendall Square, Cambridge's high-tech district, just steps from the subway and MIT. It's also a prime location for viewing July 4 fireworks. Rooms are done in the Marriott chain's signature greens, with floral spreads and drapes. A room on one of the two concierge floors nets you complimentary breakfast, hors d'oeuvres, and desserts in the lounge. **Pros:** Top-floor rooms' stunning skyline and river views, luxe bed linens, family-friendly, decent cost-saving packages on the weekends. **Cons:** High-rise chain doesn't have a lot of charm, tiny pool, parking is expensive. **Family Matters:** The big high-tech draw depends on your kids' ages; the Museum of Science is walking distance, MIT is across the street, and the somewhat wacky MIT Museum is less than a mile away. In-room, indulge your family's inner geek by signing on for the Wii package and letting the brood game to their heart's content. Cots, cribs, and fridges are free. Five will fit ultra snugly in a double room, but you'll all have to suck in those guts. ⊠*2 Cambridge Center, Cambridge* ☎*617/494–6600 or 800/228–9290* ⊕*www.marriotthotels. com* ⇋*431 rooms, 12 suites* ⌂*In-room: Internet, Wi-Fi (some). In-hotel: 2 restaurants, room service, bar, pool, gym, laundry service, Wi-Fi, parking (fee)* ⊟*AE, D, DC, MC, V* Ⓣ*Kendall/MIT.*

★ Fodor'sChoice ⊞ **Charles Hotel.** Gracious service, top-notch ame-
$$$$ nities, and a great location on Harvard Square keep this first-class hotel in high demand. The New England Shaker interior is contemporary yet homey; antique quilts and art by nationally recognized artists hang throughout. Relax in the lobby library, chock-full of titles, some autographed by authors who frequent the hotel. Also sign up for a guided art tour of the hotel or pick up a self-guided map. Guest rooms come with lots of nice touches, like terry robes, quilted down comforters, flat-screen TVs (plus LCD mirror TVs in the bathroom), and Bose radios. ■TIP→**For a river or skyline view, ask for something above the seventh floor.** Both of the hotel's restaurants—Rialto and Henrietta's Table— are excellent. **Pros:** Your wish is their command, on-site spa, health club, premier jazz club, and two of the area's top restaurants, Harvard Square is out the door, outdoor skating rink is a fun gathering spot for families during the winter months. **Cons:** Luxury comes with a price, great for

visiting Cambridge sites but less convenient to downtown Boston (though Red Line T is two blocks away). **Family Matters:** The Charles goes out of its way to take care of kids. In addition to the usual cots, cribs, and fridges for free (upon request), there are gift bags for kids at check-in, a book library and games library at their disposal, an ice-skating rink in season, and milk and cookies at turn-down. Summers, look for kid-friendly entertainment at the on-site club (extra fee), followed by a free dessert at Henrietta's Table, which also happens to have about the best brunch anywhere. For older kids, there's the College Crash Course package that includes Harvard sweatshirts, discounts in Harvard Square, and a chance to win a $3,000 scholarship to the university of one's choice. ✉*1 Bennett St., Cambridge* ☎*617/765–4515 or 800/882–1818* ⊕*www. charleshotel.com* ⤵*249 rooms, 45 suites* ♿*In-room: safe, refrigerator, Internet, Wi-Fi. In-hotel: 2 restaurants, room service, bars, pool, gym, spa, laundry service, Internet terminal, Wi-Fi, parking (fee), some pets allowed* ▭*AE, DC, MC, V* Ⓣ*Harvard.*

$$–$$$$ 🏨 **Doubletree Guest Suites.** The best things about this place: the very excellent, on-site Sculler's Jazz Club, one of the finest places in town to catch a national act, and the extra-spacious two-room suites that cost no more than a single room elsewhere. The worst thing: it's a long walk to the subway and not really within walking distance of anywhere you want to go. A courtesy shuttle van is offered, but requires a bit of planning on your part. Each unit has a living room (with refrigerator and sofa bed), a bedroom with a king-size bed or two oversize twin beds, and a bathroom with a phone. Most suites have views of the Charles River or the Cambridge or Boston skyline—along with the traffic skirting Storrow Drive. There are also smaller rooms available at reduced prices. **Pros:** After listening to top-notch jazz acts, your room is steps away; value-packed dinner, jazz, and room packages. **Cons:** You'll spend time driving or shuttling if you stay here; you have to book the hotel shuttle in advance. **Family Matters:** What you lose in location, you definitely make up for with sanity, getting your own space to recharge before the next day's activities. Count on using those shuttles, particularly if you have young kids, as the closest T stop (Central Square) is about a 15-minute walk. Cribs are available free of charge. ✉*400 Soldiers Field Rd., Allston* ☎*617/783–0090 or 800/222–8733* ⊕*www. hiltonfamilyboston.com* ⤵*22 rooms, 286 suites* ♿*In-room:*

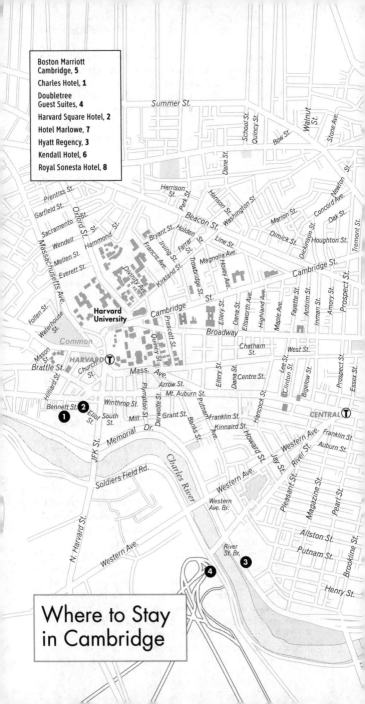

Boston Marriott Cambridge, **5**

Charles Hotel, **1**

Doubletree Guest Suites, **4**

Harvard Square Hotel, **2**

Hotel Marlowe, **7**

Hyatt Regency, **3**

Kendall Hotel, **6**

Royal Sonesta Hotel, **8**

Where to Stay in Cambridge

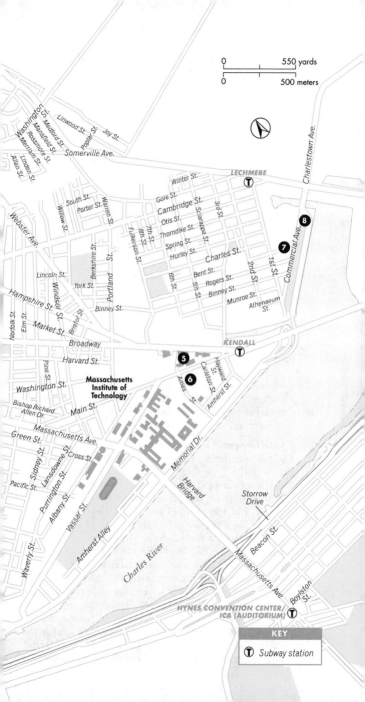

refrigerator, Internet. In-hotel: 2 restaurants, room service, bar, pool, gym, laundry facilities, laundry service, Internet terminal, parking (fee), some pets allowed ⊟*AE, D, DC, MC, V* ⊤*Central.*

$$–$$$ ⌨ **Harvard Square Hotel.** Want to be in Harvard Square and not pay the big bucks? For basic lodgings in a great location, you won't go wrong at this nondescript property that feels more dormitory than hotel. Just steps from the neighborhood's many restaurants, shops, and lively street corners, the hotel has simple but clean rooms, with refrigerators and Internet access. The desk clerks are particularly helpful, assisting with everything from sending faxes to securing dinner reservations. **Pros:** Location can't be beat, some windows open for fresh air. **Cons:** Rooms need updating and baths are small (many with exposed pipes); Wi-Fi, in-lobby computer use, and parking cost extra. **Family Matters:** It's not a luxury vacation by any means. But, older kids in particular will like the place for its proximity to the funky Harvard area. The hotel courts younger families too, by virtue of the fact that it offers cribs as well as cots (the latter for king rooms only). Rooms with two double beds feel a bit tight, but the hotel does have a limited number of connecting rooms. ⊠*110 Mt. Auburn St., Cambridge* ☎*617/864–5200 or 800/458–5886* ⊕*www.harvardsquarehotel.com* ⇗*73 rooms* ⌂*In-room: safe, refrigerator, Internet, Wi-Fi. In-hotel: laundry service, Internet terminal, Wi-Fi, parking (fee)* ⊟*AE, D, DC, MC, V* ⊤*Harvard.*

$$–$$$$ ⌨ **Hotel Marlowe.** Vivid stripes, swirls, leopard-print pillows and fake-fur throws add whimsy to the spacious rooms; many overlook the Charles River. Nice touches abound, like luscious linens, complimentary coffee and tea each morning, popular complimentary wine receptions each evening, and use of bikes and kayaks in summer. Free book readings and other literary events are held weekly in the hotel lobby. **Pros:** Luxury with below-market price tag (especially on weekends), free use of business center, very family- and pet-friendly, great money-saving packages available throughout the year. **Cons:** It's a cab ride or a walk and T ride into Boston, the wild colors and decor may not be for everyone. **Family Matters:** The hotel is close to the important stuff—namely the Museum of Science (across the street) to which you can get admission with some packages. Special deals also include goody bags for the kids, and dining at on-site Bambara. Ask about safety kits including

outlet covers, latch protectors, and a nightlight for your room. Free cots and cribs can squeeze into a standard double, but for not much more money, the King Studio suite, with pullout couch, is much roomier. There's no age range for bikes and kayaks, but Marlowe staffers will have to deem kids big enough for the equipment. Look for milk and cookies at turndown, animal-print robes (to buy or borrow), and the availability of baby gear such as strollers. ⊠ *25 Edwin H. Land Blvd., Cambridge* ☎ *617/868–8000 or 800/825–7140* ⊕ *www.hotelmarlowe.com* ⊅ *222 rooms, 14 suites* ⬧ *In-room: safe, refrigerator, Internet, Wi-Fi. In-hotel: restaurant, room service, bar, gym, bicycles, laundry service, Internet terminal, Wi-Fi, parking (fee), some pets allowed* ⊟ *AE, D, DC, MC, V* Ⓣ *Lechmere.*

$$–$$$$ ☂ **Hyatt Regency.** A dramatic ziggurat, this aging, somewhat tattered Hyatt is built around a central 16-story atrium. It's a magnet for prom nights, wedding parties, and group functions and the location is a bit out of the way; long walks or taxis are required to get around to top sites and attractions. But you can't beat the stunning views of the Charles River and the Boston skyline. Rooms that end in 06 have a river view and an interior balcony overlooking the atrium. For a small additional fee, add a large external private sundeck. **Pros:** Nice views from most rooms, look for bargain-basement Internet rates, large pool area. **Cons:** It's time to put some money into this has-been property, rooms need major freshening and updating, some bathrooms are shabby and out-of-date. **Family Matters:** For families, standard-issue rooms get a lift from on-site activities like Bike Rental (the hotel is right along the Charles River bike path) and a very nice pool. Double-queen rooms can feel a little tight for a family of four. Adding a balcony (for about $20) over the Charles makes the place feel a little roomier. Cots, cribs, and fridges are all available, free of charge. Kids age 6 and under get the breakfast buffet for free; half the $19.99 cost for kids ages 6 to 12. ⊠ *575 Memorial Dr., Cambridge* ☎ *617/492–1234 or 800/233–1234* ⊕ *www.cambridge.hyatt.com* ⊅ *459 rooms, 10 suites* ⬧ *In-room: Internet, Wi-Fi. In-hotel: 2 restaurants, room service, bar, pool, gym, bicycles, laundry service, Internet terminal, Wi-Fi, parking (fee), some pets allowed* ⊟ *AE, DC, MC, V* Ⓣ *Kendall/MIT.*

$$$ ☂ **Kendall Hotel.** You might expect a hotel in a techno-zone such as Kendall Square to be all stainless steel and chrome, but this one is quite homey and ultrafriendly. In the former

A+ AMENITIES

Beacon Hill Hotel & Bistro.
Stroll the shops on Charles Street, wander the Public Garden, and come back to the hotel for a drink on the rooftop deck.

Boston Harbor Hotel. You can park your yacht at the hotel's private marina. There's also a water taxi service.

Charles Hotel. The lending library is stuffed with titles, many autographed by authors who frequent the hotel. Art experts conduct tours of the hotel's extensive art collection.

The Colonnade. Live concerts are held at the RTP (rooftop pool), with food, drinks, and sweeping city views.

Fairmont Copley Plaza. Guests of culturally themed suites receive benefits like backstage passes to the Boston Symphony Orchestra.

Ritz-Carlton Boston Common. The Sports Club/LA, on property, offers 100,000 square feet of the latest fitness equipment. The Ritz has a bath butler who will set up a customized aromatherapy bath (think rose petals).

Royal Sonesta. The family-friendly pool has river and city views, and the New England Science Museum is right next door.

home of Engine House 7, it is stuffed with firehouse memorabilia. Owner Charlotte Forsythe loves collectibles, so an antique Chinese checkerboard and a ceramic Dalmatian add to the whimsical mix. Rooms are done up in Easter-egg hues. A seven-story addition includes an enclosed rooftop lounge, eight deluxe rooms, and four suites with kitchens, offering lots of space for families or anyone looking for a lot of room and kitchen facilities. **Pros:** Accommodating staff make guests feel right at home, extended, tasty breakfast is included, quiet rooms. **Cons:** May be too tchotchke-filled for some tastes. **Family Matters:** First up—no fire pole (kids always ask, but alas it was taken out by previous owners). Still, the firehouse theme is a treat, with lots of memorabilia to fascinate little ones. Suites are pricey, and cots cost extra, but the spacious double-queen rooms are perfect for four. Cribs are free. Most family packages include parking and all room rates include a sumptuous, homemade daily "Fireman's Breakfast." The Kendall works hard to appeal to families with packages such as a recent "Webkins" deal that included a stuffed Dalmatian named Sparky, and other goodies in a special backpack. Catch a free shuttle across the street to the CambridgeSide Galleria, which is a hop from the Museum of Science. ⊠*350*

Main St., Cambridge ☎*617/577–1300 or 866/566–1300* ⊕*www.kendallhotel.com* ⬥*73 room, 4 suites* ⚹*In-room: Internet, Wi-Fi. In-hotel: restaurant, room service, bar, laundry service, Internet terminal, Wi-Fi, parking (fee)* ⊟*AE, DC, MC, V* ❑*BP* Ⓣ*Kendall/MIT.*

★ **Fodor's**Choice ⊠**Royal Sonesta Hotel.** An impressive collection of
$$–$$$ modern art displayed throughout the hotel, sleek, updated rooms, and a friendly, professional staff make this Cambridge riverfront property a bit of a surprise. Its location next to the Museum of Science and Galleria shopping center and an attractive indoor–outdoor pool add to its appeal. Some rooms have superb views of Beacon Hill and the Boston skyline. Guest rooms are done in neutral earth tones, with modern amenities such as flat-screen TVs, Sony PlayStation consoles, high-speed Internet, and CD clock radios. The hotel has great excursion packages. **Pros:** Kids feel welcome here, easy to drive to and parking is on-site (fee), nice pool. **Cons:** A bit sterile. **Family Matters:** Family packages, particularly those offered on the Internet that often include breakfast and Museum of Science admission, can make this a great family deal. Cots fit in all the spacious rooms for an additional $25 per night. Cribs and refrigerators can be requested free of charge. The more casual Art Bar restaurant has a kids' menu, as does room service. ⊠*40 Edwin Land Blvd., off Memorial Dr., Cambridge* ☎*617/806–4200 or 800/766–3782* ⊕*www. sonesta.com/boston/* ⬥*379 rooms, 21 suites* ⚹*In-room: safe, refrigerator, Internet, Wi-Fi. In-hotel: 2 restaurants, room service, bars, pool, gym, bicycles, laundry service, Internet terminal, Wi-Fi, parking (fee)* ⊟*AE, D, DC, MC, V* Ⓣ*Lechmere.*

Performing
Arts

5

WORD OF MOUTH

"Check out what is happening at the musuems." Sometimes fabulous music! The Isabella Stewart Gardener Museum has wonderful evening performances—as does the MFA (Museum of Fine Arts)."

—escargot

Updated
by Lisa
Oppen-
heimer

WHATEVER YOUR INTEREST, YOU'RE LIKELY to find it on a Boston stage. Whether your pleasure is a touring Broadway show at the Colonial, the annual Nutcracker at the Opera House or the playful high jinks of Blue Man Group at the Charles Playhouse. Music lovers can revel in the acoustic wonders of Symphony Hall via the Boston Symphony Orchestra or the Boston Pops. Parents longing to introduce their offspring to the latter will want to check out the BSO's Youth and Family concerts. Of course, bigger, splashier, more garish musical fare can be found periodically at arenas like the TD Banknorth Garden, a popular place for the likes of the Jonas Brothers and Justin Timberlake to make tour stops.

GETTING TICKETS

Boston's supporters of the arts are an avid group; tickets often sell out well in advance, particularly for the increasing number of shows making pre-Broadway stops. Buy tickets when you make your hotel reservations if possible. Most theaters take telephone orders and charge them to a major credit card, generally with a small service fee.

BosTix is a full-price Ticketmaster outlet that sells half-price tickets for same-day performances. The "menu board" in front of the booth (corner of Boylston and Dartmouth streets) and on the Web site (⊕ *www.bostix.com*) announces the available events. Only cash and traveler's checks are accepted. On Friday, Saturday, or Sunday show up at least a half-hour early. There's a booth in Quincy Market (⊙ *10–6 Tues.–Sat., Sun. 11–4*) and a booth in Copley Square (⊙ *10–6 Mon.–Sat., Sun. 11–4*).

Broadway Across America – Boston (☎ *617/880–2400* ⊕ *www. broadwayacrossamerica.com*) brings Broadway shows to Boston and serves as a pre–New York testing ground for Broadway shows. Productions usually take place at the Colonial and Wilbur theaters, the Charles Playhouse, and the Opera House.

Live Nation/NEXT Ticketing (☎ *800/431–3462 NEXT* ⊕ *www. livenation.com*), a Boston-based outlet, handles tickets for shows at the Orpheum Theatre, Paradise Rock Club, and other nightclubs. All transactions are conducted online, but technical assistance is available Monday through Saturday 10–5.

TOP PERFORMING ARTS

- Introduction to the classics by **Boston Symphony Orchestra** via Youth and Family Concerts
- The annual classic **Nutcracker by Boston Ballet** at the Opera House
- Family-oriented performances at the **Wheelock Family Theater**
- A-one puppeteers at **Puppet Showplace** Theatre
- Kids movies and performances at **Coolidge Corner Theatre**

DANCE

Boston Dance Alliance serves as a clearinghouse for local dance information. Visit its Web site for upcoming performances and details about Boston dance companies and venues. ⊠*19 Clarendon St., South End* ☎*617/456–6295* ⊕*www.bostondancealliance.org.* Ⓣ*Back Bay.*

BALLET

★ **Boston Ballet,** the city's premier dance company, performs at the Citi Performing Arts Center from October through May. In addition to a world-class repertory of classical and high-spirited modern works, it presents an elaborate signature *Nutcracker* during the holidays at the restored downtown Opera House. ⊠*19 Clarendon St., South End* ☎*617/695–6950* ⊕*www.bostonballet.org.* Ⓣ*Back Bay.* 7 + up

FOLK/MULTICULTURAL

★ **Art of Black Dance and Music** performs the music and dance of Africa, the Caribbean, and the Americas at venues including the **Strand Theatre,** at Columbia Road and Stoughton Street in Dorchester, and local area universities. ☎*617/666–1859* Ⓣ*Andrew, then 16 or 17 bus; Ruggles, then 15 bus.* 5 + up

Cambridge Multicultural Arts Center presents local and visiting arts programs, ethnic music, and dance performances. Two galleries showcase the visual arts. ⊠*41 2nd St., Cambridge* ☎*617/577–1400* ⊕*www.cmacusa.org* Ⓣ*Lechmere.* 7 + up

Folk Arts Center of New England promotes participatory international folk dancing and music for adults and children, as well as traditional New England contra dancing at locations throughout the greater Boston area. ⊠*42 W. Foster St., Melrose* ☎*781/662–7476 recorded info, 781/662–7475* ⊕*www.facone.org* Ⓣ*No stop; Venues vary.* 7 + up

FILM

With its large population of academics and intellectuals, Boston has its share of discerning moviegoers and movie houses, especially in Cambridge. Theaters at suburban malls, downtown, and at Fenway have better screens, if less-adventurous fare. The *Boston Globe* has daily listings in the "Living/Arts" and "Sidekick" sections, and both the *Boston Herald* Friday "Scene" section and the *Boston Phoenix* "Arts" section list films for the week. Movies cost $8–$11. Many theaters have half-price matinees, but theaters sometimes suspend bargain admissions during the first week or two of a major film opening.

★ **Boston Public Library** regularly screens free family, foreign, classic, and documentary films in the Rabb Lecture Hall. ✉*700 Boylston St., Copley Sq., Back Bay* ☎*617/536–5400* ⊕*www.bpl.org* Ⓣ*Copley.* All ages

Brattle Theatre shows classic movies, new foreign and independent films, theme series, and directors' cuts. Tickets sell out every year for its acclaimed Bogart festival, scheduled around Harvard's exam period; the Bugs Bunny Film Festival in February; and *Trailer Treats,* an annual fund-raiser featuring an hour or two of classic and modern movie previews in July. It also has holiday screenings such as *It's a Wonderful Life* at Christmas. ✉*40 Brattle St., Harvard Sq., Cambridge* ☎*617/876–6837* ⊕*www.brattlefilm.org* Ⓣ*Harvard.* 5 + up

The Coolidge Corner Theatre has an eclectic and frequently updated bill of art films, foreign films, animation festivals, and classics, as well as an intimate 45-seat video-screening room for more-experimental offerings. It also holds book readings, concerts, and popular midnight cult movies. Many weekend mornings, the theater hosts performances and films especially for a family audience. Shows start at 10:30 and include magicians or features such as Willy Wonka and the Chocolate Factory. Tickets are best purchased in advance as shows are often sellouts. ✉*290 Harvard St., Brookline* ☎*617/734–2501, 617/734–2500 recorded info* ⊕*www.coolidge.org* Ⓣ*Coolidge Corner.* 5 + up

MUSIC

For its size, Boston has a great diversity and variety of live music choices. New York has more events, but 10 times the population. Most of the year the music calendar is crammed with classical, pop, and rock events. Jazz, blues, folk, and world-music fans have plenty to keep them busy as well. Supplementing appearances by nationally known artists are performers from the area's many colleges and conservatories, which also provide music series, performing spaces, and audiences.

Boston Symphony Orchestra performs at Symphony Hall October through early May and at Tanglewood Music Center in Lenox, Massachusetts, from late June through and August. The Boston Pops presents concerts of "lighter music" from May to July and during December.

CONCERT HALLS

Bank of America Pavilion gathers up to 5,000 people on the city's waterfront for summertime concerts. National pop, folk, and country acts play the tentlike pavilion from about mid-June to mid-September. ⊠*290 Northern Ave., South Boston* ☎*617/728–1600* ⊕*www.bankofamericapavilion. com* Ⓣ*South Station.* All ages

Berklee Performance Center, associated with Berklee College of Music, is best known for its jazz programs, but it's also host to folk performers such as Joan Baez and pop and rock stars such as Andrew Bird, Aimee Mann, and Henry Rollins. A diverse schedule ranges from Gospel Music to the ultra kid-friendly Wolff Brothers, famed of Nickelodeon's Naked Brothers Band. ⊠*136 Massachusetts Ave., Back Bay* ☎*617/747–2261 box office, 617/747–8890 recorded info* ⊕*www.berkleebpc.com* Ⓣ*Hynes/ICA.* 8 + up

The Boston Opera House hosts plays, musicals, and traveling Broadway shows, but also has booked diverse performers such as David Copperfield, B.B. King, and Pat Metheny. The occasional children's production may schedule a run here as well. ⊠*539 Washington St., Downtown* ☎*617/259–3400* ⊕*www.broadwayacrossamerica.com* Ⓣ*Boylston, Chinatown, Downtown Crossing, Park Street.* 7 + up

Hatch Memorial Shell, on the bank of the Charles River, is a wonderful acoustic shell where the Boston Pops perform their famous free summer concerts (including their traditional July 4 show, broadcast live nationwide on TV). Local radio stations also put on music shows and festivals here April through October. In summer, the Hatch Shell is home to Free Friday Flicks, offering family movies in the great outdoors. Shows start at roughly 8 PM, and play rain or shine. Bring a blanket, a picnic and enjoy. ⊠*Off Storrow Dr. at embankment, Beacon Hill* ☎*617/626–1470* ⊕*www.mass.gov/dcr/hatch_events.htm* Ⓣ*Charles/MGH, Arlington.* 7 + up

The Museum of Fine Arts has jazz, blues, and folk concerts in its outdoor courtyard every Wednesday evening from late June through August (bring a blanket and a picnic). During the rest of the year, the action moves inside to the Remis Auditorium on various nights of the week. ⊠*465 Huntington Ave., Fens* ☎*617/369–3300* ⊕*www.mfa.org/ concerts* Ⓣ*Museum of Fine Arts.* 7 + up

Sanders Theatre provides a jewel box of a stage for local and visiting classical, folk, and world-music performers. "The Christmas Revels," a traditional, participatory Yule celebration, delights families here each December. ⊠*Harvard University, 45 Quincy St., Cambridge* ☎*617/496–2222* ⊕*www.fas.harvard.edu/tickets* Ⓣ*Harvard.* 7 + up

Fodor'sChoice **Symphony Hall,** one of the world's best acoustical settings—if not *the* best—is home to the Boston Symphony Orchestra (BSO) and the Boston Pops. The BSO is led by the incomparable James Levine, who's known for commissioning special works by contemporary composers, as well as for presenting innovative programs such as his two-year Beethoven/Schoenberg series. The Pops concerts, led by conductor Keith Lockhart, take place in May and June and around the winter holidays. The hall is also used by visiting orchestras, chamber groups, soloists, and many local performers. Rehearsals are sometimes open to the public, with tickets sold at a discount. Youth and Family Concerts are held several times annually and designed for young audiences and shorter attention spans. Some concerts are special arrangements of old favorites, others have themes. Saturday Family Concerts also include the popular Instrument Petting Zoo. Special tours accompany those events, but regular tours are also offered on certain days. ⊠*301 Massachusetts Ave., Back Bay* ☎*617/266–1492, 617/266–2378 recorded info* ⊕*www.bostonsymphonyhall. org* Ⓣ*Symphony.* 5 + up

TD Banknorth Garden hosts concerts by big-name artists from Celine Dion to U2, ice shows, and, of course, Bruins and Celtics games. ⊠*100 Legends Way, Old West End*

CLOSE UP

Frugal Fun

See a film at the **Boston Public Library.**

Head to **Trinity Church** for free Friday organ or choir recitals at 12:15 PM.

See art in the making: check out one of the weekend **Boston Open Studios** (⊕www.bostonopenstudios.org) in neighborhoods throughout the city. Summer brings even more free activities:

Bop along with the **Boston Pops** (☎617/266–1200 or 888/266–1200 ⊕www.bso.org) at the Hatch Memorial Shell.

In July and August, the Commonwealth Shakespeare Company brings you **Shakespeare in the Park** in Boston Common.

From April to September, the Hatch Shell on the Esplanade is busy with free concerts, movie showings, and more, all part of the **Esplanade Summer Events** (☎617/626–1250 ⊕www.mass.gov/dcr/hatch_events.htm). Perennial favorites include the Boston Pops' July 4 concert and "Free Friday Flicks" outdoor movie screenings.

☎617/624–1000 ⊕www.tdbanknorthgarden.com ⊤North Station. 8 + up

CONCERT SERIES

The Bank of America Celebrity Series presents about 50 events annually—renowned orchestras, chamber groups, recitalists, vocalists, and dance companies—often at Symphony Hall or Jordan Hall. Regulars include Yo-Yo Ma and the Alvin Ailey American Dance Theater. Keep an eye out for kid-friendly performances, such as the Family Musik Green Eggs and Hamadeus. Otherwise, the vast breadth of options makes this a nice stop for adventurous families who'd like to introduce their kids to culture of all kinds. ✉20 Park Plaza, Suite 1032, Downtown ☎617/482–2595, 617/482–6661 box office ⊕www.celebrityseries.org. 5 + up

EARLY-MUSIC GROUPS

★ **Handel & Haydn Society,** America's oldest music organization, has a history of performances that dates from 1815. It presents instrumental and choral performances at Symphony Hall. The group's holiday-season performances of Handel's *Messiah* are especially popular. ☎617/266–3605 or 617/262–1815 ⊕www.handelandhaydn.org. 5 + up

ORCHESTRAS

★ **Boston Symphony Orchestra** presents more than 250 concerts annually. The season at Symphony Hall runs from October to early May. In July and August, the activity shifts to the orchestra's beautiful summer home at the Tanglewood Music Center in Lenox, Massachusetts. ☎*617/266–1200, 888/266–1200 box office* ⊕*www.bso.org.* Ⓣ*Symphony.* 7 + up

OPERA

Boston Lyric Opera stages four full productions each season at Citi Performing Arts Center, which usually include one 20th-century work. Recent highlights have included Puccini's *La Boheme* and Englebert Humperdinck's *Hansel and Gretel.* ☎*617/542–4912, 617/542–6772 audience services office* ⊕*www.blo.org* Ⓣ*Boylston.* 9 + up

THEATER

In the 1930s Boston had no fewer than 50 performing-arts theaters; by the 1980s, the city's downtown Theater District had all but vanished. Happily, in the late 1990s several historic theaters saw major restoration, opening to host pre-Broadway shows, visiting artists, and local troupes. More recently, the glorious renovation of the Opera House in 2004 has added new light to the district. Meanwhile, established companies such as the Huntington Theatre Company, near Northeastern University, and the American Repertory Theatre, in Cambridge, continue to offer premieres of works by major writers, including David Mamet, August Wilson, and Don DeLillo.

MAJOR THEATERS

The Charles Playhouse was formerly a church, a YWCA, a Prohibition-era speakeasy, and a nightclub. These days it plays host to the **Blue Man Group**, a loud, messy, (complete with a "poncho" section in the front rows) exhilarating trio of playful performance artists painted vivid cobalt. ✉*74 Warrenton St., Theater District* ☎ *617/426–6912 Blue Man Group* ⊕*blueman.com/tickets/boston* Ⓣ*Boylston.* 7 + up

Citi Performing Arts Center, formerly the Wang Center for the Performing Arts and the Shubert Theatre, is a performance space complex dedicated to both large-scale productions (at the former Wang) and more-intimate shows (at the former Shubert). Expect names such as *Riverdance* and other nationally touring Broadway shows, popular

BEST ALFRESCO ARTS EVENTS

- The Boston Pops at the Hatch Memorial Shell
- Summer rock shows at the Bank of America Pavilion
- Shakespeare in the Park on the Boston Common
- Summer concerts at the Museum of Fine Arts' Calderwood Courtyard
- Live music on summer evenings in Copley Square

comedians, and the occasional ballet. ✉*270 Tremont St., Theater District* ☎*617/482–9393* ⊕*www.citicenter.org* Ⓣ*Boylston.* 9 + up

The Colonial Theatre has ornate red wallpaper, intricately carved balconies, and stately marble columns that evoke its turn-of-the-20th-century glamour. Visiting stars from W. C. Fields to Fanny Brice to Katharine Hepburn have trod its boards. More recently, the theater welcomed Broadway productions *The Producers* and *Avenue Q.* ✉*106 Boylston St., Back Bay* ☎*617/880–2460 day, 617/880–2410 evening* ⊕*www.broadwayacrossamerica.com* Ⓣ*Boylston.* 9 + up

The Huntington Theatre Company, Boston's largest resident theater company, consistently performs a high-quality mix of 20th-century plays, new works, and classics under the leadership of dynamic artistic director Nicholas Martin, and commissions artists to produce original dramas. ✉*Boston University Theatre, 264 Huntington Ave., Back Bay* ☎*617/266–0800 box office* ⊕*www.huntingtontheatre. org* Ⓣ*Symphony* ✉*Calderwood Theatre Pavilion, Boston Center for the Arts, 527 Tremont St., South End* ☎*617/426–5000* ⊕*www.bcaonline.org* Ⓣ*Back Bay/South End, Copley.* 10 + up

★ **The Opera House** features lavish musical productions such as *The Lion King* and Boston Ballet's *The Nutcracker.* The meticulously renovated 2,500-seat, beaux arts building has $35 million worth of gold leaf, lush carpeting, and rococo ornamentation. ✉*539 Washington St., Downtown Crossing, Chinatown* ☎*617/880–2495 or 617/259–3400* ⊕*www.broadwayinboston.com* Ⓣ*Boylston, Chinatown, Downtown Crossing, Park Street.* 5 + up

SMALL THEATERS & COMPANIES

Boston Center for the Arts houses more than a dozen quirky, low-budget troupes in six performance areas, including the 300-seat Stanford Calderwood Pavilion, two black box theaters, and the massive Cyclorama, built to hold a 360-degree mural of the Battle of Gettysburg (the painting is now in a building at the battlefield). Ask about youth programs which includes offerings of discounted admission and interaction with actors at specified performances. ✉*539 Tremont St., South End* ☎*617/426–5000* ⊕*www.bcaonline.org* Ⓣ*Back Bay/South End, Copley.* 12 + up

Sports & the Outdoors

6

WORD OF MOUTH

"October is a wonderful time to see New England. Great time of the year for hiking, biking, apple picking and all that. Boston has the Head of the Charles Regatta—one of the largest rowing events in the US."

—Bennie

Updated by Lisa Oppenheimer

EVERYTHING YOU'VE HEARD ABOUT THE zeal of Boston fans is true; here, you root for the home team. You cheer, and you pray, and you root some more. "Red Sox Nation" witnessed a miracle in 2004, with the reverse of the curse and the first World Series victory since 1918. Then in 2007 they proved it wasn't just a fluke with another Series win. In 2008 the Celtics ended their 18-year NBA championship drought with a thrilling victory over long-time rivals the LA Lakers. And despite the sting of their first Super Bowl loss (in recent memory) in '08, the Patriots can still lay claim to dynasty for this decade.

Bostonians' long-standing fervor for sport is equally evident in their leisure-time activities. Harsh winters keep locals wrapped up for months, only to emerge at the earliest sign of oncoming spring, striving to push back the February blues through feverish exercise. Once the mercury tops freezing and the snows begin to thaw, Boston's extensive parks, paths, woods, and waterways teem with sun worshippers and athletes—until the bitter winds bite again in November, and that energy becomes redirected once again toward white slopes, frozen rinks, and sheltered gyms and pools.

Most public recreational facilities, including skating rinks and tennis courts, are operated by the **Department of Conservation & Recreation** (*DCR ✉251 Causeway St., Suite 600, North End ☎617/626–1250 ⊕www.mass.gov/dcr*). The DCR provides information about recreational activities in its facilities and promotes the conservation of Massachusetts parks and wilderness areas.

BEACHES

Although nearly 20 years of massive cleanup efforts have made the water in Boston Harbor safe for swimming, many locals and visitors still find city beaches unappealing since much better beaches are a short drive or train ride away.

Singing Beach (✉*Beach St., Manchester-by-the-Sea*), 32 mi north of Boston in a quiet Cape Ann town, gets its name from the musical squeaking sound its gold-color sand makes when you step on it. The beach is popular with both locals and out-of-towners in summer. It's also worth a visit in fall, when the crowds have gone home and you'll have the splendid shores all to yourself. There's a snack bar at the beach, but it's worth taking a 10-minute stroll up Beach Street

TOP BOSTON SPORTS & OUTDOORS

Charles River. Running or biking along the river banks or better yet, sailing on it with Community Boating is pure Boston.

The Emerald Necklace. Stroll or play in these lovely parks and gardens (including the Boston Common and Public Garden).

Fenway Park. Taking in a Red Sox game at the nation's oldest ballpark is an experience that can't be duplicated.

Whale Watching. Witness magnificent whales and their young close-up on a whale-watch boat tour.

into town to get a cone at Captain Dusty's Ice Cream (*60 Beach St.*). Because there's no public parking at the beach, the easiest way to get here is by Rockport commuter rail train from North Station to the Manchester stop, which is a 15-minute walk from the beach. From downtown Boston, the train takes 45 minutes and costs $7.25 each way.

Sandy Cape Cod and the rocky North Shore are studded with New England beach towns, each with its favorite swimming spot. **Nantasket Beach** (⊠ *Rt. 3A, Hull 617/727–5290*), a 45-minute drive from downtown Boston, has cleaner sand and warmer water than most local beaches. Take Route 3A South to Washington Boulevard, Hingham, and follow signs to Nantasket Avenue. Sun and sand may be plenty, but families can also enjoy the historic Paragon Carousel, the last remaining piece of what was once an entire amusement area. Part of the 1,200-acre Crane Wildlife Refuge, **Crane Beach** (⊠*Ipswich* ☎*978/356–4354*), an hour's drive to the north of Boston in the 17th-century village of Ipswich, has 4 mi of sparkling white sand that serves as a nesting ground for the threatened piping plover. From Route 128 North (toward Gloucester), follow signs for Route 1A North, 8 mi to Ipswich.

PARKS

★ **Fodor'sChoice** Comprising 34 islands, the **Boston Harbor Islands National Park Area** is somewhat of a hidden gem for nature lovers and history buffs, with miles of lightly traveled trails and shoreline and several little-visited historic sites to explore. The focal point of the national park is 39-acre Georges Island, where you'll find the partially restored

Whale Watch

Ships depart regularly for whale-watching excursions from April or May through October, from coastal towns all along the bay. Humpbacks, fin-backs, and minkes feed locally in season, so you're sure to see a few—and on a good day you may see dozens. Bring warm clothing, as the ocean breezes can be brisk; rubber-soled shoes are a good idea.

The **New England Aquarium** (⊠ *Central Wharf at end of Central St., Downtown* ☎ *617/973-5200* ⊕ *www. neaq.org. All ages*) runs daily whale-watching cruises from Central Wharf. The trip, with an aquarium staff whale expert on board, lasts three to four hours. The high-speed catamarans of **Boston Harbor Cruises** (⊠ *Long Wharf next to aquarium, Downtown* ☎ *877/733-9425* ⊕ *www. bostonharborcruises.com. All ages*) glide to the whaling banks in half the time of some other cruises, allowing nearly

as much whale time in only a three-hour tour.

The old fishing port of Gloucester is Massachusetts Bay's hot spot for whale-sighting trips. **Cape Ann Whale Watch** (⊠ *Rose's Wharf, 415 Main St., Gloucester* ☎ *800/877-5110* ⊕ *www.caww.com. 5 + up*) has run whale-watch tours since 1979. Tours with **Captain Bill's Deep Sea Fishing/Whale Watch** (⊠ *24 Harbor Loop, Gloucester* ☎ *978/283-6995 or 800/339-4253* ⊕ *www.captbill andsons.com. 5 + up*) make use of knowledgeable naturalists from the Whale Center of New England.

South of Boston, whale-watch trips leave from Plymouth and locations around Cape Cod. **Capt. John Boats** (⊠ *10 Town Wharf, Plymouth* ☎ *508/746-2643 or 800/242-2469* ⊕ *www.captjohn. com. 5 + up*) sends out several daily whale-watch cruises from Plymouth Town Wharf.

---

pre–Civil War Fort Warren that once held Confederate prisoners. Other islands worth visiting include Peddocks Island, which holds the remains of Fort Andrews, and Lovells Island, a popular destination for campers. Lovells, Peddocks, Grape, and Bumpkin islands allow camping with a permit from late June through Labor Day. There are swimming areas at the four camping-friendly islands as well, but only Lovells has lifeguards. Pets and alcohol are not allowed on the Harbor Islands. In addition to the islands' natural adventures, kids love the thrill of Boston Light. The historic lighthouse on **Little Brewster**

Island (☎617/223–8666) is open for public tours mid-June through October. Call for details. The **National Park Service** (☎617/223–8666 ⊕*www.bostonislands.com*) is a good source for information about camping, transportation, and the like. To reach the islands, take the **Harbor Express** (☎617/222–6999 ⊕*www.harborexpress.com*) from Long Wharf (Downtown) or the Hingham Shipyard to Georges Island or Spectacle Island. High-speed catamarans run daily from May through mid-October and cost $14. Other islands can be reached by the free interisland water shuttles that depart from Georges Island.

As soon as the snow begins to recede, Bostonians emerge from hibernation. Runners, bikers, and in-line skaters crowd the **Charles River Reservation** (⊕*www.mass.gov/dcr*) at the Esplanade along Storrow Drive, the Memorial Drive Embankment in Cambridge, or any of the smaller and less busy parks farther upriver. Here you can cheer a crew race, rent a canoe or a kayak, or simply sit on the grass, sharing the shore with packs of hard-jogging university athletes, in-line skaters, moms with strollers, dreamily entwined couples, and intense academics, often talking to themselves as they sort out their intellectual—or perhaps personal—dilemmas. Watching the sailboats from atop the Charlest Street footbridge is often entertainment enough. It gets better with an ice cream from Café Esplanade (near the hatch shell) and a stop at one of two playgrounds along the reservation, either at Berkeley Street, or at Deerfield.

The **Hatch Memorial Shell** (☎617/626–1250 Ⓣ*Charles/MGH*) on the Esplanade holds free concerts and outdoor events all summer. In season, activities at the Hatch Shell run the gamut from charitable walks to whiz-bang concerts. Among family favorites are the July 4 festivities, for which you should arrive early in the morning, and the family-friendly (and free) Friday Night Flicks series of films held in summer.

★ Fodor'sChoice The six large public parks known as Boston's **Emerald Necklace** stretch 5 mi from the Back Bay Fens through Franklin Park, in Dorchester. Frederick Law Olmsted's design heightened the natural beauty of the Emerald Necklace, which remains a well-groomed urban masterpiece. Locals take pride in and happily make use of its open spaces and its pathways and bridges connecting rivers and ponds. In the heart of the city, the Boston Common appeals to families for its meandering paths and playground located next to Frog Pond. In the neighboring Garden, a visit to the Duckling sculptures is a must. Look for them just inside the entrance at the corner of Charles and Beacon. The **Emerald Necklace Conservancy** (☎*617/232–5374* ⊕*www.emeraldnecklace.org*) maintains a regular calendar of nature walks and other events in the parks. Rangers with the **Boston Parks & Recreation Department** (✉*1010 Massachusetts Ave.* ☎*617/635–4505* ⊕*www.cityofboston. gov/parks/parkrangers*) lead tours highlighting the area's historic sites and surprising ecological diversity. The sumptuously landscaped **Arnold Arboretum** (✉*125 Arborway, Jamaica Plain* ☎*617/524–1718* ⊕*www.arboretum.harvard. edu* Ⓣ*Forest Hills*) is open all year to joggers and in-line skaters. Volunteer docents give free walking tours in spring, summer, and fall.

SPORTS

BASEBALL

★ **Fodor's**Choice Hide your Yankees cap and practice pronouncing "Fenway Pahk." Boston is a baseball town, where the crucible of media scrutiny burns hot, fans regard myth and superstition as seriously as player statistics, and grudges are never forgotten. The **Boston Red Sox** (✉*Fenway Park, The Fenway* ☎*617/482–4769* ⊕*www.bostonredsox.com. 5 + up*) made history in 2004, crushing the Yankees in the American League Championship after a three-game deficit and then sweeping the Cardinals in the World Series for their first title since 1918. More than 3 million fans from "Red Sox Nation" celebrated the championship team and the reversal of the "Curse of the Bambino" with a victory parade through the streets of Boston and down the Charles River. And as icing on the cake, they did it again in 2007, this time defeating the Colorado Rockies in another historic sweep. The Red Sox ownership has committed to staying in the once-threatened Fenway Park for the long term, so you can still watch a game in the country's oldest active ballpark and see (or, for a premium price, get a seat on top of) the fabled "Green Monster" (the park's 37-foot-high left-field wall) and one of the last hand-operated scoreboards in the major leagues. Baseball season runs from early April to early October. The play-offs continue several more weeks, and postseason buzz about contracts, trades, and injuries lasts all winter long. Attending a Sox game is a rite of passage, and many adults fondly recall the first time they saw the Green Monster live and in "person." For those who'd prefer their baseball a little less boisterous, the Fenway offers an alcohol-free family zone in two grandstand sections.

DID YOU KNOW? **The longest measurable home run hit inside Fenway Park—502 feet—was batted by legendary Red Sox slugger Ted Williams on June 9, 1946. A lone red seat in the right-field bleachers marks the spot where the ball landed.**

BASKETBALL

★ The **Boston Celtics** (✉*TD Banknorth Garden, Old West End* ☎*617/624–1000, 617/931–2222 Ticketmaster* ⊕*www. celtics.com.* 5 + up) have won the National Basketball Association (NBA) championship 17 times since 1957, more than any other franchise in the NBA. The mystique of the Celtics' former glory days has kept fans coming back year after year in hopes that a championship banner might again be hoisted above the court. And in 2008, after a solid defeat of long-time rivals the LA Lakers, fans got their wish and witnessed the not-a-moment-too-soon end of an 18-year championship dry spell. Basketball season runs from October to April, and play-offs last until mid-June.

BICYCLING

It's common to see suited-up doctors, lawyers, and businessmen commuting on two wheels through Downtown; unfortunately, bike lanes are few and far between. Boston's dedicated bike paths are well used, as much by joggers and in-line skaters as by bicyclists. The **Dr. Paul Dudley White Bike Path,** about 17 mi long, follows both banks of the Charles River as it winds from Watertown Square to the Museum of Science. The farther-west sections are particularly well suited for families. Artesani Park, off Soldier's Field Road in Brighton, has a great playground, plus lots of space to run around. Farther upriver, enjoy a nice 2-mi loop between Galen and Bridge Streets. In May, check out the spectacular fish run above Galen Street at the Watertown Dam. The **Minuteman Bikeway** courses 11 mi from the Alewife Red Line T station in Cambridge through Arlington, Lexington, and Bedford. The trail, in the bed of an old rail line, cuts through a few busy intersections—be particularly careful in Arlington Center. The park often teems with visitors, making it at times a bit dicey to navigate. Another bet in

Lexington, the Minute Man National Historical Park, tends to be a bit more tranquil, with off-road paths meandering through some historic Revolutionary War grounds.

For other path locations, consult the **Department of Conservation & Recreation** (*DCR* ⊕*www.mass.gov/dcr*) Web site.

The **Massachusetts Bicycle Coalition** (*MassBike* ✉*171 Milk St., Suite 33, Downtown* ☎*617/542–2453* ⊕*www.massbike. org*), an advocacy group working to improve conditions for area cyclists, has information on organized rides and sells good bike maps of Boston and the state. Thanks to MassBike's lobbying efforts, the MBTA now allows bicycles on subway and commuter-rail trains during nonpeak hours. **Community Bicycle Supply** (✉*496 Tremont St., at E. Berkeley St., South End* ☎*617/542–8623* ⊕*www.communitybicycle. com*) rents cycles from April through October, at rates of $25 for 24 hours. **Back Bay Bicycles** (✉*362 Commonwealth Ave., Back Bay* ☎*617/247–2336* ⊕*www.backbaybicycles. com*) has mountain bike rentals for $25 per day and road bikes for $35 per day. Staff members also lead group mountain bike rides on nearby trails.

BOATING

Except when frozen over, the waterways coursing through the city serve as a playground for boaters of all stripes. All types of pleasure craft, with the exception of inflatables, are allowed from the Charles River and Inner Harbor to North Washington Street on the waters of Boston Harbor, Dorchester inner and outer bays, and the Neponset River from the Granite Avenue Bridge to Dorchester Bay.

The **Charles River Watershed Association** (☎*781/788–0007* ⊕*www.charlesriver.org*) publishes a 32-page canoe and kayaking guide with detailed boating information.

LESSONS & EQUIPMENT

From May through mid-November, you can rent a canoe, kayak, paddleboat, rowboat, or rowing shell from **Charles River Canoe & Kayak Center** (✉*2401 Commonwealth Ave., Newton* ☎*617/965–5110* ⊕*www.paddleboston.com. 3 + up*). There are a variety of canoeing and kayaking classes for all skill levels, as well as organized group outings and tours. The Canoe & Kayak Center's kiosk (✉*Soldiers' Field Rd. near Eliot Bridge, Allston. 3 + up*) rents canoes and kayaks and is open Thursday evening, Friday afternoon, and weekends early May through mid-October. It's open weekdays only for group appointments. **Community Boating** (⌧*21 David Mugar Way, Beacon Hill* ☎*617/523–1038* ⊕*www.community-boating.org.* 5 + up; sailors, 10 + up), near the Charles Street footbridge on the Esplanade, is the host of America's oldest public sailing program. From April through October, $89 nets you a 30-day introductory membership, beginner-level classes, and use of sailboats and kayaks. Full memberships grant unlimited use of all facilities; splash around for 60 days for $159 or all season long for $229. Experienced sailors short on time can opt for a two-day sailboat rental for $100.

From April to October, the **Jamaica Pond Boat House** (⌧*Jamaica Way and Pond St., Jamaica Plain* ☎*617/522–5061.* 5 + up) provides lessons and equipment for rowing and sailing on its namesake pond.

EVENTS
In mid-October more than 7,500 male and female athletes
★ from all over the world compete in the annual **Head of the Charles Regatta** (☎*617/868–6200* ⊕*www.hocr.org.* All ages). Thousands of spectators line the banks of the Charles River with blankets and beer (although the police disapprove of the latter), cheering on their favorite teams and generally using the weekend as an excuse to party. Limited free parking is available, but the chances of finding an open space close to the race route are slim, so take public transportation if you can. During the event, free shuttles run between the start and end point of the race route on both sides of the river.

FISHING

Efforts to clean up the city's waterways have heightened the popularity of recreational fishing in and around Boston. For saltwater fishing, locals cast their lines from the **John J. McCorkle Fishing Pier** on Castle Island off Day Boulevard in South Boston and **Tenean Beach** and **Victory Road Park** off Morrissey Boulevard in Dorchester. The **Boston Harbor Islands National Park Area** (☎*617/223–8666* ⊕*www.bostonislands. com*) is also known for great fishing, although note no public piers are available.

You can try to catch freshwater fish in **Jamaica Pond** (⌧*Jamaica Way and Pond St., Jamaica Plain*); Turtle Pond in **Stony Brook Reservation** (⌧*Turtle Pond Pkwy., Hyde Park*); Quarter Mile Pond and Dark Hollow Pond in **Middlesex Fells**

Reservation (⊠*Off Rte. 93, Stoneham*); or Houghton's Pond in **Blue Hills Reservation** (⊠*Off Rte. 128, Milton*).

Nonresidents can purchase a three-day Massachusetts fishing license for $23.50 at the **MassWildlife Boston Office** (⊠*251 Causeway St., North End* ☎*617/626–1590* ⊕*www.mass. gov/dfwele*), Brookline Town Hall, and some sporting-goods stores around the city. No license is required for recreational ocean angling.

FOOTBALL

Since 2002, Boston has been building a football dynasty, starting with the **New England Patriots'** (⊠*Gillette Stadium, Rte. 1, off I–95 Exit 9, Foxborough* ☎*617/931–2222 Ticketmaster* ⊕*www.patriots.com.* 3 + up) come-from-behind Super Bowl victory against the favored St. Louis Rams. Coach Bill Belichick and heartthrob quarterback Tom Brady then brought the team two more Super Bowl rings, in 2004 and 2005, and have made Patriots fans as zealous as their baseball counterparts. The team's heartbreaking Super Bowl loss in 2008 has only increased fan fervor for coming seasons. Exhibition football games begin in August, and the season runs through the play-offs in January. The state-of-the-art Gillette Stadium is in Foxborough, 30 mi southwest of Boston. The long-time kid favorite Patriots Experience, where kids can try out their future NFL arms, currently operates only during training camp. It may reappear during the regular season once construction on the next-door shopping/entertainment complex, Patriot's Place, is complete. Kids and adults can pay homage to their hometown heroes at the newly opened Patriots Hall of Fame.

DID YOU KNOW? The New England Patriots, formerly the Boston Patriots, played in Fenway Park from 1963 to 1968 before moving to Foxborough.

With the only Division 1A football program in town, the **Boston College Eagles** (⊠*Alumni Stadium, Chestnut Hill* ☎*617/552–3000*) play against some of the top teams in the country.

Built in 1903, Harvard Stadium is the oldest concrete stadium in the country and the home of the **Harvard University Crimson** (⊠*Harvard Stadium, N. Harvard St. and Soldiers Field Rd., Allston* ☎*877/464–2782*), who went undefeated in 2001 and 2004. The halftime shows of the Harvard Band make any game worth the trip.

GOLF

Although you'll need to know someone who knows someone who *is* someone to play at Brookline's **Country Club,** one of the nation's top-rated private courses, anyone can use the public courses in Boston, which are among the best in the country.

Donald Ross crafted the 6,009-yard, par-70 **Franklin Park Golf Course** (⊠*1 Circuit Dr., Dorchester* ☎*617/265–4084.* 10 + up) in the early 1900s. It's open year-round, weather permitting. Greens fees without a cart are $17.50 for 9 holes and $30 for 18 holes on weekdays, and $19.50 and $34, respectively, on weekends. (You can play 9 holes only after 1 PM on weekends.) If you're not a Boston resident, the course ups the ante by $5 to $7; charges for a golf cart tend to run about $10 to $11 more. Club rentals run $10 for 9 holes and $18 for 18 holes. The course is part of a delightful city park with picnic facilities and jogging paths. Festivals and other outdoor activities take place all year.

The hilly **George Wright Golf Course** (⊠*420 West St., Hyde Park* ☎*617/364–2300.* 12 + up) is more challenging than the other Donald Ross–designed course at Franklin Park. The par-70, 6,096-yard course is open for the season starting in April each year. Weekend 18-hole greens fees are $42; weekday fees are $36. Tee times are necessary on weekends. How hard is this course? Let's just say USGA qualifiers are run here. It's a tough one for young juniors. Teens, on the other hand, may actually enjoy the challenge.

The **Massachusetts Golf Association** (⊠*300 Arnold Palmer Blvd., Norton* ☎*800/356–2201* ⊕*www.mgalinks.org.* 3 + up) represents 400 clubs in the state and has information on courses that are open to the public. The MGA owns the par-3 MGA Links at Mamantapett in Norton. It's an especially family-friendly course that welcomes the youngest of wannabe golfers as long as they're supervised by an adult.

HIKING

With the Appalachian Trail just two hours' drive from Downtown and thousands of acres of parkland and trails encircling the city, hikers will not lack for options in and around Boston.

★ A 20-minute drive south of Boston, the **Blue Hills Reservation** (⊠*695 Hillside St., Milton* ☎*617/698–1802*) encompasses

7,000 acres of woodland with about 125 mi of trails, some ideal for cross-country skiing in winter, some designated for mountain biking the rest of the year. Although only 635 feet high, Great Blue Hill, the tallest hill in the reservation, has a spectacular view of the entire Boston metro area. It's open daily, and maps are available for purchase at the reservation headquarters or the Blue Hills Trailside Museum. To get there, take Route 93 South to Exit 3, Houghton's Pond. All ages

The **Blue Hills Trailside Museum** (✉ *1904 Canton Ave., Milton* ☎ *617/333–0690*), which is managed by the Massachusetts Audubon Society, organizes hikes and nature walks. Open Wednesday through Sunday 10–5, the museum has natural-history exhibits and live animals. Admission is $3. Take Route 93 South to Exit 2B and Route 138 North. If you're planning to hike, this is a good place to pick up information and get trail facts, such as which ones are appropriate for strollers.

Just a few miles north of Boston, the 2,575-acre **Middlesex Fells Reservation** (☎ *617/727–1199*) has well-maintained hiking trails that pass over rocky hills, across meadows, and through wetland areas. Trails range from the quarter-mile Bear Hill Trail to the 6.9-mi Skyline Trail. Mountain bikers can ride along the reservation's fire roads and on a designated loop trail. This sprawling reservation covers areas in Malden, Medford, Stoneham, Melrose, and Winchester. To get to the western side of the reservation from Boston, take Route 93 North to Exit 33, and then take South Border Road off the rotary.

Easily accessible from downtown Boston, the **Boston Harbor Islands National Park Area** is seldom crowded. The park maintains walking trails through diverse terrain and ecosystems (⇨ *Parks, above*).

Rangers with the **Boston Parks & Recreation Department** (✉ *1010 Massachusetts Ave.* ☎ *617/635–7383* ⊕ *www.cityof boston.gov/parks/parkrangers*) lead walks through the Emerald Necklace parks.

HOCKEY

Boston hockey fans are informed, vocal, and extremely loyal. Despite frequent trades of star players, disappointing losses, high ticket prices, and the complete lockout of the 2004–05 season, the stands are still packed at Bruins games.

That said, local college hockey teams tend to give spectators more to celebrate at a much more reasonable price.

The **Boston Bruins** (⊠*TD Banknorth Garden, 100 Legends Way, Old West End* ☎*617/624–1000, 617/931–2222 Ticketmaster* ⊕*www.bostonbruins.com.* 5 + up) are on the ice from September until April, frequently on Thursday and Saturday evenings. Play-offs last through early June.

Boston College, Boston University, Harvard, and Northeastern teams face off every February in the **Beanpot Hockey Tournament** (☎*617/624–1000.* 5 + up) at the TD Banknorth Garden. The colleges in this fiercely contested tournament traditionally yield some of the finest squads in the country.

ICE SKATING

The Department of Conservation & Recreation operates more than 20 **public ice-skating rinks** (☎*617/626–1250* ⊕*www.mass.gov/dcr*); hours and season vary by location. Call for a complete list of rinks and their hours of operation.

Thanks to a refrigerated surface, the **Boston Common Frog Pond** (⊠*Beacon Hill* ☎*617/635–2120* ⊕*www.boston commonfrogpond.org.* 3 + up) transforms into a skating park from November to mid-March, complete with a warming hut and concession stand. Admission is $4 for adults; kids 13 and under skate free. Skate rentals cost $8 and lockers are $1. Frog Pond hours are Monday 10–5, Tuesday through Thursday and Sunday 10–9, and Friday and Saturday 10–10.

Skaters flock to the frozen waters of the lagoon at **Boston Public Garden.** Ice on one side of the bridge is theoretically reserved for figure skating and the other for faster-paced ice hockey, though most ignore the rule during slow times.

SKATE RENTALS

Beacon Hill Skate Shop (⊠*135 Charles St., off Tremont St., near Wang Center for the Performing Arts, South End* ☎*617/482–7400*) rents skates for use in the Frog Pond and Public Garden for $10 per hour or $20 per day. A credit card is required; call in advance and they'll have the skates sharpened and ready for you.

RUNNING

EVENTS

Every Patriots' Day (the third Monday in April), fans gather along the Hopkinton–to–Boston route of the **Boston Marathon** to cheer on more than 20,000 runners from all over the world. The race ends near Copley Square in the Back Bay. For information, call the **Boston Athletic Association** (☎617/236–1652 ⊕*www.bostonmarathon.org*).

In October women runners take the spotlight on Columbus Day for the **Tufts Health Plan 10K for Women** (☎888/767–7223 *Registration* ⊕*www.tufts-healthplan.com/tufts10k*), which attracts 7,000 participants and 20,000 spectators. Four American records have been set at this race since it began in 1977.

SKIING & SNOWBOARDING

CROSS-COUNTRY

From mid-December to March, the **Weston Ski Track** (⊠*200 Park Rd., Weston* ☎781/891–6575 ⊕*www.skiboston.com*. 4 + up) provides cross-country skiers and snowshoers with 9 mi of groomed, natural trails and a snowmaking area with a lighted 1-mi ski track. Rentals and basic instruction are available. Ski rentals are available for skiers as young as age 3. If your tykes are too little to get around on their own, you can rent a PULK, a little sled that can be towed behind.

DOWNHILL

The closest downhill skiing to Boston is at the **Blue Hills Ski Area** (⊠*Blue Hills Reservation, 4001 Washington St., Canton* ☎781/828–5070 ⊕*www.ski-bluehills.com*. 3 + up). It has 60 acres of skiing terrain and 10 trails to choose from. There's a snow sports school, equipment rentals, and a restaurant. Off-peak and group rates are available. Take Route 93 South to Exit 2B and Route 138 North.

On weekends and holidays, serious skiers and snowboarders head north to the mountain resorts along I–93 in New Hampshire. The first big resort off the interstate, **Waterville Valley Resort** (⊠*Rte. 49, off I–93 Exit 28, Waterville Valley, NH* ☎603/236–8311 or 800/468–2553. 3 + up), is one of the state's most popular ski destinations with 52 trails and a terrain park with a 400-foot half pipe.

Nearby **Loon Mountain Resort** (⊠*Off I–93 Exit 32, Lincoln, NH* ☎603/745–8111 or 800/229–5666 ⊕*www.loonmtn.com*) has 53 trails spanning more than 2,100 vertical feet and six terrain parks. Farther north in Franconia Notch, the historic **Cannon Mountain Resort** (⊠*Off I–93 N Exit 34A, B, or C, Franconia, NH* ☎*603/823–8800* ⊕*www. cannonmt.com.* 3 + up) is the site of North America's first aerial tramway and home to the New England Ski Museum. There are 60 trails and nine lifts. **Ski NH** (☎*603/745–9396 or 800/887–5464* ⊕*www.skinh.com*) is a good source for local ski information.

SOCCER

New England's major-league soccer team, **New England Revolution** (⊠*Gillette Stadium, Foxborough* ☎*800/543–1776, 617/931–2222 Ticketmaster* ⊕*www.nerevolution.com.* All ages), plays from late March to late October.

On any clear weekend morning, pickup games at most of Boston's parks, especially the fields at the western end of **Back Bay Fens Park** and at **Mayor Thomas W. Danehy Park** near the Alewife transit center in Cambridge, become meeting places for amateur soccer players and fans.

TENNIS

The **Department of Conservation & Recreation** (☎*617/626–1250* ⊕*www.mass.gov/dcr*) maintains more than 25 public tennis courts throughout the greater Boston area. These operate on a first-come, first-served basis. Lighted courts are open from dawn to 10 PM; other courts are open from dawn to dusk.

Some of Boston's most popular lighted courts are those at **Charlesbank Park** (⊠*Storrow Dr. opposite Charles St., Beacon Hill*); **Marine Park** (⊠*Day Blvd., South Boston*); and **Weider Playground** (⊠*Dale St., Hyde Park*).

Shopping

WORD OF MOUTH

". . . For an authentic Boston shopping experience, on a Friday or Saturday, walk . . . from Quincy Market to Haymarket. Pushcarts with veggies, cheeses, and all sorts of piles of fish on ice. Probably not a good place for a souvenir home, but still fun since it is real. "

—gail

Updated
by Lisa
Oppen-
heimer

SHOPPING IN BOSTON IS A lot like the city itself: a mix of classic and cutting-edge, the high-end and the handmade, and international and local sensibilities. Though many Bostonians think too many chain stores have begun to clog their distinctive avenues, there remains a strong network of idiosyncratic gift stores, handicrafts shops, galleries, and a growing number of savvy, independent fashion boutiques. For the well-heeled, there are also plenty of glossy international designer shops. Parents looking to outfit their tykes in designer gear will have no shortage of places to look. For kids, the most popular items come from the plentiful supply of logo merchandise, with everything from sports teams to university names to just plain "Boston" splashed across the front (and back) of T-shirts, sweatshirts, and sweatpants. Such merchandise is peddled everywhere (kiosks, store fronts) and seems to draw young ones like magnets.

Boston's shops are generally open Monday through Saturday from 10 or 11 until 6 or 7 and Sunday noon to 5. Many stay open until 8 PM one night a week, usually Thursday. Malls are open Monday through Saturday from 9 or 10 until 8 or 9 and Sunday noon to 6. Most stores accept major credit cards and traveler's checks. There's no state sales tax on clothing. However, there's a 5% luxury tax on clothes priced higher than $175 per item; the tax is levied on the amount in excess of $175.

MAJOR SHOPPING DISTRICTS

Boston's shops and department stores are concentrated in the area bounded by Quincy Market, the Back Bay, and Downtown, with the carts of bric-a-brac at the former a particular hot spot for families. There are plenty of bargains in the Downtown Crossing area. The South End's gentrification creates its own kind of consumerist milieus, from housewares shops to avant-garde art galleries. In Cambridge, student sensibilities are catered to via lots of shopping around Harvard and Central squares, with independent boutiques migrating west along Massachusetts Avenue (or Mass Ave., as the locals and almost everyone else calls it) toward Porter Square and beyond.

TOP BOSTON SHOPPING

Harvard Square: Worlds collide in Harvard Square, where the funky jam, the politically minded pontificate, and the merely hungry grab a burger (or more likely a veggie burger) at a greasy spoon or eco-friendly café.

Newbury Street: The tony Ave is the place to indulge, where the fashionable and fabulous dangle shopping bags from Armani and Chanel. Don't be intimidated—sprinkled in is a healthy dose of affordable shops and restaurants.

Prudential Center: Bad weather? No problem. The citified mall connects upscale department stores (Neiman Marcus, Saks, Lord & Taylor) to dining, hotels, and boutiques via skybridge. No galoshes required.

Quincy Market: Hard to know what the revolutionaries would think, but the historic spot that sparked a political uprising is now a retail/dining/entertainment Mecca. In season, look for Ben Franklin, who might just be leading a tour.

BOSTON

Pretty **Charles Street** is crammed beginning to end with top-notch antiques stores such as Judith Dowling Asian Art, Eugene Galleries, and Devonia as well as a handful of independently owned fashion boutiques (including a children's store) whose prices reflect their high Beacon Hill rents. River Street, parallel to Charles Street, is also an excellent source for antiques. Both are easy walks from the Boston Common and the Charles Street T stop on the Red Line.

Copley Place. This indoor shopping mall in the Back Bay includes such high-end shops as Christian Dior, Louis Vuitton, and Gucci, anchored by the pricey but dependable Neiman Marcus and the flashy, overpriced Barneys. ✉*100 Huntington Ave., Back Bay* ☎*617/369–5000* Ⓣ*Copley.*

Downtown Crossing. A pedestrian mall with a Macy's and a handful of decent outlets. Millennium Place, a 1.8-million-square-foot complex with a Ritz-Carlton Hotel, condos, a massive sports club, a 19-screen Loews Cineplex, and a few upscale retail stores, seems to be transforming the area, as promised, from a slightly seedy hangout to the newest happening spot. ✉*Washington St. from Amory St. to about Milk St., Downtown* Ⓣ*Downtown Crossing, Park St.*

Faneuil Hall Marketplace. A huge complex that is hugely popular, even though most of its independent shops have given way to Banana Republic, Build-a-Bear, and other chains. The place has one of the area's great à la carte casual dining experiences (Quincy Market), and carnival-like trappings: pushcarts sell everything from silver jewelry to Peruvian sweaters, and buskers carry out crowd-pleasing feats such as balancing wheelbarrows on their heads. ✉ *Bounded by Congress St., Atlantic Ave., the Waterfront, and Government Center, Downtown* ☎ 617/338–2323 Ⓣ *Government Center.*

★ **Newbury Street.** Boston's version of New York's 5th Avenue. Upscale clothing stores, up-to-the-minute art galleries, and dazzling jewelers line the street near the Public Garden. As you head toward Mass Ave., Newbury gets funkier and the cacophony builds, with skateboarders zipping through traffic and garbage-pail drummers burning licks outside the hip boutiques. Parallel to Newbury Street is **Boylston Street,** where a few standouts, such as Shreve, and Crump & Low, are tucked among the other chains and restaurants. Ⓣ *Arlington, Copley, Hynes/ICA.*

Prudential Center. A skywalk connects Copley Place (⇨ *above*) to the Pru, as it's often called. You'll find moderately priced chain stores such as Ann Taylor and the Body Shop. ✉ *800 Boylston St., Back Bay* ☎ 800/746–7778 Ⓣ *Copley, Prudential Center.*

CAMBRIDGE

CambridgeSide Galleria. Here is your basic three-story mall with a food court. Macy's makes it a good stop for appliances and other basics; it's a big draw for local high-school kids. ✉ *100 CambridgeSide Pl., Kendall Sq.* ☎ 617/621–8666 Ⓣ *Lechmere, Kendall/MIT via shuttle.*

Central Square. This fun spot has an eclectic mix of furniture stores, used-record shops, ethnic restaurants, and small, hip performance venues. ✉ *East of Harvard Sq.* Ⓣ *Central.*

Harvard Square. Cambridge's most famous square takes up just a few blocks but holds more than 150 stores selling clothes, books, records, furnishings, and specialty items. Ⓣ *Harvard.*

Porter Square. There are distinctive clothing stores, as well as crafts shops, coffee shops, natural-food stores, restaurants, and bars with live music in this slightly less touristy alternative to Harvard Square. ⊠ *West on Mass Ave. from Harvard Sq.* Ⓣ *Porter.*

DEPARTMENT STORES

Lord & Taylor. This is a reliable, if somewhat overstuffed with merchandise, stop for classic clothing by such designers as Anne Klein and Ralph Lauren, along with accessories, cosmetics, and jewelry. The children's department is also a dependable staple, and, even better, less expensive than some of its Back Bay department-store brethren. ⊠ *760 Boylston St., Back Bay* ☎ *617/262–6000* Ⓣ *Prudential Center.*

Macy's. Three floors offer men's and women's clothing and shoes, housewares, and cosmetics. Although top designers and a fur salon are part of the mix, Macy's doesn't feel exclusive; instead, it's a popular source for family basics. Away from the hoity-toity sections, Macy's stands out as one of the most accessible of the area's department-store destinations, with a sprawling children's department and racks that have enough to suit any age. ⊠ *450 Washington St., Downtown* ☎ *617/357–3000* Ⓣ *Downtown Crossing.*

Neiman Marcus. The flashy Texas-based retailer known to many as "Needless Markup" has three levels of swank designers such as Gaultier, Gucci, Ferragamo, and Calvin Klein, as well as cosmetics and housewares. While some Neiman Marcus stores cater to children as well as adults, the Boston branch is strictly for grownups only. That doesn't mean you can't shop with the little ones, but you won't find anything for them, unless their tootsies are already fitting into Jimmy Choos. ⊠ *5 Copley Pl., Back Bay* ☎ *617/536–3660* Ⓣ *Back Bay/South End.*

Saks Fifth Avenue. The clothing and accessories at Saks run from the traditional to the flamboyant. It's a little pricey, but an excellent place to find high-quality merchandise, including shoes and cosmetics. ⊠ *Prudential Center, 1 Ring Rd., Back Bay* ☎ *617/262–8500* Ⓣ *Prudential Center.*

7

SPECIALTY STORES

BOOKS

If Boston and Cambridge have bragging rights to anything, it's their independent bookstores, many of which stay open late and sponsor author readings and literary programs.

Inside the Prudential Center is **Barnes & Noble** (✉*800 Boylston St., Back Bay* ☎*617/247–6959* Ⓣ*Prudential Center* ✉*660 Beacon St., Kenmore Sq.* ☎*617/267–8484* Ⓣ*Kenmore*). The company now runs the Harvard Coop. **Borders** (✉*10–24 School St., Downtown* ☎*617/557–7188* Ⓣ*Government Center* ✉*511 Boylston St., Back Bay* ☎*617/236–1444*) is also prominent.

SPECIALTY

Ars Libri Ltd. The rare and wonderful books on display here make it easy to be drawn in. The airy space is filled with books on photography and architecture, out-of-print art books, monographs, and exhibition catalogs. ✉*500 Harrison Ave., South End* ☎*617/357–5212* Ⓣ*New England Medical Center.*

★ Fodor'sChoice **Barefoot Books.** Don't come looking for the same old kids' books; Barefoot is full of beautifully illustrated, creatively told reading for kids of all ages. These are the kind of books that kids remember and keep as adults. ✉*1771 Massachusetts Ave., Cambridge* ☎*617/349–1610* Ⓣ*Porter.*

Brattle Bookshop. The late George Gloss built this into Boston's best used- and rare-book shop. Today, his son Kenneth fields queries from passionate book lovers. If the book you want is out of print, Brattle has it or can probably find it. ✉*9 West St., Downtown* ☎*617/542–0210 or 800/447–9595* Ⓣ*Downtown Crossing.*

Globe Corner Bookstore. Hands down, this is the best source for domestic and international travel books and maps. The store also has very good selections of books about New England and by New England authors. ✉*90 Mt. Auburn St., Cambridge* ☎*617/497–6277 or 800/358–6013* Ⓣ*Harvard.*

Grolier Poetry Bookshop. Proprietor Louisa Solano is an outspoken proponent of all things poetic—and her dog, Jessie, is one of the friendliest shopkeepers in Harvard Square. The store, founded in 1927, carries in-print poetry from all eras and from all over the world. ✉ *6 Plympton St., Cambridge* ☎*617/547–4648 or 800/234–7636* Ⓣ*Harvard.*

★ **Harvard Book Store.** The intellectual community is well served here, with a slew of new titles upstairs and used and remaindered books downstairs. The collection's diversity has made the store a frequent destination for academics. ✉*1256 Massachusetts Ave., Cambridge* ☎*617/661–1515* Ⓣ*Harvard.*

Kate's Mystery Books. A favorite Cambridge haunt, Kate's is a good place to track down mysteries by local writers; look for authors in the flesh at the shop's frequent readings and events. ✉*2211 Massachusetts Ave., Cambridge* ☎*617/491–2660* Ⓣ*Porter.*

Trident Booksellers & Café. Browse through an eclectic collection of books, tapes, and magazines; then settle in with a snack. It's open until midnight daily, making it a favorite with students. ✉*338 Newbury St., Back Bay* ☎*617/267–8688* Ⓣ*Hynes/ICA.*

CHILDREN'S BOUTIQUES

Bonpoint. The famed French maker of super high-end children's clothing, Bonpoint is for the baby who wants for nothing, with a sparsely stocked store aimed squarely at the well-heeled. For most of us, the three-digit sweaters and coats are akin to museum pieces. Hats and tops, however, can be found for mere high double digits. ✉*16 Arlington St., Back Bay* ☎*617/267–1717* Ⓣ*Back Bay.*

Lester Harry's. Trendy babies will want to bring their moms to this friendly second-floor shop along Newbury Street. In addition to ultraswank buggies and diaper bags, tots can be outfitted with designed duds from Juicy Couture, Marc Jacobs and more. ✉*115 Newbury St., Back Bay* ☎*617/927–5400* Ⓣ*Back Bay.*

Red Wagon. The cute and happy store is packed with little designer duds like Me Too and Juicy. Head upstairs for a small but well thought out selection of children's books, and downstairs for a small toy area including cute finger puppets that, at $6.50, are sure to appease the kids. ✉*69 Charles Street., Beacon Hill* ☎*617/523–9402* Ⓣ*Beacon Hill.*

7

Boston Shopping

CAMBRIDGE

Broadway

Main St.

KENDALL

0   275 yards
0   250 meters

Memorial Dr.

Charles River Basin

Byron

Storrow Dr.

Back St.

Marlborough St.

Beacon St.

BACK BAY

Commonwealth Ave.

Newbury St.

Boylston St.

Blagden St.

COPLEY

Stuart St.

HYNES CONVENTION CENTER/ ICA (AUDITORIUM)

PRUDENTIAL CENTER

BACK BAY

PRUDENTIAL

SYMPHONY

MASSACHUSETTS AVE.

Columbus Ave.

Appleton St.

Warren Ave.

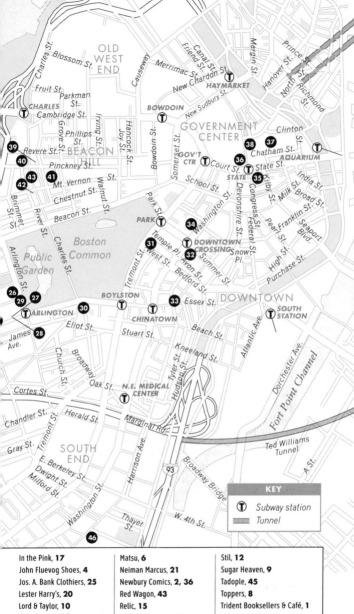

In the Pink, **17**	Matsu, **6**	Stil, **12**
John Fluevog Shoes, **4**	Neiman Marcus, **21**	Sugar Heaven, **9**
Jos. A. Bank Clothiers, **25**	Newbury Comics, **2, 36**	Tadople, **45**
Lester Harry's, **20**	Red Wagon, **43**	Toppers, **8**
Lord & Taylor, **10**	Relic, **15**	Trident Booksellers & Café, **1**
Louis Boston, **23**	Saks Fifth Avenue, **11**	Urban Outfitters, **3**
Macy's, **32**	Society of Arts & Crafts, **13**	
Marc Jacobs, **28**		

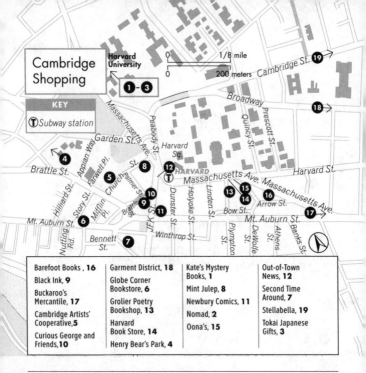

Barefoot Books , **16**	Garment District, **18**	Kate's Mystery Books, **1**	Out-of-Town News, **12**
Black Ink, **9**	Globe Corner Bookstore, **6**	Mint Julep, **8**	Second Time Around, **7**
Buckaroo's Mercantile, **17**	Grolier Poetry Bookshop, **13**	Newbury Comics, **11**	Stellabella, **19**
Cambridge Artists' Cooperative, **5**	Harvard Book Store, **14**	Nomad, **2**	Tokai Japanese Gifts, **3**
Curious George and Friends, **10**	Henry Bear's Park, **4**	Oona's, **15**	

CLOTHING & SHOES

The terminally chic shop on Newbury Street, the hip hang in Harvard Square, and everyone goes Downtown for the real bargains. This just may be the part of your trip that the little ones will have to endure while you indulge.

★ **Alan Bilzerian.** Satisfying the Euro crowd, this store sells luxe men's and women's clothing by such fashion darlings as Yohji Yamamoto and Ann Demeulemeester. ⊠ *34 Newbury St., Back Bay* ☎ *617/536–1001* Ⓣ*Arlington.*

Anne Fontaine. You can never have too many white shirts—especially if they're designed by this Parisienne. The simple, sophisticated designs are mostly executed in cotton and priced around $160. ⊠ *318 Boylston St., Back Bay* ☎ *617/423–0366* Ⓣ*Arlington, Boylston.*

Betsy Jenney. Ms. Jenney herself is likely to wait on you in this small, personal store, where the well-made, comfortable lines are for women who cannot walk into a fitted size-4 suit—in other words, most of the female population. The designers found here, such as Philippe Adec, Teenflo, and

Nicole Miller, are fashionable yet forgiving. ✉*114 Newbury St., Back Bay* ☎*617/536–2610* Ⓣ*Copley.*

Brooks Brothers. Founded in 1818, Brooks still carries the classically modern styles that made them famous—old faithfuls for men such as navy blazers, seersucker in summer, and crisp oxford shirts. Its Newbury Street store offers a similar vibe for women as well. ✉*46 Newbury St., Back Bay* ☎*617/267–2600* Ⓣ*Arlington* ✉*75 State St., Government Center* ☎*617/261–9990* Ⓣ*Government Center.*

Calypso. The women's and children's clothing here bursts with bright colors, beautiful fabrics, and styles so fresh you might need a fashion editor to help you choose. ✉*114 Newbury St., Back Bay* ☎*617/421–1887* Ⓣ*Copley.*

Chanel. Located at No. 5 in honor of its famous perfume, this branch of the Parisian couture house carries suits, separates, bags, shoes, cosmetics, and, of course, a selection of little black dresses. ✉*5 Newbury St., Back Bay* ☎*617/859–0055* Ⓣ*Arlington.*

Dress. True to its name, this shop owned by two young local women carries a number of great party dresses as well as flattering tees, pretty tops, and shoes from emerging designers. ✉*221 Newbury St., Back Bay* ☎*617/424–7125* Ⓣ*Copley, Hynes/ICA.*

DSW. Major discounts on high-quality (and big-name) shoes for men and women are what draw much of Boston to DSW, also known as Designer Shoe Warehouse. Everything from Nike to Prada can be found at varying discounts—sometimes up to 90% off. ✉*385 Washington St., Downtown* ☎*617/556–0052* Ⓣ*Downtown Crossing.*

Giorgio Armani. This top-of-the-line Italian couturier is known for his carefully shaped jackets, soft suits, and mostly neutral palette. ✉*22 Newbury St., Back Bay* ☎*617/267–3200* Ⓣ*Arlington.*

Grettaluxe. Drop by Copley's sassy little boutique and pick up the latest "it" pieces—from velour hoodies by Juicy Couture to the must-have Stella McCartney design du moment. There's also jewelry, handbags, and other accessories. ✉*Copley Place, 100 Huntington Ave., Back Bay* ☎*617/536–1959* Ⓣ*Copley.*

Helen's Leather Shop. Choose from half a dozen brands of boots (Lucchese, Nocona, Dan Post, Tony Lama, Justin, and Frye); then peruse the leather sandals, jackets, briefcases, luggage, and accessories. ✉*110 Charles St., Beacon Hill* ☎*617/742–2077* Ⓣ*Charles/MGH.*

Holiday. A stockpile of flirty and feminine getups—from dresses to denim—are the rage here. Cult lines such as Rock and Republic, Mint, Eberjey, and Tracy Reese are in regular rotation among the fashionable racks. ✉*53 Charles St., Beacon Hill* ☎*617/973–9730* Ⓣ*Charles/MGH.*

In the Pink. Don't be caught dead in Palm Beach this year without your Lilly Pulitzer resort wear, available here along with shoes, home decor, and children's clothing. ✉*133 Newbury St., Back Bay* ☎*617/536–6423* Ⓣ*Copley.*

John Fluevog Shoes. Many club goers have at least one pair of these oh-so-hip shoes in their closets, perhaps because of the company's claim that their Angel soles repel all kinds of nasty liquids "and Satan." ✉*302 Newbury St., Back Bay* ☎*617/266–1079* Ⓣ*Copley.*

Jos. A. Bank Clothiers. Like Brooks Brothers, Joseph Bank is well known to the conservatively well dressed everywhere. ✉*399 Boylston St., Back Bay* ☎*617/536–5050* Ⓣ*Arlington.*

★ Fodor'sChoice **Louis Boston.** Impeccably tailored designs, subtly updated classics, and the latest Italian styles highlight a wide selection of imported clothing and accessories. Visiting celebrities might be trolling the racks along with you as jazz spills out into the street from the adjoining Restaurant L. ✉*234 Berkeley St., Back Bay* ☎*617/262–6100* Ⓣ*Arlington.*

Marc By Marc Jacobs. The celebrated designer recently changed the Boston outpost from high-end couture to the somewhat less astronomically priced "urban chic." ✉*81 Newbury St., Back Bay* ☎*617/425–0707* Ⓣ*Copley.*

Matsu. This shop trends toward the funkier with edgy pieces from designers like Lilith and Rozae Nichols. Look for a well-edited jewelry selection as well as high-end handbags and accessories. ✉*259 Newbury St., Back Bay* ☎*617/266–9707* Ⓣ*Copley, Hynes/ICA.*

Mint Julep. Cute dresses, playful skirts, and form-fitting tops make up the selection here. The Cambridge location is a little larger and easier to navigate, but Brookline houses the original. ✉*6 Church St., Cambridge* ☎*617/576–6468* Ⓣ*Harvard* ✉*1302 Beacon St., Brookline* ☎*617/232–3600* Ⓣ*Coolidge Corner.*

Queen Bee. Only clothes from the hottest, most youthful lines—Mint, Tibi, Shoshana—pass through this boutique's doors. Even if you wouldn't wear most of this stuff, it's fun just to see the latest and maybe pick up an accessory. ⊠*85 Newbury St., Beacon Hill* ☎*617/859–7999* Ⓣ*Arlington, Copley.*

Relic. This ultrahip subterranean shop sells designer denim such as Miss Sixty and Meltin' Pot. The interior is a work of art; a few local artists designed the space with pieces of metal culled from the city's Big Dig project and hand-painted wall murals. ⊠*116 Newbury St., Back Bay* ☎*617/437–7344* Ⓣ*Copley.*

Stil. Local designers such as Daniela Corte and Elaine Perlov share rack space with cutting-edge Scandinavian labels such as Rutzou and Bruun's Bazaar—all of it at surprisingly earthly prices. ⊠*170 Newbury St., Back Bay* ☎*617/859–7845* Ⓣ*Copley.*

Toppers. Nothing old hat about this place, where you can cover your head in anything from a tam-o'-shanter to a 10-gallon. ⊠*151 Tremont St., Back Bay* ☎*617/859–1430* Ⓣ*Back Bay.*

Urban Outfitters. At the funky end of Newbury Street at Mass Ave., this huge emporium is enormously popular with teens (male and female) for hip lines at chain-store prices. The tchotchke collection on the first floor is always entertaining for its off-color sensibility. Fun to browse. ⊠*361 Newbury St., Back Bay* ☎*617/236–0088* Ⓣ*Arlington* ⊠*Faneuil Hall Marketplace* ☎*617/523–0651* Ⓣ*Government Center.*

CRAFTS

Beadworks. Find beads of every color, texture, size, and material in the tiny bins in Back Bay's do-it-yourself jewelry store. The prices are reasonable, the staff is helpful and friendly, and there's a worktable to assemble your masterpiece in the center of the shop. ⊠*167 Newbury St., Back Bay* ☎*617/247–7227* Ⓣ*Copley.*

Cambridge Artists' Cooperative. The ceramics, weavings, jewelry, and leather work here can be pricier than most, but they're all one-of-a-kind or limited edition. ⊠*59A Church St., Cambridge* ☎*617/868–4434* Ⓣ*Harvard.*

Society of Arts & Crafts. More than a century old, this is the country's oldest nonprofit crafts organization. It displays a fine assortment of ceramics, jewelry, glass, woodwork, and furniture by some of the country's finest craftspeople. The retail gallery on the first floor includes some one-of-a-kind children's items like handmade, knitted stuffed animals that come with names and back stories, as well as baby spoons made from toy magic wands (perhaps they'll magically get your kids to eat). ✉*175 Newbury St., Back Bay* ☎*617/266–1810* Ⓣ*Copley.*

GIFTS

Black Ink. A wall full of rubber stamps stretches above unusual candles, cookie jars, and other home accessories and gift items. Apart from traditional gift ware, the store includes a hefty amount of kid-centric stuff, such as comics, games, and toys. ✉*101 Charles St., Beacon Hill* ☎*617/723–3883* Ⓣ*Charles/MGH* ✉*5 Brattle St., Cambridge* ☎*617/497–1221* Ⓣ*Harvard.*

Buckaroo's Mercantile. It's Howdy Doody time at Buckaroo's—a great destination for the kitsch inclined. Find pink poodle skirts, lunch-box clocks, Barbie lamps, *Front Page Detective* posters, and everything Elvis. The Central Square emporium may not have children's merchandise per se, but that doesn't mean it's not any fun. Teens especially will love the vintage wares and merchandise offerings that range from cheeky to blush inducing. ✉*5 Brookline St., Cambridge* ☎*617/492–4792* Ⓣ*Central.*

The Flat of the Hill. There's nothing flat about this fun collection of seasonal items, toiletries, pillows, and whatever else catches the fancy of the shop's young owner. Her passion for pets is evident—pick up a Fetch & Glow ball and your dog will never again have to wait until daytime to play in the park. Tots can be amply outfitted with the store's selection of super soft blankies and stuffed toys, plus Noodle & Boo's brand of baby bubble baths and lotions. ✉*60 Charles St., Beacon Hill* ☎*617/619–9977* Ⓣ*Charles/MGH.*

★ **Fresh.** You won't know whether to wash with these soaps or nibble on them. The shea-butter-rich bars come in such scents as clove-hazelnut and orange-cranberry. They cost $6 to $7 each, but they carry the scent to the end. ✉*121 Newbury St., Back Bay* ☎*617/421–1212* Ⓣ*Copley.*

★ **Nomad.** Low prices and an enthusiastic staff are just the beginning at this imports store; it carries clothing as well as Indian good-luck *torans* (wall hangings), Mexican *milagros* (charms), mirrors to keep away the evil eye, silver jewelry, and curtains made from sari silk. In the basement you'll find kilims, hand-painted tiles, and sale items. ⊠*1741 Massachusetts Ave., Cambridge* ☎*617/497–6677* Ⓣ*Porter.*

Tokai Japanese Gifts. Chopstick rests, origami paper, Yukata cotton robes, and high-end kimonos are among the wares here. ⊠*1815 Massachusetts Ave., Cambridge* ☎*617/864–5922* Ⓣ*Porter.*

MUSIC

As befitting a town with so many colleges and universities, live music of all kinds is never far away. Unfortunately, the market for recorded music has diminished over the years and CD and record stores are disappearing fast.

★ **Newbury Comics.** These local outposts for new rock and roll carry especially good lineups of independent pressings. Frequent sales keep prices down. Kids who haven't discovered music yet will enjoy browsing the large supply of pop-culture items. In addition to CDs, the retail chain is known for throwback items like vintage-style lunch boxes, Star Wars toys, and gag toys galore. ⊠*332 Newbury St., Back Bay* ☎*617/236–4930* Ⓣ*Hynes/ICA* ⊠*36 JFK St., Cambridge* ☎*617/491–0337* Ⓣ*Harvard* ⊠*1 Washington Mall, Government Center* ☎*617/248–9992* Ⓣ*Government Center.*

ODDS & ENDS

Boston Campus Gear. Sweatshirts, Ts, and more from local institutions of higher ed—Harvard, Boston college, MIT, among them—but at a savings of about $200,000 over the alumni price. Gear is sold in sizes small enough to fit the tiniest tots—consider it inspirational. ⊠*Faneuil Hall Marketplace, Government Center* ☎*617/367–9339* Ⓣ*Central.*

Essex Corner. Colorful wares in this cute Chinatown shop are of every variety. Pass the stone dragons on the stairs (yep—they're for sale) and browse shelves lined with jewelry and decorative items like lanterns, pottery, and watercolors. Kids will have a ball ogling the large selection of trinkets like silk-jacket key chains and scads of Sanrio—definitely the place to come for some inexpensive souvenirs. ⊠*50 Essex St., Chinatown* ☎*617/338–8882* Ⓣ*Chinatown.*

Grasshopper Shops. The souvenirs in this little collection of independently owned shops in historic Faneuil Hall are Boston-centric but not cheesy. The **Bostonian Society Museum Shop** (☎617/720–3284) has history books for children and adults. At **Explore Boston** (☎617/725–1055) you can buy saltwater taffy or a Boston-in-a-Box board game. **Out of Left Field** (☎617/722–9401) sells Red Sox gear. ✉*Faneuil Hall Sq., Government Center* Ⓣ*Government Center.*

Out-of-Town News. Smack in the middle of Harvard Square is a staggering selection of the world's newspapers and magazines. The stand is open daily 6 AM–10:30 PM. ✉*0 Harvard Sq., Cambridge* ☎*617/354–7777* Ⓣ*Harvard.*

Sugar Heaven. The newish kid on the Newbury block stocks about 3,500 ways to satisfy your sweet tooth, whether it's the kids' taste for the ubiquitous gummy, or grandpa's yen for hard-to-find Chuckles. Despite its tony address, Heaven's prices start at a mere few cents for certain candies, making it a great stop for kids. The exceptions are imported chocolates, and bulk goodies that are priced by quarter pound. ✉*218 Newbury St., Boston* ☎*617/491–6290* Ⓣ*Back Bay.*

THRIFT SHOPS

Garment District. This warehouselike building is crammed with vintage, used, and new clothing and accessories. Students crowd the store year-round, and everyone comes at Halloween for that perfect costume. ✉*200 Broadway, Cambridge* ☎*617/876–5230 or 617/876–9795* Ⓣ*Kendall/MIT.*

Oona's. Crowded racks of cared-for, secondhand clothing for women and men are reason enough to browse through the multiple rooms of reasonably priced stock. A helpful staff and fun, eclectic vibe just make doing so that much more fun. ✉*1210 Massachusetts Ave., Cambridge* ☎*617/491–2654* Ⓣ*Harvard.*

Second Time Around. OK, so $700 isn't all that cheap for a used suit—but what if it's Chanel? Many of the items here, from jeans to fur coats, are new merchandise; the rest is on consignment. The staff takes periodic markdowns, ranging from 20% to 50% over a 90-day period. ✉*176 Newbury St., Back Bay* ☎*617/247–3504* Ⓣ*Copley* ✉*8 Eliot St., Cambridge* ☎*617/491–7185* Ⓣ*Harvard.*

TOYS

The Boston Baked Bean. The item for which "beantown" is nicknamed takes on life in all forms—figurines of all ilk, key chains, and in plush. The upside of the kitschy store: it's an inexpensive way for kids to bring home a vacation keepsake—and one from Newbury Street at that! ✉*291 Newbury St., Cambridge* ☎*617/266–0050* Ⓣ*Central.*

Curious George and Friends. Time can really slip away from you in this jungle of kids' books and gifts. Decorated with tropical plants, a fake hut, and tot-size chairs, and equipped with puzzles, toys, activity sets, and books of all kinds for all ages, this store is a wonderland for kids and a parent's salvation on a rainy day. ✉*1 JFK St., Harvard Sq., Cambridge* ☎*617/498–0062* Ⓣ*Harvard.*

Henry Bear's Park. The specialty at this charming neighborhood store is huggable bears and collectible dolls, although it also sells books, toys, and games. ✉*361 Huron St., Cambridge* ☎*617/547–8424* Ⓣ*Porter* ✉*19 Harvard St., Brookline* ☎*617/264–2422* Ⓣ*Brookline Village.*

Magic Beans. The friendly store is an institution in Brookline, where parents find everything from a marble roller coaster for the school-age set, to Bugaboo Strollers for tots. Books, puzzles, CDs . . . you could be in here for days. ✉*312 Harvard St., Brookline* ☎*617/264–2326* Ⓣ*Brookline Village.*

Stellabella. Creative toys are the draw here—books and games to stimulate kids' imaginations and get their brains going without relying on TV or violence. No gun or weapon toys are sold. ✉*1360 Cambridge St., Cambridge* ☎*617/491–6290* Ⓣ*Central.*

Tadpole. The latest in the South End's boutiques focuses on trendy parents and their well-heeled kids, with eco-friendly wooden toys and dollhouses, organic gear and bubble baths, plus the latest in diaper bags and strollers. ✉*37 Clarendon St., Boston* ☎*617/778–1788* Ⓣ*South End.*

7

FAMILY FUN

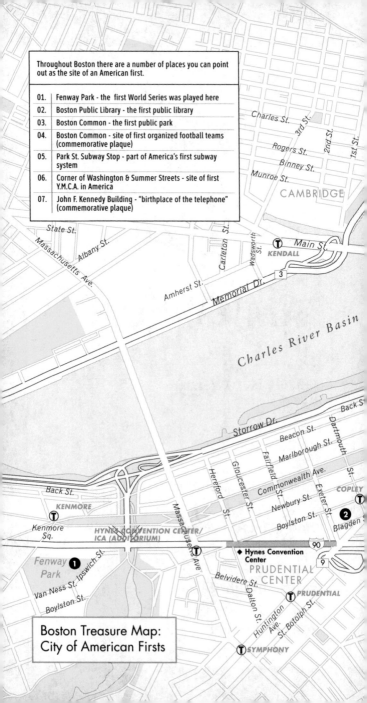

Throughout Boston there are a number of places you can point out as the site of an American first.

01.	Fenway Park - the first World Series was played here
02.	Boston Public Library - the first public library
03.	Boston Common - the first public park
04.	Boston Common - site of first organized football teams (commemorative plaque)
05.	Park St. Subway Stop - part of America's first subway system
06.	Corner of Washington & Summer Streets - site of first Y.M.C.A. in America
07.	John F. Kennedy Building - "birthplace of the telephone" (commemorative plaque)

Boston Treasure Map:
City of American Firsts

THE CLASSICS

"I'm thinking of an animal . . ."

With older kids you can play 20 Questions: Have your leader think of an animal, vegetable, or mineral (or, alternatively, a person, place, or thing) and let everybody else try to guess what it is. The correct guesser takes over as leader. If no one figures out the secret within 20 questions, the first person goes again. With younger children, limit the guessing to animals and don't put a ceiling on how many questions can be asked. With rivalrous siblings, just take turns being leader. Make the game's theme things you expect to see at your day's destination.

"I see something you don't see and it is blue."

Stuck for a way to get your youngsters to settle down in a museum? Sit them down on a bench in the middle of a room and play this vintage favorite. The leader gives just one clue—the color—and everybody guesses away.

FUN WITH THE ALPHABET

Family Ark

Noah had his ark—here's your chance to build your own. It's easy: Just start naming animals and work your way through the alphabet, from antelope to zebra.

"I'm going to the grocery . . ."

The first player begins, "I'm going to the grocery and I'm going to buy..." and finishes the sentence with the name of an object, found in grocery stores, that begins with the letter "A." The second player repeats what the first player has said, and adds the name of another item that starts with "B." The third player repeats everything that has been said so far and adds something that begins with "C," and so on through the alphabet. Anyone who skips or misremembers an item is out (or decide up front that you'll give hints to all who need 'em). You can modify the theme depending on where you're going that day, as "I'm going to X, and I'm going to see..."

"I'm going to Asia on an ant to act up."

Working their way through the alphabet, players concoct silly sentences stating where they're going, how they're traveling, and what they'll do.

What I See, from A to Z

In this game, kids look for objects in alphabetical order—first something whose name begins with "A," next an item whose name begins with "B," and so on. If you're in the car, have children do their spotting through their own window. Whoever gets to Z first wins. Or have each child play to beat his own time. Try this one as you make your way through zoos and museums, too.

JUMP-START A CONVERSATION

What if . . .?

Riding in the car and waiting in a restaurant are great times to get to know your youngsters better. Begin with imaginative questions to prime the pump.

• If you were the tallest man on earth, what would your life be like? The shortest?

• If you had a magic carpet, where would you go? Why? What would you do there?

• If your parents gave you three wishes, what would they be?

• If you were elected president, what changes would you make?

• What animal would you like to be and what would your life be like?

• What's a friend? Who are your best friends? What do you like to do together?

• Describe a day in your life 10 years from now.

Druthers

How do your kids really feel about things? Just ask. "Would you rather eat worms or hamburgers? Hamburgers or candy?" Choose serious and silly topics—and have fun!

Faker, Faker

Reveal three facts about yourself. The catch: One of the facts is a fake. Have your kids ferret out the fiction. Take turns being the faker. Fakers who stump everyone win.

KEEP A STRAIGHT FACE

"Ha!"

Work your way around the car. First person says, "Ha." Second person says, "Ha, ha." Third person says "Ha" three times. And so on. Just try to keep a straight face. Or substitute, "Here, kitty, kitty, kitty!"

Wiggle & Giggle

Give your kids a chance to stick out their tongues at you. Start by making a face, then have the next person imitate you and add a gesture of his own—snapping fingers, winking, clapping, sneezing, or the like. The next person mimics the first two and adds a third gesture, and so on.

Junior Opera

During a designated period of time, have your kids sing everything they want to say.

Igpay Atinlay

Proclaim the next 30 minutes Pig Latin time, and everybody has to talk in this fun code. To speak it, move the first consonant of every word to the end of the word and add "ay." "Pig" becomes "igpay," and "Latin" becomes "atinlay." For words that begin with a vowel, just add "ay" as a suffix.

MORE GOOD TIMES

Build a Story

"Once upon a time there lived . . ." Finish the sentence and ask the rest of your family, one at a time, to add another sentence or two. Bring a tape recorder along to record the narrative—and you can enjoy your creation again and again.

Not the Goofy Game

Have one child name a category. (Some ideas: first names, last names, animals, countries, friends, feelings, foods, hot or cold things, clothing.) Then take turns naming things that fall into that category. You're out if you name something that doesn't belong in the category—or if you can't think of another item to name. When only one person remains, start again. Choose categories depending on where you're going or where you've been—historic topics if you've seen a historic sight, animal topics before or after the zoo, upside-down things if you've been to the circus, and so on. Make the game harder by choosing category items in A-B-C order.

Color of the Day

Choose a color at the beginning of your outing and have your kids be on the lookout for things that are that color, calling out what they've seen when they spot it. If you want to keep score, keep a running list or use a pen to mark points on your kids' hands for every item they spot.

Click

If Cam Jansen, the heroine of a popular series of early-reader books, says "Click" as she looks at something, she can remember every detail of what she sees, like a camera (that's how she got her nickname). Say "Click!" Then give each one of your kids a full minute to study a page of a magazine. After everyone has had a turn, go around the car naming items from the page. Players who can't name an item or who make a mistake are out.

The Quiet Game

Need a good giggle—or a moment of calm to figure out your route? The driver sets a time limit and everybody must be silent. The last person to make a sound wins.

Travel Smart
Boston with Kids

WORD OF MOUTH

"We ended up parking at the Pru[dential Center] and walking to Fenway and back . . . The best part of parking at the Pru was that, if you show them your game tickets, the parking charge is only $15 (it would have been $34 for all of the hours we were there.) There was also very little traffic getting back onto 93, compared to the chaos around Fenway."

–lvk

GETTING HERE & AROUND

▮ BY AIR

Flying to Boston takes about 1 hour from New York, 1½ hours from Washington, DC, 2¼ hours from Chicago, 3¾ hours from Dallas, 5½ hours from Los Angeles, 7½ hours from London, and 21–22 hours from Sydney (including connection time). Delta, US Airways, and jetBlue have many daily shuttle flights from New York and Washington.

■TIP→ **The Boston Convention and Visitor Bureau's Web site,** ⊕*www.bostonusa.com,* **has direct links to 19 airlines that service the city. You can book flights here, too.**

Airlines & Airports **Airline and Airport Links.com** (⊕www.airlineandairportlinks.com) has links to many of the world's airlines and airports.

Airline Security Issues **Transportation Security Administration** (⊕www.tsa.gov) has answers for almost every question that might come up.

AIRPORTS

Boston's major airport, Logan International (BOS), is across the harbor from Downtown, about 2 mi outside the city center, and can be easily reached by taxi, water taxi, or subway (called the "T") via the Silver or Blue Line. Logan has five terminals, identified by letters A through E. A free airport shuttle runs between the terminals and airport hotels. Some airlines use different terminals for international and domestic flights. Most international flights arrive at Terminal E. Most charter flights arrive at Terminal D. A visitor center in Terminal C offers tourist information. Green Airport, in Providence, Rhode Island, and the Manchester Airport in Manchester, New Hampshire, are both about an hour from Boston.

■TIP→ **If you travel frequently, look into the TSA's Registered Traveler program. The program, which is still being tested in several U.S. airports, is designed to cut down on gridlock at security checkpoints by allowing prescreened travelers to pass quickly through kiosks that scan an iris and/or a fingerprint. How sci-fi is that?**

Airport Information **Green Airport** (⊠Off I–95, Exit 13, Providence, RI ☎888/268–7222 or 401/737–8222 ⊕www.pvdairport.com). **Logan International** (⊠I–90 east to Ted Williams Tunnel ☎800/235–6426 ⊕www.massport.com ⊤Airport). **Manchester Airport** (⊠Off I–293/Rte. 101, Exit 2, Manchester, NH ☎603/624–6556 ⊕www.flymanchester.com).

TRANSFERS—BY BUS OR SHUTTLE VAN

Several companies offer shared-van service to many Boston-area destinations. J. C. Transportation, Logan/Boston Hotel Shuttle, and Ace American provide door-to-door service to several major

Back Bay and Downtown hotels. (Check their Web sites for a listing of hotels.) Reservations are not required, because vans swing by all terminals every 20 minutes to a half hour. One-way fares are $14 per person. Easy Transportation is also a shared-van service, which runs from the airport to the Back Bay Hilton, Radisson, and Lenox hotels from 7 AM to 10 PM. Star Shuttle operates shared vans from the airport to the Marriott Copley Place and Sheraton Copley, every hour on the half hour, from 5:30 AM to 11:30 PM. Logan Express buses travel from the airport to the suburbs of Braintree, Framingham, Peabody, and Woburn. One-way fares are $11.

Contacts Ace American (☎800/517–2281). **Easy Transportation** (☎617/869–7760). **J. C. Transportation** (☎800/517–2281 ⊕www.jctransportationshuttle. com). **Logan/Boston Hotel Shuttle** (☎617/331–8388). **Logan Express** (☎800/235–6426 ⊕www. massport.com). **Star Shuttle** (☎617/230–6005).

TRANSFERS — BY CAR OR TAXI

For recorded information about traveling to and from Logan Airport, as well as details about parking, contact the airport's ground-transportation hotline. Traffic can be maddening; it's a good idea to take public transportation to and from the airport.

When driving from Logan to downtown Boston, the most direct route is by way of the Sumner Tunnel ($3 toll inbound; no toll outbound). On weekends and holidays and after 10 PM weekdays, you can get around Sumner Tunnel backups by using the Ted Williams Tunnel ($3 toll inbound; no toll outbound), which will steer you onto the Southeast Expressway south of downtown Boston. Follow the signs to I–93 northbound to head back into the downtown area.

Taxis can be hired outside each terminal. Fares to and from Downtown should be about $15–$18, including tip. Taxis must pay an extra toll of $4.50 and a $2 airport fee when leaving the airport (but not going in) that will be tacked onto your bill at the end of the trip. (Major traffic jams or taking a longer route to avoid traffic will add to the fare.)

Contact Logan Airport Customer Information Hotline (☎800/235–6426).

TRANSFERS — BY SUBWAY

The Blue and Silver lines on the subway, commonly called "the T" (and operated by the MBTA), run from the airport to downtown Boston in about 20 minutes. The Blue Line is best if you're heading to North Station, Faneuil Hall, North End/Waterfront, or Back Bay (Hynes Convention Center, Prudential Center area). Take the Silver Line to South Station, Boston Convention and Exhibition Center, Seaport World Trade Center, Chinatown Theater, and South End areas. From North and South stations, you can reach the Red, Green, or Orange lines, or commuter rail. For adults, the T costs $2 for in-town travel if you're paying in cash or $1.70 if you purchase a CharlieCard (a prepaid stored-value card). On school days, student fares are discounted by 50 percent, but require an ID card from participating schools, meaning it's likely only a local perk. Children under 11 are always free (no ID required) when riding with a paying adult (maximum 2 children per adult). *See By Subway, Train, and Trolley, below for more information.* Free 24-hour shuttle buses connect the subway station with all airline terminals. Shuttle Bus 22 runs between the subway and Terminals A and B, and Shuttle Bus 33 runs between the subway and Terminals C, D, and E.

Contact **MBTA** (☎800/392–6100 or 617/222–3200, 617/222–5146 TTY ⊕www.mbta.com).

FLIGHTS

Airline Contacts **Alaska Airlines** (☎800/252–7522 ⊕www.alaskaair.com). **American Airlines** (☎800/433–7300 ⊕www.aa.com). **Continental Airlines** (☎800/523–3273 for U.S. and Mexico reservations, 800/231–0856 for international reservations ⊕www.continental.com). **Delta Airlines** (☎800/221–1212 for U.S. reservations, 800/241–4141 for international reservations ⊕www.delta.com). **jetBlue** (☎800/538–2583 ⊕www.jetblue.com). **Northwest Airlines** (☎800/225–2525 ⊕www.nwa.com). **Southwest Airlines** (☎800/435–9792 ⊕www.southwest.com). **Spirit Airlines** (☎800/772–7117 ⊕www.spiritair.com). **United Airlines** (☎800/864–8331 for U.S. reservations, 800/538–2929 for interna-

tional reservations ⊕www.united.com). **US Airways** (☎800/428–4322 for U.S. and Canada reservations, 800/622–1015 for international reservations ⊕www.usairways.com).

▌ BY BOAT

Rowes Wharf Water Taxi shuttles from Logan Airport to Rowes Wharf, Downtown for $10 per person. It operates daily year-round between 7 AM and 7 PM, and from April through October, 7AM to 10 PM, Monday to Saturday and 7AM to 8PM on Sunday.

Harbor Express water taxis take passengers from Logan Airport to Long Wharf, Downtown ($10) and to Quincy and Hull on the South Shore ($12). Boats leave approximately every 40–45 minutes 6:20 AM–10:20 PM Monday through Thursday, 6:20 AM–11 PM Friday, 8:30 AM–10:30 PM Saturday, and 8:30 AM–9 PM Sunday.

City Water Taxi has an on-call boat service between the airport and 16 downtown locations that operates from 7 AM to 10 PM Monday through Saturday and 7 AM to 8 PM on Sunday year-round. One-way fares to or from the airport are $10, and round-trip tickets are $17. Children under 12 ride free.

MBTA commuter boat service operates weekdays between several downtown harbor destinations and quite a few locations on the South Shore. One-way fares range from $1.50 to $6 depending on destination. Children under 11 are free with paying adults. Schedules change seasonally, so call ahead.

By Bus > **193**

Several boat companies make runs between the airport and downtown destinations. Take the free Shuttle Bus 66 from any terminal to the airport's ferry dock to catch Boston's water taxis.

Information **City Water Taxi** (☎617/422–0392 ⊕www.citywatertaxi.com). **Harbor Express** (☎617/222–6999 ⊕www.harborexpress.com). **MBTA** (☎617/222–5000 ⊕www.mbta.com). **Rowes Wharf Water Taxi** (☎617/406–8584 ⊕www.roweswharfwatertaxi.com).

▌BY BUS

ARRIVING & DEPARTING
Greyhound has buses to Boston from all major cities in North America. Besides its main location at South Station, Greyhound has suburban terminals in Newton, Framingham, and Worcester. Peter Pan Bus Lines connects Boston with cities elsewhere in Massachusetts, Connecticut, New Jersey, New York, and Maryland.

Concord Trailways heads to Maine and New Hampshire. C&J Trailways sends buses up the New Hampshire coast to Dover. All of the above-mentioned bus companies leave from South Station, which is connected to the Amtrak station. The station is clean and safe. Many bus lines also make stops at Logan Airport; check individual lines for up-to-date schedules.

The Fung Wah bus offers inexpensive (very) low-maintenance service between the Chinatown neighborhoods of Boston and New York.

COMMUTING WITH A VIEW

The Rowes Wharf Water Taxi offers a stunning glimpse of the city's skyline as it makes seven-minute trips across Boston Harbor between Logan Airport and Rowes Wharf in downtown Boston.

If you want to travel in style, the LimoLiner provides luxury bus service (with television, movies, high-speed Internet, and food-and-drink service) between Boston's Hilton Back Bay and Manhattan's Hilton New York for $79 each way. This service is open to the general public, not just guests of the Hilton. Reservations are a good idea.

Fares and schedules for all buses except LimoLiner are posted at South Station, at many of the tourist kiosks, and online.

Major credit cards are accepted for all buses. You can usually purchase your tickets online.

Bus Information **C&J Trailways** (☎800/258–7111 ⊕www.cjtrailways.com). **Concord Trailways** (☎800/639–3317 ⊕www.concordtrailways.com). **Fung Wah Bus** (☎617/345–8000 ⊕www.fungwahbus.com). **Greyhound** (☎800/231–2222 ⊕www.greyhound.com). **LimoLiner** (☎888/546–5469 or 339/502-6411 ⊕www.limoliner.com). **Peter Pan** (☎800/343–9999 ⊕www.peterpanbus.com). **Plymouth & Brockton** (☎508/746–0378 ⊕www.p-b.com).

Station Information **South Station** (✉700 Atlantic Ave., at Summer St., Downtown Ⓣ South Station).

BY TRAIN

Boston is served by Amtrak at North Station, South Station, and Back Bay Station, which accommodate frequent departures to and arrivals from New York, Philadelphia, and Washington, DC. Amtrak's pricey high-speed Acela train cuts the travel time between Boston and New York from 4½ hours to 3½ hours. South Station is also the eastern terminus of Amtrak's *Lake Shore Limited*, which travels daily between Boston and Chicago by way of Albany, Rochester, Buffalo, and Cleveland. An additional Amtrak station with ample parking is just off Route 128 in suburban Westwood, southwest of Boston.

Amtrak tickets and reservations are available at Amtrak stations, by telephone, through travel agents, or online. Amtrak schedule and fare information can be found at South Station, Back Bay Station, or the Route 128 station in suburban Westwood, as well as online. The 24-hour hotline is another good source for route, schedule, fare, and other information. Free maps are available at the MBTA's Park Street Station information stand.

Amtrak ticket offices accept all major credit cards, cash, traveler's checks, and personal checks when accompanied by a valid photo ID and a major credit card. You may pay on board with cash or a major credit card, but a surcharge may apply. MBTA commuter-rail stations generally accept only cash. You may also pay in cash on board commuter trains, but there may be a $1–$2 surcharge.

Amtrak has both reserved and unreserved trains. During peak times, such as a Friday night, get a reservation and a ticket in advance. Trains at nonpeak times are unreserved, with seats assigned on a first-come, first-served basis.

Train Information **Back Bay Station** (✉145 Dartmouth St., Back Bay). **North Station** (✉Causeway and Friend Sts., North End). **South Station** (✉Atlantic Ave. and Summer St., Downtown).

GETTING AROUND BOSTON

The best form of transportation within Boston or Cambridge/Somerville is the MBTA system, or the T, as it's known locally. Five separate lines run through the entire city and out toward the outlying suburbs. The system of underground trains, aboveground trolleys, and buses will take you to every major point of interest. A car is only necessary for getting out of town.

In most cases, address numbers are listed in even numbers on one side of the street and odd number on the opposite side.

▪TIP→ **Ask the local tourist board about hotel and local transportation packages that include tickets to major museum exhibits or other special events.**

Buses of the Massachusetts Bay Transportation Authority (MBTA) crisscross the metropolitan area and travel farther into suburbia than subway and trolley lines. Buses run roughly from 5:30 AM to 12:30 AM.

At this writing, fares are $1.50 if paying in cash, $1.25 if paying with a prepurchased CharlieCard for trips within the city; you often pay an extra fare for longer lines that run to the suburbs. As with all MBTA fares, children 11 and under ride free with paying adults. The SmarTraveler information line provides service updates.

CharlieCards (prepaid stored-value fare cards), sold at all subway terminals, can be purchased with cash or with debit or credit cards. To pay the bus fare, either flash your pass or pay in cash when you enter. Drivers accept dollar bills but don't have change.

Bus Information **MBTA** (☎617/222–3200, 617/222–5146 TTY ⊕www.mbta.com). **SmarTraveler** (☎617/494–5200 ⊕www.smartraveler.com).

▌ BY CAR

Driving isn't easy in Boston. It's important to plan out a route in advance if you're unfamiliar with the city. There's a profusion of one-way streets, so always keep a detailed map handy. It's also a good idea to pay extra attention to other drivers. Boston drivers have a bad reputation, and you should watch out for those using the emergency breakdown lanes (illegal unless posted otherwise), passing on the right, or turning from the wrong lane.

NAVIGATING BOSTON

Boston is a walkable city but since its streets were originally laid out as cow paths leading from the waterfront to spots around the city, they are sometimes tricky to navigate.

■ Head toward Boston Common or the Public Garden. It's a central spot in the city and there are maps around the park to help direct you around the city. Or, if you're near the waterfront, head towards Quincy Market where there are also maps to help you navigate.

■ The Financial District and Downtown Crossing are part of Downtown. Since the streets here are part of that circuit of former cow paths, they have no rhyme or reason and often run only one way. Bring a map.

■ In general, signage in Boston is hard to come by, especially on roadways. But the city has done a great job of posting street maps at major visitor points throughout the city. If you're lost, ask for directions. Most residents are familiar with how difficult it is to find your way around.

■ The public transportation system, the T, offers easy-to-read navigation guides and maps in every station. It stops at all major points of interest throughout the city and just beyond the city limits, too.

It's best to park in lots or garages rather than on the street. You're more likely to avoid tickets, accidents, or theft. Remember that the Central Artery/Tunnel Project, a massive highway reconstruction effort in downtown Boston that's also known as the "Big Dig," continues to cause traffic snarls. The latest information on the construction is available on the project's Web site, ⊕*www.masspike. com/bigdig.*

GASOLINE

Gas stations are not plentiful in downtown Boston. Try Cambridge Street (behind Beacon Hill, near Massachusetts General Hospital), near the airport in East Boston, along Commonwealth Avenue or Cambridge Street in Allston/ Brighton, or off the Southeast Expressway just south of downtown Boston.

Cambridge service stations can be found along Memorial Drive, Massachusetts Avenue, and Broadway. In Brookline, try Commonwealth Avenue or Boylston Street. Gas stations with 24-hour service can be found at many exits off Route 3 to Cape Cod, suburban Route 128 and Interstate 95, and at service plazas on the Massachusetts Turnpike. Many offer both full and self-service.

PARKING

Parking on Boston streets is tricky. Some neighborhoods have strictly enforced residents-only rules, with just a handful of two-hour visitors' spaces; others have meters, which usually cost 25¢ for 15 minutes, with a one- or two-hour maximum.

Keep a few quarters handy, as most city meters take nothing else.

Parking-police officers are ruthless—it's not unusual to find a ticket on your windshield five minutes after your meter expires. However, most on-street parking is free after 8 PM in the city and on Sunday. Repeat offenders who don't pay fines may find the "boot" (an immovable steel clamp) secured to one of their wheels.

Major public lots are at Government Center and Quincy Market, beneath Boston Common (entrance on Charles Street), beneath Post Office Square, at the Prudential Center, at Copley Place, and off Clarendon Street near the John Hancock Tower. Smaller lots and garages are scattered throughout Downtown, especially around the Theater District and off Atlantic Avenue in the North End. Most are expensive; expect to pay up to $8 an hour or $24 to park all day. The few city garages are a bargain at about $7–$11 per day. Theaters, restaurants, stores, and tourist attractions often provide customers with one or two hours of free parking. Most downtown restaurants offer valet parking.

ROAD CONDITIONS

Bostonians tend to drive erratically. These habits, coupled with inconsistent street and traffic signs, one-way streets, and heavy congestion, make it a nerve-wracking city to navigate. Many roadways in the city are under construction or in need of repairs. Potholes and manhole covers sticking up above the street are the most common hazards. In general, err on the side of caution.

Dial 911 in an emergency to reach police, fire, or ambulance services. If you're a member of the AAA auto club, call their 24-hour help bureau.

Emergency Services **AAA** (☎800/222–4357).

▌ BY SUBWAY, TRAIN & TROLLEY

The Massachusetts Bay Transportation Authority (MBTA)—or "T" when referring to the subway line—operates subways, elevated trains, and trolleys along five connecting lines. A 24-hour hotline and the MBTA Web site offer information on routes, schedules, fares, wheelchair access, and other matters. Free maps are available at the MBTA's Park Street Station information stand, open daily from 7 AM to 10 PM. They're also available online at ⊕*www.mbta.com*. Those traveling with the stroller set will find foldable strollers quite manageable. Subways/Trolley cars require a few steps up, making the bulky variety somewhat impractical.

"Inbound" trains head into the city center and "outbound" trains head away from downtown Boston. If you get on the Red Line at South Station, the train heading toward Cambridge is inbound. But once you pass the Park Street station, the train becomes an outbound train. The best way to figure out which way to go is to know the last stop on the train, which is usually listed on the front of the train. So,

from Downtown, the Red Line to Cambridge would be the Alewife train and the Green Line to Fenway would be the Boston College or Cleveland Circle train.

Trains operate from about 5:30 AM to about 12:30 AM. T fares are $2 for adults paying in cash or $1.70 with a prepurchased CharlieCard. There are CharlieCard dispensing machines at almost every subway stop. Children under age 11 ride free and senior citizens pay 60¢. An extra fare is required outbound on the most distant Red Line stops (for example, the fare each way from Braintree is $2.50). Fares on the commuter rail—the Purple Line—vary widely; check with the MBTA.

One-day ($9) and seven-day ($15) passes are available for unlimited travel on subways, city buses, and inner-harbor ferries. You must pay a double fare if you're headed to some suburban stations such as Braintree; pay the second fare as you exit the station. Buy passes at any full-service MBTA stations. Passes are also sold at the Boston Common Visitor Information Center (⇨ *Visitor Information*) and at some hotels.

The Red Line originates at Braintree and Mattapan to the south; the routes join near South Boston and continue to suburban Arlington. The Green Line operates elevated trolleys in the suburbs that dip underground in the city center. The line originates at Cambridge's Lechmere, heads south, and divides into four routes that end at Boston College (Commonwealth Avenue),

Cleveland Circle (Beacon Street), Riverside, and Heath Street (Huntington Avenue). Buses connect Heath Street to the old Arborway terminus.

The Blue Line runs weekdays from Bowdoin Square and weeknights and weekends from Government Center to the Wonderland Racetrack in Revere, north of Boston. The Orange Line runs from Oak Grove in north suburban Malden to Forest Hills near the Arnold Arboretum. The Silver Line consists of two transit lines. One connects Downtown Crossing and Boylston to Dudley Square. The other runs from South Station down the waterfront to City Point. Park Street Station (on the Common) and State Street are the major downtown transfer points.

The MBTA runs commuter trains to points south, west, and north. Those bound for Worcester, Needham, Forge Park, Providence (RI), and Stoughton leave from South Station and Back Bay Station; those to Fitchburg, Lowell, Haverhill, Newburyport, and Rockport operate out of North Station.

TICKET/PASS	PRICE
Single Fare	$2
Day Pass	$9
Weekly Pass	$15
Monthly Unlimited Pass	$59

Contact **MBTA** (☎800/392–6100 or 617/222–3200, 617/222–5854 TTY ⊕www.mbta.com).

▌ BY TAXI

Cabs are available around the clock. You can also call for a cab or find them outside most hotels and at designated cab stands around the city that are marked by signs. Taxis generally line up in Harvard Square, around South Station, near Faneuil Hall Marketplace, at Long Wharf, near Massachusetts General Hospital, and in the Theater District. A taxi ride within the city of Boston starts at $1.75, and costs 30¢ for each mi thereafter. Licensed cabs have meters and provide receipts. An illuminated rooftop sign indicates an available cab. If you're going to or from the airport or to the suburbs, ask about flat rates. Cabdrivers sometimes charge extra for multiple stops. One-way streets often make circuitous routes necessary and increase your cost. Cabs are exempt from the car-seat requirement, however all vehicles have seatbelts in the back.

Taxi Companies **Boston Cab Association** (☎617/536–3200). **Checker Cab** (☎617/536–7000). **Green Cab Association** (☎617/625–5000). **Independent Taxi Operators Association (ITOA)** (☎617/825–4000). **Town Taxi** (☎617/536–5000).

ESSENTIALS

▌ BABYSITTING

Decidedly not a beach-resort type of destination, Boston does not offer many decked-out kids' clubs. Those looking for childcare will likely have to contract through their hotels. Concierges can usually arrange something, but there's often a premium for the convenience. The organization Parents in a Pinch works with many hotels but can also be contacted by parents directly. Service requires a $45 referral fee (paid advance with a credit card) plus hourly rates (paid directly to sitter) that begin at $15, slightly more for newborns zero to four months or twins. Visiting parents will have to contract as nonmembers, meaning they're limited to evening and weekend hours. Twenty-four to 48-hours notice is recommended.

Contact **Parents in a Pinch**
(⊠45 Bartlett Crescent, Brookline, MA 02446 ☎617/739–5437 or 800/688–4697).

▌ COMMUNICATIONS

INTERNET

Most downtown hotels have started offering either free or fee-based wireless in their rooms and common areas. Call your hotel before arriving to confirm.

There are also a small number of Internet cafés on Newbury Street and scattered Downtown that charge a small fee ($2 and up) depending on how many minutes you use. Most Starbucks locations and locally based coffee shops, such as Espresso Royale, have Wi-Fi service.

Contacts **Cybercafes** (⊕www.cybercafes.com) lists more than 4,000 Internet cafés worldwide. **WiFi Free Spot** (⊕www.wififreespot.com/mass.html) lists hundreds of spots where you can connect to free Wi-Fi around the state.

▌ DAY TOURS & GUIDES

All of Boston's excellent orientation tours stop at spots along the Freedom Trail. Bus tours, which cost around $25 and run daily from mid-March to early November, traverse the main historic neighborhoods in less than four hours. Reserve bus tours at least a day in advance. Narrated trolley tours, which usually cost $26 or so, don't require reservations and are more flexible; you can get on and off as you wish. A full trip normally lasts 1½–2 hours. All trolleys run daily, though less frequently off-season. Because they're open vehicles, be sure to dress appropriately for the weather. Boston Private Tours has customized van tours of the Greater Boston area.

RECOMMENDED TOURS/ GUIDES

BOAT TOURS

Boston has many waterways that offer stunning views of the city skyline. Narrated sightseeing water tours generally run from spring through early fall, daily in summer, and on weekends in the shoulder seasons. (Labor Day weekend is often the cutoff point.) These trips normally last ¾–1½ hours and cost a little more than $20. Many companies also offer sunset or evening cruises with music and other entertainment.

The kid-favorite Boston Duck Tours, which gives narrated land-water tours on a World War II amphibious vehicle, are particularly popular. After driving past several historic sights, the vehicle dips into the Charles River to offer a view of the Boston skyline. These tours, costing $34.95 per person ($25.95 children 3 to 11, $6.95 children 2 and under), run later than most, through late November.

June through September, you can relive the Golden Age of Sail aboard the *Liberty Clipper,* a replica two-masted gaff-rigged schooner that operates midday harbor tours and romantic sunset cruises from Long Wharf.

Boston Harbor Cruises and Massachusetts Bay Lines have tours around the harbor. Trips with Boston Duck Tours and the Charles Riverboat Company are along the Charles River Basin.

Fees & Schedules **Boston Duck Tours** (⊠Departures from Prudential Center, Huntington Ave. in front of Shaw's supermarket, and from Museum of Science ☎617/267–3825 ⊕www.bostonducktours.com). **Boston Harbor Cruises** (⊠1 Long Wharf ☎877/733–9425 or 617/227–4321 ⊕www.bostonharborcruises.

com). **Charles Riverboat Company** (⊠100 Cambridge Pl., Suite 320, Cambridge ☎617/621–3001 ⊕www.charlesriverboat.com). Liberty Clipper (☎617/742–0333 ⊕www.libertyfleet.com).

Massachusetts Bay Lines (⊠60 Rowes Wharf ☎617/542–8000 ⊕www.massbaylines.com).

BUS TOURS

Boston Private Tours has customized tours in vans or limousines. Brush Hill has more-traditional charter bus tours as well as smaller tours, with lots of prepackaged options and add-ons.

Both Brush Hill and Old Town Trolley have 1½-hour narrated tours. Old Town Trolley tours focus on history.

Fees & Schedules **Boston Private Tours** (☎800/620–1136 ⊕www.bostonprivatetours.com). **Brush Hill Tours** (⊠Transportation Bldg., 16 Charles St. S ☎800/343–1328 or 781/986–6100 ⊕www.brushhilltours.com).

TROLLEY TOURS

Old Town Trolley (⊠380 Dorchester Ave., South Boston ☎800/868–7482 or 617/269–7150 ⊕www.historictours.com/boston).

THEME TOURS

Hear spine-tingling tales about Boston's famous cemeteries; or tour (for free) the offices and printing plant of the *Boston Globe.* These tours are often given a few days a week. Some organizations have age restrictions. Many tours are free, but you'll often need to make a reservation at least a few days in advance and call ahead for schedules.

Bike Tours **Boston Bike Tours** (✉Meet at Boston Common near Visitor Information Center ☎617/308–5902 ⊕www.boston biketours.com).

Children's Tours **Boston by Little Feet** (✉Meet at Samuel Adams statue in front of Faneuil Hall ☎617/367–2345 ⊕www.bostonby foot.com).

Gardens & Parks Tours **Beacon Hill Garden Club Tours** (✉Charles and Beacon Sts., Beacon Hill ☎617/227–4392 ⊕www.beacon hillgardenclub.org). **Boston Park Rangers** (✉Parks and Recreation Dept. kiosk in Boston Common ☎617/635–4505 ⊕www.cityof boston.gov/parks).

History Tours **Bay Colony Historical Tours** (✉1 Cordis St., Charlestown ☎617/523–7303). The **Literary Trail of Greater Boston** (✉One Broadway, Suite 600, Cambridge ☎617/621–4020 ⊕www.literarytrailofgreaterboston.org).

Movie Tours **Boston Movie Tours** (✉Meet at Shaw Memorial in front of State House ☎866/668–4345 ⊕www.bostonmovietours.net).

WALKING TOURS

Boston is the perfect city for walking tours, to explore topics ranging from history and literature to ethnic neighborhoods. Most tours cost less than $20 and last one to two hours. Guides prefer to keep groups at fewer than 20 people, so always reserve ahead. Several organizations give tours once or twice a day spring through fall and by appointment (if at all) in winter. Others run tours a few days a week, spring through fall.

The Women's Heritage Trail, the Freedom Trail, and the Black Heritage Trail can be completed as self-guided tours. Maps for the Women's Heritage Trail are available online and at the Old State House and the National Park Service Visitor Center (⇨ *Visitor Information*). The Boston Common Visitor Information Center (⇨ *Visitor Information*) has maps of the Freedom Trail, which is indicated with a red line painted on the ground. The Freedom Trail and the Black Heritage Trail can also be completed with a ranger-led group. The Boston and Cambridge centers for Adult Education lead in-depth educational tours on many topics, most of them centered on art, architecture, and literature.

Harvard Square is the starting point for free student-led campus tours.

Fees & Schedules **Black Heritage Trail** (☎617/725–0022 ⊕www.afroammuseum.org). **Boston by Foot** (✉77 N. Washington St. ☎617/367–2345 ⊕www.bostonby foot.com). **Boston Center for Adult Education** (✉5 Commonwealth Ave. ☎617/267–4430 ⊕www.bcae.org). **Cambridge Center for Adult Education** (✉42 Brattle St., Cambridge ☎617/547–6789 ⊕www.ccae.org). **Freedom Trail** (☎617/357–8300 ⊕www.the-freedomtrail.org). **Harvard Campus Tours** (☎617/495–1573 ⊕www.harvard.edu/community/visitors.html).

Historic New England (✉141 Cambridge St. ☎617/227-3956 ⊕www.historicnewengland.org/about). **North End Market Tour** (✉6 Charter St. ☎617/523-6032 ⊕www.northendmarkettours.com). **Women's Heritage Trail** (⊕www.bwht.org).

▌HOURS OF OPERATION

Banks are generally open weekdays 9–4 or 5, plus Saturday 9 AM–noon or 1 PM at some branches. Public buildings are open weekdays 9–5.

Although hours vary quite a bit, most museums are open Monday through Saturday 9 or 10 AM–5 or 6 PM and Sunday noon–5 PM. Many are closed one day a week, usually Monday.

The major pharmacy chains—Brooks, CVS, and Walgreens—are generally open daily between 7 or 9:30 AM and 8 or 10 PM; independently owned pharmacies usually close earlier. Several pharmacies are open 24 hours a day.

Boston stores are generally open Monday through Saturday 10 or 11 AM–6 or 7 PM, closing later during the holiday-shopping season. Mall shops often stay open until 9 or 10 PM; malls and some tourist areas may also be open Sunday noon–5 or 6 PM.

▌MONEY

Prices are generally higher in Beacon Hill, the Back Bay, and Harvard Square than elsewhere. You're more likely to find bargains in the North End, Kenmore Square, Downtown Crossing, and Cambridge's Central Square. Many museums have one evening of free admission each week. There are no "happy hours" at any Boston bars due to a state law ("blue laws") that forbids promotions of discounted liquor.

ITEM	AVERAGE COST
Cup of Coffee	$1–$2
Glass of Wine	$6 and up
Glass of Beer	$3.50 and up
Slice of Pizza	$1.50–$2.50
One-Mile Taxi Ride	$3.50–$4
Museum Admission	$7–$15

Prices throughout this guide are given for adults. Substantially reduced fees are almost always available for children, students, and senior citizens.

CREDIT CARDS

Throughout this guide, the following abbreviations are used: **AE,** American Express; **D,** Discover; **DC,** Diners Club; **MC,** MasterCard; and **V,** Visa.

It's a good idea to inform your credit-card company before you travel, especially if you're going abroad and don't travel internationally very often. Otherwise, the credit-card company might put a hold on your card owing to unusual activity—not a good thing halfway through your trip. Record all your credit-card numbers—as well as the phone numbers to call if your cards are lost or stolen—in a safe place, so you're prepared should something go wrong. Both

MasterCard and Visa have general numbers you can call (collect if you're abroad) if your card is lost, but you're better off calling the number of your issuing bank, since MasterCard and Visa usually just transfer you to your bank; your bank's number is usually printed on your card.

Reporting Lost Cards **American Express** (☎800/528–4800 in U.S., 336/393–1111 collect from abroad ⊕www.americanexpress.com). **Diners Club** (☎800/234–6377 in U.S., 303/799–1504 collect from abroad ⊕www.dinersclub.com). **Discover** (☎800/347–2683 in U.S., 801/902–3100 collect from abroad ⊕www.discovercard.com). **MasterCard** (☎800/622–7747 in U.S., 636/722–7111 collect from abroad ⊕www.mastercard.com). **Visa** (☎800/847–2911 in U.S., 410/581–9994 collect from abroad ⊕www.visa.com).

▎ PACKING

The principal rule on Boston weather is that there are no rules. A cold, overcast morning can become a sunny, warm afternoon—and vice versa. Thus, the best advice on how to dress is to layer your clothing so that you can remove or add garments as needed for comfort. Rain often appears with little warning, so remember to pack a raincoat and umbrella. But if you're coming in winter, a warm jacket is crucial. Because Boston is a great walking city—with some picturesque but uneven cobblestone streets—be sure to bring comfortable shoes. This is particularly important advice for teens who will be miserable taking the long, steep Freedom Trail trek in their generation's ubiquitous flip-flop. Most rental-car companies offer car-seats for a fee, the price of which can add up if you're staying many days. Of course, now that airlines are charging for every bit of checked luggage, bringing your own car seat will be most economical if your child occupies it on the plane. In Massachusetts, child passenger restraints are required until age 8 or 57 inches. Please note: the law does not require children to be in restraints while in taxis, but it's never a good idea to travel with a child on your lap. Some hotels (mostly the high-end ones) have also gotten into the business of renting/loaning baby gear, but you'll have to call ahead to be sure. In all seasons, remember it's often breezier along the coast; always carry a windbreaker and fleece jacket or sweatshirt to the beach.

SHIPPING LUGGAGE AHEAD

Imagine globe-trotting with only a carry-on in tow. Shipping your luggage in advance via an air-freight service is a great way to cut down on backaches, hassles, and stress—especially if your packing list includes strollers, car seats, etc. There are some things to be aware of, though.

First, research carry-on restrictions; if you absolutely need something that isn't practical to ship and isn't allowed in carry-ons, this strategy isn't for you. Second, plan to send your bags several days in advance to U.S. destinations and as much as two weeks in advance to some international destinations. Third, plan to spend some money: it will cost least $100 to send a small piece of luggage, a golf bag, or a pair of skis to a domestic destination, much more to places overseas.

Some people use Federal Express to ship their bags, but this can cost even more than air-freight services. All these services insure your bag (for most, the limit is $1,000, but you should verify that amount); you can, however, purchase additional insurance for about $1 per $100 of value.

Contacts **Luggage Concierge** (☎800/288–9818 ⊕www.luggage concierge.com). **Luggage Express** (☎866/744–7224 ⊕www.usx-pluggageexpress.com). **Luggage Free** (☎800/361–6871 ⊕www. luggagefree.com). **Virtual Bellhop** (☎877/235–5467 ⊕www.virtual bellhop.com).

▌RESTROOMS

Public restrooms outside of restaurants, hotel lobbies, and tourist attractions are rare in Boston, but you'll find clean, well-lighted facilities at South Station, Faneuil Hall Marketplace, and the Visitor Information Center on Boston Common. Quarter-operated, self-cleaning public toilets can be found at Puopolo Park in the North End, near Faneuil Hall, at Central Wharf, and near the Boston Public Library. (⇨*See also "Where Can I find . . ." charts in chapters 1 and 2*).

Find a Loo **The Bathroom Diaries** (⊕www.thebathroomdiaries.com) is flush with unsanitized info on restrooms the world over—each one located, reviewed, and rated.

▌SAFETY

With their many charming neighborhoods, Boston and Cambridge often feel like small towns. But they're both cities, subject to the same problems plaguing other urban communities nationwide. Although violent crime is rare, residents and tourists alike sometimes fall victim to pickpockets, scam artists, and car thieves. As in any large city, use common sense, especially after dark. Stay with the crowds and walk on well-lighted, busy streets. Look alert and aware; a purposeful pace helps deter trouble wherever you go. Take cabs or park in well-lighted lots or garages.

Store valuables in a hotel safe or, better yet, leave them at home. Keep an eye (and hand) on handbags and backpacks; do not hang them from a chair in restaurants. Carry wallets in inside or front pockets rather than back pockets. Use ATMs in daylight, preferably in a hotel, bank, or another indoor location with security guards.

Subways and trolleys tend to be safe, but it's wise to stay on your guard. Stick to routes in the main Boston and Cambridge tourist areas—generally, the downtown stops on all lines, on the Red Line in Cambridge, on the Green Line through the Back Bay, and on the Blue Line around the New England Aquarium. Know your itinerary and make sure you get on the right bus or train going in the right direction. Avoid empty subway and trolley cars and lonely station hallways and platforms, especially after 9 PM on weeknights. The MBTA has its own police officers; don't hesitate to ask them for help.

■TIP→ **Distribute your cash, credit cards, IDs, and other valuables between a deep front pocket, an inside jacket or vest pocket, and a hidden money pouch. Don't reach for the money pouch once you're in public.**

▌ TAXES

Hotel room charges in Boston and Cambridge are subject to state and local taxes of up to 12.45%.

A sales tax of 5% is added to restaurant and take-out meals and to all other goods except nonrestaurant food and clothing valued at less than $175.

▌ VACATION PACKAGES

Packages *are not* guided excursions. Packages combine airfare, accommodations, and perhaps a rental car or other extras (theater tickets, guided excursions, boat trips, reserved entry to popular museums, transit passes), but they let you do your own thing. During busy periods, packages may be your only option, as flights and rooms may be sold out otherwise.

Packages will definitely save you time. They can also save you money, particularly in peak seasons, but—and this is a really big "but"—you should price each part of the package separately to be sure. And be aware that prices advertised on Web sites and in newspapers rarely include service charges or taxes, which can up your costs by hundreds of dollars.

■TIP→ **Some packages and cruises are sold only through travel agents. Don't always assume that you can get the best deal by booking everything yourself.**

Each year consumers are stranded or lose their money when packagers—even large ones with excellent reputations—go out of business. How can you protect yourself?

First, always pay with a credit card; if you have a problem, your credit-card company may help you resolve it. Second, buy trip insurance that covers default. Third, choose a company that belongs to the United States Tour Operators Association, whose members must set aside funds to cover defaults. Finally, choose a company that also participates in the Tour Operator Program of the American Society of Travel Agents (ASTA), which will act as mediator in any disputes.

You can also check on the tour operator's reputation among travelers by posting an inquiry on one of the Fodors.com forums.

Traveling to Boston on a package tour makes it quite convenient for those interested only in hitting the highlights or major historic sites such as the Freedom Trail, Faneuil Hall, the Bunker Hill Memorial, Quincy Market, and Harvard Square. If you're interested in exploring more neighborhoods, a tour will likely not give you access to these.

Organizations **American Society of Travel Agents** (ASTA ☎800/965-2782 or 703/739-2782 ⊕www.astanet.com). **United States Tour Operators Association** (USTOA ☎212/599-6599 ⊕www. ustoa.com). ■TIP→**Local tourism boards can provide information about lesser-known and small-niche operators that sell packages to only a few destinations.**

▍ VISITOR INFORMATION

Contact the city and state tourism offices for general information, details about seasonal events, discount passes, trip planning, and attraction information. The National Park Service has a Boston office where you can watch an eight-minute slide show on Boston's historic sites and get maps and directions. The Welcome Center and Boston Common Visitor Information Center offer general information.

Contacts **Boston Common Visitor Information Center** (⊠148 Tremont St. where Freedom Trail begins, Downtown ☎617/426-3115). **Boston National Historical Park Visitor Center** (⊠15 State St., Downtown ☎617/242-5642 ⊕www.nps.gov/bost). **Cambridge Tourism Office** (⊠4 Brattle St., Harvard Sq., Cambridge ☎800/862-5678 or 617/441-2884 ⊕www. cambridge-usa.org). **Greater Boston Convention and Visitors Bureau** (⊠2 Copley Pl., Suite 105, Back Bay ☎888/733-2678 or 617/536-4100 🖷617/424-7664 ⊕www.bostonusa. com). **Massachusetts Office of Travel and Tourism** (⊠State Transportation Bldg., 10 Park Plaza, Suite 4510, Back Bay ☎800/227-6277 or 617/973-8500 🖷617/973-8525 ⊕www.massvacation.com).

INDEX

NOTES

NOTES

NOTES

NOTES

NOTES

NOTES

NOTES

NOTES

NOTES

NOTES

NOTES

NOTES

ABOUT OUR WRITER

A native New Yorker, Lisa Oppenheimer has settled into Boston suburbia, where writing local travel pieces has helped her fully appreciate the flavor of her adoptive home. She now wholeheartedly roots for the Patriots, the Celtics, the Bruins and even the Red Sox—just don't tell her family. In addition to Fodor's guides, Lisa has written about travel, parenting, and family entertainment for *Parents*, *Parenting*, *Family Fun*, and the online parenting resource, Family.com.